IIII III IIIIIIIIIIIIII I III IIIIIIIIIIIIIIIIIIIIIIIIII I III

W9-CCB-661

To Pam ~ June 7, 1987
who pulls out my fire !!!
anytime
xxxx
[signature]

REPORT FROM ENGINE CO. 82

REPORT FROM
ENGINE CO. 82

DENNIS SMITH

With a New Introduction
by the Author

Bonanza Books
New York

Copyright © MCMLXXII by Dennis Smith
All right reserved

This 1983 edition is published by Bonanza Books,
distributed by Crown Publishers, Inc., by arrangement with Dennis Smith

Manufactured in the United States of America

Library of Congress Cataloging in Publication Data

Smith, Dennis, 1940–
  Report from Engine Co. 82.

  1. New York (N.Y.). Fire Dept.   2. New York (N.Y.)—
Fires and fire prevention.   I. Title.   II. Title: Report
from Engine Company eighty-two.
TH9505.N5S63   1983   628.9'2'097471   83-15034

ISBN: 0-517-420635
h g f e d c b a

For Deirdre and Aislinn.

INTRODUCTION

There is an inherent immodesty in writing an introduction to a new edition of a book that is eleven years old. It says, "This book still means something, still has value, so it is being reissued."

This immodesty notwithstanding, I will tell you the story of *Report from Engine Co. 82* in as modest and as thankful a voice as possible. I remember a writer saying that Dennis Smith came to writing the way a starlet comes to stardom by way of Schwab's Drugstore. Well, he wasn't very far off the mark because he was saying that I got lucky, and I do very much believe that luck played a principal part in the development of my writing career.

I was lucky in the following innocuous way: One Sunday in 1970, I, like several million others, read the *New York Times Book Review.* There I came across an essay by Joyce Carol Oates, a writer of novels and poetry, on the Irish poet William Butler Yeats, an essay which took a very strong position on the universality of Yeat's poetry. I took issue with that essay and wrote a letter to the *New York Times* saying that Yeats was not fundamentally a universal poet, but an Irish poet, and an extraordinarily nationalistic Irish poet at that. The letter I wrote to the *Times* was, I can confess now that I look back on it, somewhat presumptuous and pedantic. Yet for all of that, I continue to believe it was a letter that at least made an intelligent observation.

Not long thereafter, I received many letters—many being twelve to fifteen, which in response to a letter in a newspaper I am told is quite a lot. These letters were from college professors and students from across the country, all of them agreeing with the conclusion about Yeats that I had made.

I also received two letters that proved to have extraordinary consequence. The first was a letter from the now-defunct *True Magazine* that commented on the astuteness of my observations about Irish poetry. You may wonder why *True Magazine* would have sent a letter of congratulations to me. The reason is that I had signed my communication to the *New York Times Book Review:* "Dennis Smith, New York City Fireman." I've always been extremely proud to be a part of New York's Bravest, yet looking back, I suppose that the *New York Times* must have been inspired not a little by the reverse snob appeal of having in their very prestigious *Book Review* a presumptuous, pedantic letter signed by a fireman from the Bronx.

The letter from *True Magazine*, after delivering a safe number of compliments to what its author presumably thought was a tall and tough South Bronx firefighter, asked if I had ever thought of writing about my life as a fireman.

The fact is that I had been writing rather consistently since I was a teenager, and as I was 30 in 1970, I was well practiced in part-time writing. Yet I had never seriously thought about writing an account of being a firefighter in the South Bronx. I thought that being a firefighter in the South Bronx was simply what I did for a living, and I thought of writing as something that belonged within quotation marks, as in "writing." I viewed writing in a way that perhaps carried a little too much reverence—the kind of attitude that some people might bring to poetry or even to driving a fancy car. My work until that time had been very literary—again a word that belongs in quotes. Safe to say that the early novels I had worked on and the short stories and the poetry were all presumptuous and pedantic, but that is the price—or the dues—that most young writers have to pay.

I replied to the editor from *True Magazine*, saying that I would be happy to meet with him, and it was not long thereafter that I experienced my first of what now seems to be thousands of professional publishing luncheons. I remember that we met in a restaurant on the corner of 47th Street and Madison Avenue in New York, a restaurant that, like much of the South Bronx, is no longer there. We discussed my writing a 2000-word first-person article on the life of a firefighter in the South Bronx. I was told then, and it nearly knocked me off the leather banquette, that *True Magazine* would pay me the grand sum of $2000 for such an article. Think of that—one dollar a word—for a firefighter who was earning at that time about four dollars an hour for fighting fires in what was then the busiest firehouse in the world.

I was also contacted at that time by a woman named Susan Sheehan, who was writing "Talk of the Town" pieces for *The New Yorker*. She asked to meet with me, and I met her in the very same 47th Street restaurant where I had a lunch that would be better suited to the term "literary" than to "publishing." We discussed Irish literature in general and William Butler Yeats in specific, and Mrs. Sheehan seemed to enjoy it very much. Several months then passed —"Talk of the Town" pieces in *The New Yorker* have a long pre-publication shelf life—before an article entitled "Fireman Smith" was published.

The article was the direct link between a fireman fighting fires in the South Bronx and the publication of *Report from Engine Co. 82*, for not long after *The New Yorker* appeared on the stands I received a letter from the McCall Publishing Company that asked if I had ever thought of writing a book-length account of the life of a firefighter in New York's South Bronx.

I responded to this letter with the alacrity of, well, a fireman responding to an alarm.

I next remember a group of very ragged, tired, smoke-saturated firemen standing around outside the firehouse on Intervale Avenue in the South Bronx. A taxicab pulled up in front, a yellow taxicab that came from "downtown," unlike the beat-up gypsy cabs that were common to the neighborhood. I remember particularly the way the firefighters' eyes widened as a young woman from the McCall Publishing Company stuck an unusually handsome leg from the back seat of the cab and placed it on the garbage-strewn cobblestones of Intervale Avenue.

Stephanie Erickson was her name, and she was sent to the South Bronx on a beyond-the-call-of-duty mission by Charlie Sopkin, the editor-in-chief of McCall Books. I greeted her, showed her around the firehouse, and brought her to the kitchen at the back of the apparatus floor for a cup of coffee, all the time being followed by a group of soot-stained firefighters. Would I be interested, she asked, in trying to write a book about what I did, for it seemed apparent to her, from reading *The New Yorker* "Talk of the Town" piece, that I was an "intelligent" firefighter who "might be able to write a book." I told her that I already was an accomplished author, having published an article in a national magazine. I also told her that I had been paid at the rate of one dollar a word, and having been made newly rich I had junked the old Volkswagen and bought a new fire-engine-red Ford sedan. Being disinclined to have her think I was concerned only with the rewards of my labor, I added that I was (1) married and the father of three young boys (two girls have since been added); (2) working in the busiest fire station in the history of the New York City Fire Department; and (3) working on my Master's degree in communications at New York University—all of which left me little time to write a book for the McCall Publishing Company.

Unless, of course, they were willing to pay me money for the value of my time and labor, for even then I remembered Dr. Johnson's adage that only a fool writes for things other than money. The McCall Publishing Company, in consideration of my talent, experience, and need, granted me a contract valued at $2000, the same amount of money to write a 70,000-word book as *True Magazine* offered me to write a 2000-word article. And so my value as a writer diminished considerably from the one-dollar-a-word mark. Yet for all of that it was a good start.

I don't remember very much about the actual writing of *Report from Engine Co. 82* except that in explication of the woman with the handsome legs on the cobblestones of Intervale Avenue, I let it be known in the firehouse that I was writing a book. The men in the firehouse were very accommodating toward their fellow firefighter who had set about to write a book, in much the same ironic way they would be accommodating toward one who was, say, about to star in a major motion picture or about to perform brain surgery at Massachusetts General. In other words, they endured a small vanity.

It soon became something of a pervasive and continuous joke, though, for each time thereafter that I entered the firehouse kitchen or the firehouse office or the firehouse bunkroom someone would inevitably say, "Uh oh, watch what you're saying. Here comes Smith —he's got a pencil in his ear."

In fact, I am not a note taker. What I did, simply, was to think very carefully about the events I experienced each day in the South Bronx, and then tried to integrate them with my knowledge of the social structure of what can safely be called the ghetto of the South Bronx, and with the emotions I felt at what I had seen. When I went home each day I would write a vignette of my tour of duty. It was these vignettes, these day-to-day, hour-to-hour accounts of my experiences as a firefighter that made up the chapters of the book.

The actual writing of the book took place in the smallest bedroom of our family residence in a place called Washingtonville, New York. We had four small bedrooms in that house and three young boys, each of whom had his own room. When I began to write the book I moved my youngest son, Sean, out of his bedroom and into his brother's room, which they then shared for the next six months. It was a small inconvenience, and he remembers it hardly at all.

I, though, remember very distinctly the day I thought I had written the last sentence of *Report from Engine Co. 82*. I gathered the three boys together, held before them the pile of manuscript pages which was about two-and-half-inches thick, and said, "Well, boys, this book which has preoccupied me and consumed most of our lives in the last six months is now finished." It was to me a terribly important and terribly romantic moment, an image that was soon shattered by my son Sean, who said, perhaps with justifiable enthusiasm, "Good. Now can I have my room back?"

The names—I am reluctant to say of the "characters," because they are more clearly and truthfully participants—used in the book were changed only because of an inconvenient legal mandate. In order to publish a day-to-day account of not only my life but also of the lives of the men with whom I worked, I had to receive their written permission to use their names or likenesses. And, since the book was, in the publisher's mind, just one on a long list of books to be published the following year, there were no extraordinary steps taken to secure the proper and legal permissions. Also, there were not enough pre-publication galley proof copies to go around to each of the many firefighters to read, and certainly I would not have asked them to sign a release for a book they had not read. So the most practical solution to the legal problem was to change the names of the participants, but to change them in such a way so that they would be immediately recognizable to each other and to their families.

Consequently, I changed the names in the very slightest way. For instance, Charlie McCarty is in fact Charlie McCarthy; Bill Knipps is Bill Knapp; and Bill Kelsey is Billy Kelly. Benny Carroll is Benny Cassidy; Captain Albergray is Al Gray; and finally, Billy O'Mann is in fact Billy O'Meara. These men played a very important part in my life then as indeed they do today. They are the kind of people with whom one does not develop transient friendships. When they do things they do them for keeps and with their whole heart.

The launch of the book when it was finished was not very auspicious. The book simply was an unpublished collection of bound pages one day, and then the next day it was a published book, albeit published with very little—in fact, no—fanfare. No publication party, no press conference.

Not long thereafter Bella Abzug, who was at the time, a member of Congress, wrote a book about her life, and there was a rather large, very pretty, very expensive garden party in the back of a fancy Italian restaurant in New York. I mention this fact only to illustrate that there is a significant difference between the way the world perceives members of Congress and the way the world perceives firefighters—the world in this case being people of position, influence and conse-quence. If I sound a little scarred, it's because I am, for I have found many times in the years since this book was published that the gen-eral observation of firefighters by most members of the management class in America is that, when everything is said and done, they are not very much different from any other blue-collar worker. Not that I think there's anything wrong with that observation. It's just that most blue-collar workers in this country stand head and shoulders over most of our Congressmen and -women.

I remember, as well as I remember yesterday's weather, a tele-phone call I received from Stephanie Erickson one day, just prior to the book's publication, when I was working at the firehouse. Bells were ringing and people were running from one end of the place to the other. The ladder company and the chief were responding to some alarm, Engine 82 was standing fast, and Stephanie Erickson said, "Today I received the first review of your book and I don't know how to tell you this, but it's not very good." And I said, "Stephanie, I've been in a lot of fires and I'm not too worried about book reviews." Though in truth, I *was* worried, for I had put so much of my life into writing the book.

She responded by reading a line from *Publisher's Weekly,* a magazine for the publishing trade, which said, "It is pretty obvious that Dennis Smith is a much better firefighter than he is a writer."

However, most of the other reviews were very positive, not only in reference to the information I had to convey but in the way I chose to convey it.

What did the publication of *Report from Engine Co. 82* do? Cer-tainly, it changed my life. And it changed the lives of my family. It became an immediate best seller; it climbed very rapidly to the number 3 position on the *New York Times* best seller list and stayed there for a long time. In all it was on the *Times* list for 16 weeks. The good reviews were very reassuring to me because I had tried to paint a very honest canvas of what I saw in the South Bronx and what I experienced there. William Buckley, in a review in *New York* magazine said, "I think fireman Smith has written a masterpiece." The vice-president of CBS said on the radio that the book was "a moving profile of the people who keep America's big cities from falling apart or burning down. It reads like a good war novel written by a soldier who, unlike the journalist, cannot escape the battle." And then a review in the *Catholic Transcript* said, "An extraordinary book. A young New York City fireman, Dennis Smith by name, is destined for fame."

I fooled this last reviewer, though, because I never did become famous. Of course I'm not entirely certain about this. Fame is often mistaken in today's world for celebrity. I am in no way a celebrity. While fame is generally a consequence of accomplishment, celebrity is an accomplishment of mere exposure to the electronic media, a consequence of the number of one's photographs that appear in places like *People* magazine. I don't think of myself as famous, and I suppose only time will tell if I acquire the longevity of an author's reading worthiness that brings fame. By this I mean that a writer can be famous because a book he wrote is still worthy of being read, long after publication.

While I'm never recognized in restaurants or walking down the street as being somebody well known, I have undoubtedly become, among the firefighters of this nation, famous for what I am—a firefighter, a writer, an editor of a magazine for firefighters. That is a kind of fame of which I am very proud, and of which my children will be proud in the years to come.

Report from Engine Co. 82 did do something of consequence in that it showed America what firefighters are truly like, what kind of work they actually do, the dangers they are continually exposed to, and the superhuman efforts they will go to in saving the life of another human being. And since the book was translated into nine languages, it also showed these things to people all over the world.

Its past success notwithstanding, why reprint a book like this one? Normally a book has its time in the sun and then it is consigned forever to the musty bins of libraries or someone's bookshelf. But *Report from Engine Co. 82* has, I have found in my experience, a unique audience, a fan club if those words can properly be used here. I continually meet people who tell me they have recently read or reread *Report from Engine Co. 82*. And people are always asking me where they can buy the book. More importantly, I've received letters from educators at both the high school and the college level who tell me that they would like to use *Report from Engine Co. 82* in their classes—their sociology classes, their urban studies classes, and their history classes—but they cannot find it for purchase anywhere.

In addition, I find that there is a whole new generation of firefighters who, while they may have heard of *Report from Engine Co. 82*, have not read it and I think that the book is a valuable tool for new firefighters in helping them understand the extraordinary variety of demands that will be placed upon them in the future. Consequently, I have decided to issue a new edition for both old and new readers.

There is also another reason: the more things change, the adage goes, the more they stay the same. Recently, I had the opportunity to spend the evening riding from alarm to alarm with a friend who is now a deputy chief, or division chief, in the South Bronx. It is curious that the area we call the South Bronx has moved ever northward in the last ten to fifteen years. At one time the South Bronx was the area from 138th Street and below, then it was raised to 161st Street and below, then it was raised to that whole area below the intersection of Boston Road and Southern Boulevard, then it was raised to the area below the Cross-Bronx Expressway at 174th Street, and now it seems to go clear up to Yonkers. In point of fact, the South Bronx is defined by any large area of devastation in the borough of the Bronx.

In any case, the area through which I was riding was in the more northern part of the Bronx, 180th Street and thereabouts, and that area today looks and feels and smells and vibrates with the same kind of malcontent, disadvantage, and cultural deprivation as the streets surrounding 169th Street and Intervale Avenue—the area that police come to refer to as Fort Apache—as it did eleven years ago, when *Report from Engine Co. 82* was first published. The firefighters there are still fighting fires in the same kinds of buildings, still crawling through garbage-strewn hallways, still responding to those terribly frustrating alarms at two, three, four, and five o'clock in the morning, and still crawling down those endless, lethal, mortally dangerous

hallways of abandoned buildings, buildings whose destruction trans-
lates directly into dollars for the true leeches of our society—the
depraved, immoral, firesetting landlords of our big cities.

The poverty of today is not much different from the poverty of
eleven years ago. Not much has changed after the social policy positions of the Nixon, Ford, Carter, and Reagan administrations. Today,
a prototypical young man might be seen walking down a pockmarked
street of the Bronx with a two-hundred-dollar sound system perched
on his shoulder, but he is no better educated than he was eleven
years ago, he is no better prepared to be employed than he was
eleven years ago. He does not feel himself any more a part of the
greater society in which he lives. And that is a great tragedy still.
Poverty and disenfranchisement, of course, have a direct relationship
to the number of fires and false alarms in an area. And the Bronx
today is still among the very highest fire hit areas of the world.

It must be said, though, that while many things remain the same,
the level of tragedy, the level of false alarms, the level of deaths and
injuries to the Bronx population is not as great as it was in 1972. During the years that I worked on Intervale Avenue and 169th Street,
from 1966 to 1973, Engine Co. 82 and Ladder Co. 31 were responding
to about 40 alarms a day. Of these alarms about one-third were false
alarms, about one-third were what we called nuisance fires (backyard
garbage fires, mattress fires, car fires), and the last third were serious
building fires. The fire rate of the South Bronx is still enormous but
that kind of extraordinarily heavy fire load does not exist for the fire
companies in today's Bronx. And we all hope it never will again.

It is important to remember that during the years I worked in the
South Bronx there was a pervasive negative social psychology, a kind
of "Burn, baby, burn" syndrome that operated on the streets in many
of our cities. It was during the age of riots, it was during the age when
people looked at firefighters and policemen—white or black—as
occupying forces, as people who did not live in the neighborhood
and, consequently, had no business being there. It was a period of
great self-destruction, a period that moved Senator Daniel Moynihan
and others to call for a new period, one of benign neglect.

It was because we paid so much attention, particularly during the years of The Great Society, to the problems of the minority poor in places like the South Bronx, that the continual media coverage of those problems created each day a stronger and stronger resentment for the society that permitted those problems to exist.

However, while the fire rates don't exist in as great a number now as they did during the late sixties and early seventies, they still exist at unconscionable levels and that is something that we should be reminded of daily.

Still, fire is not something that will pass away. It will always be with us in all parts of America, at every social level. We have the highest fire rate in the world. And since Americans, like their pioneer ancestors of old, tend to meet crises head on rather than plan for them, I do not see a radical diminishment in the number of fires or the number of fire mortalities in the near future. The firefighters of America will continue to be as crucial to the well-being and safety of the American public in the future as they have been in the past.

But back to the firefighters of *Report from Engine Co. 82*. What has happened to them, the firefighters with whom I worked side by side during all of those years while the South Bronx burned down? Men like Charlie McCarty and Billy O' and Knipps and Kelsey and Benny Carroll? For the readers who have grown to know and to love these men as I have, I think it will be interesting for them to know the changes that occurred over the years in the lives of these valiant firefighters.

Charlie McCarty, or Charles McCarthy, was promoted to the rank of lieutenant. At a fire in an abandoned building, he fell through a floor and hurt his knee and was retired from service in the New York City Fire Department on a medical disability pension in 1981. He is now, as I write this, in college studying to be a registered nurse.

Billy O', or Bill O'Meara was also promoted to lieutenant and was retired from the New York City Fire Department after 20 years of service. He was working in Rescue Company 3 in the Bronx one night a little more than two years ago when a firefighter was trapped at a window on the fourth floor of a burning tenement in Harlem. Billy O' supervised one of his firefighters in a roof-rope rescue operation. The man, Larry Fitzpatrick, was tied to the end of a one-half-inch nylon rope and was lowered from the roof to pick up the trapped firefighter as heat and smoke poured out the window in which he was framed. The trapped man, firefighter Frisby, was made frantic by the encroaching fire, and wrapped his arms about Larry Fitzpatrick, who had been lowered to his level. At that moment the rope broke and both men toppled to the hard concrete of the yard below. Both men were killed instantly. Billy O' watched from the roof and quickly ran to the backyard. But it was too late. There was nothing to do except console the other members of his company and the families of his fallen brothers. It was not long after that fire that Billy O'Meara submitted his retirement papers to the city's Fire Commissioner.

Billy Knipps, or Bill Knapp, is still working as a firefighter in Engine Co. 82 on Intervale Avenue and 169th Street, along with Lieutenant Tom Walsh, who still plays the guitar, and Jerry Albert, who is the first whip of Ladder Co. 31, and Billy Valenzano who still smiles continually. They are standard fixtures in the firehouse, like plaques on the wall. Valiant, respected "old-timers" now, though still relatively young, they are the men who will get things done. Bill Knapp, consistent in his personality and the level of enthusiasm with which he dedicates his life to good and decent things, spends almost all of his spare time as a volunteer emergency medical technician with an ambulance corps in the small upstate town in which he lives—Washingtonville—the very same town in which I spent three very happy years living as his next-door neighbor.

My other Washingtonville neighbor, Bill Kelsey or Bill Kelly, also continued to work in Engine Co. 82 and in his spare time became a volunteer fireman with the Monell Volunteer Fire Department in Washingtonville. Then one day in 1981, Bill Kelly went to the hospital to have a routine, uncomplicated operation, and he died inexplicably on the operating table at 43 years of age.

Benny Carroll, or Ben Cassidy, is now a captain of one of the busiest engine companies in the Bronx. He became a marathon runner and ran in the famous 26-mile New York City Marathon. More importantly, especially to his wife and six children, he has passed the examination for battalion chief and will soon be appointed to that rank in the New York City Fire Department.

Others, like Chief Kelso and Chief Neibrock, have also retired as did my old captain, Al Gray and good friend Don Butler. Vinny Bollon, Ed Penna, Bob Beatty, and the rest of the firefighters I wrote about are still running into burning buildings. I wish them all the only decent thing to wish a firefighter: good health and lots of laughs.

And I? I continued to work as an active firefighter, going from Engine Co. 82 to a ladder company in a place called City Island in the Bronx and finally to another ladder company, Ladder Co. 61 in Co-op City, the Bronx. I founded *Firehouse Magazine* in 1975 and it began to take a great deal of my time and interest until finally, in December of 1980, after nearly 18 years of active service with New York's Bravest, the responsibilities of the magazine became so great that I could not continue to work 40 hours on a fire truck in the Bronx and handle a magazine that had grown enough to have readers in every state in the Union and in many foreign countries, the largest circulating magazine of its kind in the world. I, like Billy O', forwarded my retirement papers with great reluctance, some misgivings, and considerable sadness to the New York City Fire Commissioner. And as I reflect on all the years of being a firefighter and being a writer, there is not a thing that I would change.

The writing of one book changed my life utterly. It provided me with a voice and an audience and a stepping stone to do other things. I have since written and published seven additional books, and I am now completing my ninth, a new novel called *Steely Byrnes. Firehouse Magazine* has become an important voice in the world of the fire service, a voice that is as far-reaching as anything I dreamed possible.

Now it is my profound hope that this new edition of *Report from Engine Co. 82* will reach and inspire and motivate the courage of firefighting in a new generation of America's firefighters. This book has no meaning unless it is read in relation to the memory of those firefighters.

Dennis Smith

New York
1983

This book seems to be about a particular group of firefighters working in the South Bronx, but the incidents described here tell the story of all firefighters working in this country. The problems in Boston, Cleveland, Chicago, Detroit, and Los Angeles are the same, only the names change.

REPORT FROM
ENGINE CO. 82

1

The Late, Late Show is on the television and most of us are sitting in the kitchen when the bells start to ring. I take a last sip of tea as I count onetwo onetwothreefourfive one onetwothreefourfive. The kitchen chairs empty as the last number comes in. Box 2515. Intervale Avenue and Kelly Street.

We can smell the smoke as the pumper turns down Intervale, and hands automatically start pulling boot-tops to thighs, clipping coat-rings closed, and putting on gloves. The pumper stops in front of a building just before we reach Kelly Street. We're about to stretch the hose when there is an anguished scream from inside the building. A boy is running out of the doorway, his shirt and hair aflame.

Ladder 31 and Chief Solwin are right behind us, and one of the ladder men goes rapidly to the boy's assistance. Willy Knipps takes the first folds of the hose and heads into the building. Carroll and I follow, dragging the rest of the hose with us. Royce and Boyle are still on the sidewalk donning masks.

Lieutenant Welch is waiting for us on the second floor, crouched low by a smoking door. There are four apartments on the floor, and three of the doors are open, their occupants fleeing. Chief Solwin arrives, stops for a moment at the top of the stairs, and then rushes into the apartment adjoining the rooms on fire. He starts kicking through the wall with all his strength. The smoke rushes through the hole, darkening the apartment and the hall. Knipps and I are coughing and have to lie on our bellies as we wait for the water to surge through the hose. Carroll has gone down for another mask. He can tell it's going to be a tough, snotty job.

Billy-o and Artie Merritt start to work on the locked door. It's hard for me to breathe with my nose to the marble floor of the hall, and I think of the beating Artie and Billy-o must be taking as they stand where the smoke is densest, swinging on the ax, hitting the door with the point of the halligan tool. The door is tight and does not give easily.

Captain Frimes arrives with Charlie McCartty behind him. "Give me a man with a halligan," Chief Solwin yells, and Captain Frimes and McCartty hustle into the adjoining apartment.

"I'm sure I heard someone in there," Chief Solwin says.

Charlie widens the hole in the wall. The Chief and Captain Frimes are on their knees as Charlie works. After furious hacking, the hole is through to the next apartment. Charlie tries to squeeze through the bay—the sixteen-inch space between the two-by-fours. He can't make it. Not with his mask on. He turns to take the mask off, but before he can get it off Captain Frimes enters through the hole.

The front door has still not been opened, and Frimes knows that only luck or the help of God will keep the whole place from lighting up. He crawls on the floor toward the front door, swinging his arms before him as if swimming the breast stroke. His hand is stopped by the bulk of a body, lying on the floor. It's a big frame, and Captain Frimes struggles to drag it toward the hole in the wall. The fire is raging in three rooms at the end of the hall, and spreading fast toward the front of the building.

McCartty is just crawling through the hole as the Captain passes by with the body. "Here, Cap, here," McCartty yells. The smoke is so thick that Captain Frimes missed the hole. McCartty grabs the body under the arms, and pulls.

Captain Frimes can hear Billy-o and Artie working on the door, and he makes a desperate effort back down the hall. He reaches the front door and feels the long steel bar of a Fox lock. Like a flying buttress, the bar reaches up from the floor and braces the door closed. Captain Frimes knows locks as well as he knows his own kids' names, and he kneels and turns the bolt of the lock. He jumps back, and the door swings open. Billy-o and Artie grab the Captain, who is overcome by smoke and can barely move now, and pull him out of the apartment.

Charlie McCartty walks past us with the body in his arms. It is a boy, about sixteen or seventeen years old. He is a strapping black youth, but McCartty is a powerful man, and carries him easily to the street. The boy is still breathing, but barely. McCartty knows that he has to get some oxygen into him if he is to live, and begins mouth-to-mouth resuscitation.

The hose comes to life with water as Billy-o and Artie pull the Captain down the stairs. Lieutenant Welch gives the "okay" to Knipps, and we start crawling down the hall. We reach the first burning room, and Knipps opens the nozzle. The room is filled with the crackling of fire, and as the water stream hits the ceiling the sound is made louder by falling plaster, steaming and hissing on the wet floor.

The fire darkens quickly, and the smoke banks to the floor. There is no escape from it, and Knipps knows that he has to push into the last room for a rest. "Give me some more line!" he yells, and his order is relayed back through the hall by Lieutenant Welch's voice: "Lighten up on the inch-and-a-half." The hose moves forward, and Knipps with it.

Boyle moves up, breathing easily in his mask. He is going to relieve Knipps on the line, but he trips in the middle of the room.

He feels around the floor to see what tripped him, and his hands sink into another body. "I got a victim here!" he yells through the mouthpiece of the mask. Carroll joins him quickly, and they carry the body out.

Royce moves up to the nozzle, and Knipps says that he thinks he can make it. But Lieutenant Welch orders him to take a blow, and Royce takes the nozzle. Knipps stands to make a quick exit to clean air, but the smoke has gotten to him. He vomits, and the stream of food and acid falls over the back of my coat and boots. He doesn't stop to apologize.

Vinny Royce moves slowly and deliberately through the second and third rooms. Lieutenant Welch is next to him all the while, saying, "You got it, Vinny. You got it," and coughing continuously. I am right behind humping the hose and leaning into it to relieve the fifty-pound-per-square-inch back pressure that is straining Vinny's arms. As the third room darkens down completely, I run to the fire-escape window and climb out of it. I lie on my back on the narrow steel strips of the fire escape, taking the air, sucking the oxygen from it, not taking the time to look at anything.

Boyle and Carroll lay the second body on the sidewalk, next to the boy McCartty carried out and is now using the mechanical resuscitator on. Carroll looks at the body before him. He is a teenager also, and his clothes are like charred bits of paper sticking to his skin. He is badly burned, and the flesh on parts of his face has opened so that it looks like there are pink patches woven into his black skin. Boyle turns away and vomits as Benny plugs the face-piece connection into the regulator of the resuscitator. He puts his finger into the face piece, testing it, making sure there is the quick, clicking sound of air being pushed and relieved—in and out, in and out. The mechanical apparatus forces pure oxygen into the lungs until they expand and build up enough pressure to push the air out again. Benny tilts the boy's head back, and fits the face piece onto the burned face. He holds the mouthpiece tightly with both hands to ensure a good seal, because the thing doesn't work if the oxygen escapes. Boyle places one hand over the other on the boy's chest. And he pumps. Like a heart. Sixty times a minute. "He's as dead as a board," Boyle says.

"Yeah," Benny says, "but we have to try."

Engine 73 stretched a line to the floor above the fire. One room was lost, but they stopped the fire there. Now they have taken up their hose, and are on their way back to their Prospect Avenue firehouse. Ladder 31 and Ladder 48 are still here, pulling the ceilings and walls. Vinny has taken his mask off, and is waiting for the men of the truck companies to finish their work. One quick bath, a final wash down, and we'll take up.

Chief Solwin is supervising the operation, and Allen Siebeck asks him, between pulls on his hook, "What happened to that guy who was on fire, Chief?"

"The police put him in the car and rushed him to the hospital, but I understand he didn't make it. The doctor pronounced him DOA."

"How the hell did he get out?" Allen asks.

"The only thing I can figure is that he got out the fire-escape window, and went downstairs and through the hall, burning all the while."

Bill Finch, Chief Solwin's aide, enters the room. "What should I do with the gas cans, Chief?" he asks.

"Just leave them here. The fire marshals will be here shortly."

While Billy-o was searching the rooms, he found two gas cans, and Artie found a third in the hall. The one in the hall was still half full.

"That's somethin', isn't it?" Vinny says, making a facial gesture of disgust and dejection. "These kids were probably torching the place, and it lit up on them. I know it sounds lousy to say, but if it happened more often people would learn, and we wouldn't have so many torch jobs."

Lieutenant Welch joins us, and we begin to talk about the fire, as we do after each job. "Did you notice that the whole place was charred?" he asks, as he leads us to the front of the apartment. We look at the walls in all of the rooms, and they are bubbled and crisp. "You can see," he says, "that there was a great amount of intense heat here, but when we got here there were only three rooms going. The kids must have spread gasoline all over, and there was a flash fire. It probably burned through the whole place for a few moments, and then burned itself out, except, of course, in the front three rooms, where there was enough oxygen to keep the fire going. It's like lighting a candle in a mayonnaise jar, and then putting the top on; the candle will burn until the flame eats all the oxygen in the jar, and then it will go out."

Two fire marshals arrive and begin to question the Chief, Captain Frimes, and Lieutenant Welch. They are dressed in wide-lapeled jackets and colorful ties. If I were in a downtown bar I would figure them for detectives, because they wear their jackets opened and have tough but handsome faces. Their job is essentially that of a police detective, but they are responsible only for crimes connected with fires. They're firefighters just like us, but they would rather wear a gun at their side than have a nozzle in their hands. I was asked once if I would like to be a marshal, but I figured that I applied to be a firefighter because I wanted to fight fires. If I had wanted to investigate crimes I would have applied to be a policeman. The marshals take down the information they think necessary, and leave for the hospital. One of the teenagers is still living, and they want to see if he can answer some questions before he dies. They take the gas cans with them.

The truckmen are finished with their overhauling work, and Vinny gives the rooms a last spray. We drain the hose, repack it, and head back to the firehouse. It is near six o'clock now, and the brightness of the day begins to invade the South Bronx.

In the kitchen again. The men haven't bothered to wash up, and they sit before their steaming cups of coffee, with smoke- and mucus-stained faces. They are talking about the ironic justice of the fire, although they don't call it ironic justice but "tough shit." None of us want to see anyone killed, but there is a sad kind of "it's either you or me" irony here. We remember

[8]

all the obvious torch jobs we have been called into, all the vacant buildings, the linoleum placed over holes in the floor so the firefighters would fall to the floor below, the people killed in the rooms above a fire because the tenant below had a fight with his wife and set the place up, and the burns, cuts, and broken limbs we have suffered because of them. Any one of us could have been killed in that fire. But it was the arsonists who were killed this time.

Willy Knipps comes into the kitchen, and I remember Vinny Royce washing the vomit from my coat and boots. I had forgotten about it, but Vinny noticed it and put the nozzle on me, washing me clean. Ordinarily I would say something funny about this, something like, "Hey, Knipps, next time you go into a fire bring a bucket with you. Huh?" But I'm too tired.

It was four days later that Benny Carroll asked me, "Did you hear about the fire we had the other night, the one where the two kids were killed?"

"I was there, Benny, don't you remember?"

"I don't mean it that way, dummo, I mean about the investigation."

"No. Tell me about it."

"Well, the marshals were here last night, and told the story. It seems that the landlord wanted that apartment vacant, and he knew that the people wouldn't be there that night. So he hired some guy to torch the place. The guy then hires the three kids to light it up, and when they were in there spreading the gasoline the guy threw a match in and locked the door on them. They're looking for the guy now for a double murder. It looks like the kid Captain Frimes got out is gonna live."

Benny was going to continue with the story, but the bells came in. Now I am on the back step of the pumper, and thinking that it wasn't ironic justice at all. It's what always happens in the South Bronx. The real devil gets away without a burn, and the children of the South Bronx are the victims.

[9]

2

My name is Dennis Smith, and I'm a New York City fireman—one of New York's bravest. "New York's bravest," that's what the writers of newspaper editorials call us. There are almost eight million people in this city, and twelve thousand of us are firemen. We are different from the rest of the people who work in this town: bankers, ad-men, truck drivers, secretaries, sellers and buyers, all have a high degree of assurance that they will return home from work in the evening the same way they left in the morning—on their feet. A little tired perhaps, but on their feet. Firemen are never sure. When a fireman's wife kisses him as he leaves for work, she makes a conscious wish that he will return to her. She hopes that she will not have to make those fast, desperate arrangements for a baby-sitter so that she can visit him in the hospital, and each time the doorbell rings she hopes that there will not be a chief, a chaplain, and a union official there, all coming to say kind things about her husband, how good he was, how dedicated, how brave.

I'm part of Engine Company 82. The firehouse I work out of is on Intervale Avenue and 169th Street in a ghetto called the South Bronx. Of the three biggest ghettos in New York City, the South Bronx is the least talked about. You've heard of Harlem, Adam Clayton Powell came from Harlem; and you may have heard of Bedford-Stuyvesant, Shirley Chisholm comes from Bedford-Stuyvesant. Nobody you've ever heard of comes from the South Bronx.

Around the corner from the firehouse is the Forty-first Precinct House. It is the busiest police station in the city. There are more homicides per square mile in this precinct than anywhere in the United States, more drug traffic, more prostitution.

There are four companies working out of the firehouse on Intervale Avenue. Engine 82 and Engine 85 do the hose work in the district. Ladder Company 31 and Tactical Control Unit 712 do the rescue work, the ladder work, and the ax work.

Until recently my company and Engine 85 responded to many of the same alarms. Then, two years ago, we responded a record number of times. Engine 85 went out 8,386 times in a twelve month period. Ladder Company 31 went to 8,597 alarms, and my company, Engine 82, went to 9,111. The Fire Department saw that a change was needed, and arranged that engines 82 and 85 would not respond to the same alarms. The plan worked. Last year my company's responses dropped to 6,377, and Engine 85's to 5,012. But the plan worked only for the engine companies; Ladder Company 31's responses increased to 8,774. Another plan was then devised, and Tactical Control Unit 712 was created to respond only within the high incidence hours between three in the afternoon and one in the morning. The four companies on Intervale Avenue are now each averaging 700 runs a month. It is safe to say that ours is the busiest firehouse in the city—and probably the world.

An average of eight firemen die each year while doing their duty in New York City. Only six died last year, and I don't want to think about how many will die this year, or next. Almost five thousand firemen were injured in the line of duty last year. The injuries cost the city 65,000 days in medical leaves.

There is a sign in the kitchen of my firehouse. It is inconspicuously hung, and it reads with a proper amount of ambiguity: THIS COULD BE THE NIGHT! We don't talk about the hazards of the trade in the firehouse. There is no sense in talking about what we hope never becomes a reality for us, and for our families. It's all part of the job, and like committed Calvinists we accept what's written in the cards for us.

Just yesterday a man was killed. He was assigned to Rescue Company 1, and he was working on the roof of a burning warehouse. The roof had been weakened by the fire, and it gave in. The man fell through the roof and into an air shaft. He passed eight floors before he hit the bottom.

I was sitting in the kitchen of the firehouse when the bells came in. First five short rings, a pause, five more, a pause, another five, another pause, and the final five. Signal 5-5-5-5 has a special meaning to us. Put the flag at half mast, and listen to the department radio for the message.

There is a five-by-five cubicle at the front of the firehouse. Inside the small partition there is a man writing the signal in the department company journal. He turns the volume of the department radio up as we gather around it. This is the man assigned housewatch duty, and he knows what he has to do. After recording the signal, he moves to the outside of the firehouse and brings the colors to half-mast. He returns to the watch-desk and prepares to write the message in the company journal. His face is pensive, and he is asking himself the same question we all ask ourselves: I wonder if I know the guy?

The radio begins to squawk the message, and the housewatchman begins to write. *"The signal 5-5-5-5 has been transmitted, and the message is as follows: It is with deep regret that the department announces the death of Fireman 1st Grade Edward Tuite which occurred while operating at Box 583, at 1125 hours this date."*

None of us there knew the man personally, but we all felt the loss. We went about our work for the rest of the day without talking about it.

I had a friend we don't talk about either. His name was Mike Carr, and he was an upstanding kind of a guy. He was the union delegate of Engine 85. Only a few days before his death I had mentioned to him that we should clean out an old locker and use it for our union business. It was a shabby old locker, but it could be used to store medical forms, work contracts, information bulletins, and other union material. Mike thought it was a good idea, and within the hour he had the locker cleared and had begun painting it. Anything that had the smallest benefit for firemen would interest Mike, and he worked untiringly for the men in the firehouse.

Then a nine-year-old boy reached up and pulled the alarm-box handle. Kids do this a lot in the South Bronx. His friends giggled, and they all ran up the street to watch the fire engines come. The box came in on the bells—2787—Southern Boulevard and 172nd Street. Mike pulled himself up on the side step of the apparatus. The heavy wheels turned up Intervale Avenue, the officer's foot pressing hard on the siren. At Freeman Street the apparatus turned right, and Mike lost his grip. He spun from the side step like a top. Marty Hannon and Juan Moran jumped off the apparatus even before it came to a screeching stop. There was blood all over. They could see that Mike had stopped breathing. Marty cleared some of the blood away with a handkerchief, and began mouth-to-mouth resuscitation. He told me all he remembers of those agonizing minutes was the Battalion Chief's voice blaring over the Department radio: *"Transmit signal ten ninety-two for Box 2787. Malicious false alarm."*

The following day the city's newspapers ran the story stating that the Uniformed Firefighters Association was offering a thousand dollars reward for information leading to the arrest of the person who pulled the box. That afternoon a nine-year-old boy was led through the heavy iron doors of the Forty-first Precinct

[13]

House. News spreads quickly in the South Bronx, and the boy's friends told their parents, who called the cops.

While the boy was being questioned at the police station, people from the Hoe Avenue Association, a neighborhood action group, painted alarm box number 2787 black, and hung a sign around it. The sign was in two parts, the top half in Spanish, and the bottom in English. It read: A FIREMAN WAS KILLED WHILE COMING HERE TO A FALSE ALARM. Before the paint was dry another false alarm was pulled at the same box, and the men of Engine 85 took the sign down.

Mike had two sons, one seven, the other nine—two brave and frightened boys now walking on either side of their mother, walking slowly behind a shining red fire engine that moves between endless rows of their school chums, and hundreds of firemen. They look up at the flag-draped casket on top of the fire engine and feel proud that their daddy is the cause of all this ceremony, but they are also frightened because they are old enough to realize that there is a tomorrow, and it is going to be different without him.

The young boy in the police station is frightened too, but in a different way. He is confused, and wonders why everyone is so upset. All the kids pull false alarms. At least the kids he pals around with do. He came to this country from Puerto Rico five years ago, and the kids on the block taught him that you have to make your own fun in the South Bronx. You can play in the abandoned buildings, they told him, or on the towering trash heaps in the backyards, or in musty, rat-infested cellars. There used to be a boys' club in the neighborhood, but it burned down and never reopened. He learned, too, that pulling the handle of a fire-alarm box causes excitement, and a certain pleasure that comes with being responsible for all the noise, the sirens, the air horns. Why is everyone so upset?

I know why I am upset. My company alone, Engine 82, responded to over two thousand false alarms last year. Many of them were caused by kids like this. Kids with no place to go, nothing to do. Kids whose parents never talk to them, never have a surprise gift for them, or a warm squeeze. Kids whose real meaning in the family is that they symbolize a few extra dollars in the welfare check each month. Kids whose parents did not know anything about contraception to begin with, and never learned to love what they did not ask for. Kids born of poverty and ignorance into a system of deprivation.

What do you do with a nine-year-old boy who has pulled a false alarm that has resulted in a death? It is easy to say that the death was unfortunate, but peripheral to the crime of pulling a false alarm. It is even easier to say that the perpetrator is only nine years old, and so should be made aware of the severity of his actions merely by being given over to the social services for guidance care. This, in fact, is what happened to the child.

I do not advocate cutting off the child's hand, but I do think he should have been institutionalized for a year. I understand the sad social conditions in which this child has been forced to live, but I have lost sympathy for the cry that poverty founded the crime, not the boy. Anyone found guilty of pulling a malicious false alarm should be sent to jail for a year, or, if under sixteen, to a reform school. But, in the eight years I have been a fireman, I have seen only one man jailed, and I have responded to thousands of alarms that proved to be maliciously false.

In the city of New York last year, firemen responded to 72,060 false alarms—an average of 197 daily. Yet, the courts and the Police Department do not look on the pulling of a false alarm as a serious offense. Few are arrested, fewer are found guilty, and fewer still are punished.

Besides Mike Carr, I know of two other firemen who were killed en route to false alarms in New York City in the past eight years. But, it is not just firemen who are victimized by false alarms. Often while firemen are answering a false alarm at one end of their district, a serious fire breaks out at the other end. Time is the most important factor in fighting fires. I can remember many fires where, had we been there a minute or two sooner, we probably would have saved someone's life. Three hundred and seven people died in New York City fires last year. Statistics are not available, but you can be sure that some of those deaths could have been avoided if firemen had not been answering a false alarm minutes before.

Mike Carr is dead, and his widow will have to make it on just half the salary she was used to. It's strange, but had Mike come through the accident with a disabling injury, he would have been pensioned off with three-fourths of his salary. His wife would have been happy to have him alive. But he died, and she gets half his salary to support his family. The same will go to the widow of the man who fell through the roof yesterday.

We don't talk about Mike Carr in the firehouse. We think about him often, but we don't talk about him. Words of sentiment and emotion do not come easily.

The day following Mike's death the firehouse was busy with journalists and television news camera crews. Marty Hannon and Juan Moran were not working, and the television people decided to film an interview with Charlie McCartty, who is the biggest man in Ladder 31. And he is as tough a fireman as he is big. He is respected around the firehouse, not only because of his size and his ability as a fireman, but also because he is known to do the right thing—always. Never pretentious, McCartty is willing to stand up for anything or anyone when he thinks the cause is right.

Charlie applied the mechanical resuscitator to Mike Carr as the ambulance careened its way to the hospital. He stayed with Mike the whole time the doctors worked on him. He tried to make small talk with the members of Engine 85 at the hospital, to take their minds off Mike. He tried to console Nick Riso, who was punishing himself because he was driving the apparatus from which Mike fell. He said, "God Almighty, Nick, how many times did you turn that corner before when nothing ever happened? The Big Guy upstairs called the shots, that's all. You gotta look at it that way." But Nick just sobbed, with his face in his hands.

Charlie understood what was happening, and he had full control over his own feelings. Now, though, the television people wanted to film him, and I could see his lips moving in that uncontrollable way a person's lips do when he is nervous.

"You knew Mike Carr?" The television commentator pushed the microphone to Charlie's twitching lips.

"Yes, I knew him. I worked with him here for the past three years," Charlie said, looking directly at the ground.

"What did you think of him, and what do you think of what's happened?"

"He was a great guy," Charlie answered, still looking at the ground. "It's a shame this had to happen, and, and . . ." Charlie turned away, his shoulders shaking. He turned back, tears were running from his eyes, and said, "I'm sorry—I just can't do this," and the toughest guy in the firehouse walked away.

I am sitting now, along with eight other men, in the kitchen of the firehouse. It is a long, narrow room at the rear of the apparatus floor. The walls are tiled brown, and there are four tables set against the side wall, with room enough to seat twenty-eight men. A soda machine and a refrigerator are set against the opposite wall. A sink, a stove, and another refrigerator are at the front of the room, at the entrance.

Billy O'Mann is at the stove preparing the night's meal—tenderloin, boiled potatoes, and cabbage. A couple of men are playing cards, a few read magazines, and the rest are watching the television, which is sitting on a shelf in the corner.

Charlie McCartty has forgotten about the accident, the funeral, the news telecaster. It is almost time to eat, and he is yelling over the sound of the T.V.

"Yessir, men, Mrs. O'Mann is cooking Irish footballs tonight, and she requests that you clean off the tables."

Billy-o hears the remark, and approaches waving a long-pronged fork in his hand. "Listen, Charlie," he says, "I don't mind you calling me Mrs. O'Mann, just as long as you don't try to touch my body."

"He doesn't need you Billy-o," Jerry Herbert says, "because

[17]

he can get his own Mrs. McCartty for a deuce anytime he wants."

Everyone laughs. Charlie makes a motion as if he was pulling a spear from his chest. "Got me," he says. "But, a deuce is a lot of money. It doesn't cost that much, does it?"

"Well, it depends on whether you want coupons or not," Billy-o says.

"Ahh, got me again."

Charlie, Billy-o, and Jerry have worked together for the past seven years—in fires and above fires, where it is roughest. Each has saved the other's life at one time or another, and they can say anything about each other, or each other's family, with impunity.

The laughing over, the men in the kitchen begin to gather empty coffee cups and soda cans from the tables. One man goes to the sink to wash the cups and the pots Billy-o has finished with. Another sweeps the floor. It is ten minutes after nine, and we'll eat early.

There is a list of men on the kitchen blackboard. Twenty-four men are eating tonight, and the price of the meal is seventy-five cents. I go to the cabinet and count twenty-four plates.

As I arrange the plates on the table I think of how slow it has been since I began duty at six o'clock. We answered three alarms—a false alarm and two garbage fires burning in corner trash cans. The plates arranged, I go to count the silverware. I count off twenty-four forks, and begin counting knives when the bells start ringing. I count each gong: two—five—nine—six. Box 2596.

"That's right up the block," Jerry says. "Home and Simpson."

The housewatchman begins yelling, "Eighty-two and seven twelve, get out. Chief goes too." Men scramble out of the kitchen and run to the apparatus, passing others who are sliding down the brass poles. The Battalion Chief, who has an office on the top floor of the firehouse, watches as 712's truck and 82's pumper leave the house. He will respond behind us.

As we leave the firehouse we can see a large crowd of people standing in the middle of Home Street. We pass the intersection of Simpson Street, but that is as far as we are going to get. The sirens are screaming, but the crowd won't move. We get off the rigs and push our way through.

The attraction is a ten-year-old boy lying on the street. He is in great pain, but he is not crying. A handsome boy, with long, wavy, black hair. His face is tense, and he is biting his teeth together with all his energy. The cause of his pain is his leg, which is broken and lying under him like a contortionist's trick. He has been hit by a car.

The Chief sees what the conditions are, and uses his walkie-talkie to tell his aide to call for an ambulance and for the cops to control the crowd. Chief Niebrock has been around for a long time, almost thirty years, and nothing shakes him. He spent all his time as a fireman in Harlem, and as a fire officer in the South Bronx. He has seen it all, and if the whole block were burning he would act as he acts now—with cool and confidence. "Make the kid comfortable," he says, "but don't move him. And try to move this crowd back a bit." He is not talking to anyone in particular, but we all move to do as he says.

I take off my rubber coat, fold it, and place it under the boy's head. John Nixon, of Ladder 712, is feeling around his body for other injuries. The boy is really in pain, and I feel sorry for him, but I can't help thinking how lucky the boy is that he seems to have only a broken leg.

There is a lot of hysterical screaming and yelling. A woman is trying to get close to the boy, but she is being restrained by three men. She is a heavy woman, and the men are finding it difficult to hold her. They are screaming at her in Spanish. It is the boy's mother, and she wants to pick her son up. Luckily, the men understand that the boy should not be moved, and they carry her away.

Soon Spanish passion infects two other women who evidently know the boy, and they, too, are carried from the street by their neighbors. There are about three hundred people gathered now in the middle of Home Street. The boy seems confused by the crowd and the noise, but he still doesn't cry. I lean down close to him, and ask, "Does it hurt anywhere else?"

"No, just my leg," he replies in a mild Spanish accent.

"Just hold on, son. The ambulance will be here soon."

John Nixon covers him with a blanket, and starts to say those reassuring words kids need to hear. There is nothing to do now but wait for the ambulance, so I push my way through to the rim of the crowd.

I put a cigarette between my lips, and I'm about to ask Bill Valenzio, the chauffeur of our pumper, for a light when I hear an urgent cry: "Hey Dennis. Bill. Here, quick!"

It is our captain, Al Albergray, and he has his arm around a bleeding man. It is the driver of the car that hit the boy. His eye is closed, and blood drips from his lip. Captain Albergray has managed to get him away from a group of eight men who have beaten him. The leader of the group reminds me of a Hollywood stereotype of the Mexican bandito. His eyes are close together, and one is slightly turned. He has a wide, thick mustache on his dark face, and he wears a bandanna around his forehead. He stands squarely in front of the others, in a flowered wool jacket, yelling "Peeg, peeg," but I'm not sure at whom.

"These guys are looking to kill this man," Captain Albergray says. "Put him in the cab of the pumper, and sit in there with him. And call for police assistance." As Bill and I hustle the man into the pumper, I can see Captain Albergray trying to talk to the group of men, but they want nothing to do with him and walk away.

A police car arrives. Bill and I take the man from the pumper and put him in the back seat of the squad car. Captain Albergray tells the cops what has happened. The eight men have now been joined by others, and there is a crowd of hostile people surrounding the car. The cops put in a call for additional assistance.

The early winter cold is penetrating my sweatshirt, and I silently wish that the ambulance would get there so I could get my coat back. Many of the men around the car have cans of beer in their hands, and they are screaming for the man sitting in the back seat. Their words fly into the night in English and Spanish. I can understand only the English. "Give 'im to us, man, he needs a lesson, give 'im to us," they are saying.

Suddenly, the man in the flowered wool jacket jerks open the rear door and begins to swing wildly at the man in the back seat. The two cops struggle with him, and the crowd surges toward the car on all sides. Captain Albergray and I are pressed against the rear door on the other side of the car, and people are trying to push us away so they can get at him. But we stand firm. As long as the punches don't fly at us, it is a little like playing tug of war.

The man in the back seat is crying, but his tears come more from fear than pain. Just a few minutes before he was speeding happily through the streets of the South Bronx in a souped-up Chevy sedan, and now he sits in the back of a police car, looking out at a panorama of hating eyes. He came close to killing a boy who doesn't cry, and now he sobs because he is not sure if a few cops and firemen can hold off the crowd that wants to kill him.

It is not very long before two more squad cars arrive at the scene. The noise of their screaming sirens alarms the crowd, and they back off. The newly arrived cops clear a path between the people, and the beleaguered squad car backs out of the street carrying the sobbing driver to safety. The disappointed crowd returns to mill around the boy.

The ambulance finally appears. It has been thirty minutes since the Chief's aide called for it. The attendant pulls out a stretcher and hands it to Benny Carroll, one of the men in my company. John Nixon, two other firemen, and I carefully lift the boy as Benny shoves the stretcher beneath him. The boy cries out in agony as he feels his leg being moved. "It's all right, Joseph," John says. "In a little while it will be all over, and all the kids on the block will want to sign their names on the big white cast the doctor will fix you up with." The boy feels reassured, and he holds John's hand as we lift him into the ambulance.

Our job is done as we watch the ambulance carry little Joseph Mendez away. Captain Albergray will make an entry in the company journal: "*Assisted injured civilian, rendered first aid, 35 minutes.*"

Most of the people have re-entered the buildings now, and the street is near normal as we drive up toward Southern Boulevard. On the way back to the firehouse, Benny Carroll says to me, "A lady back there told me why they were trying to do that guy in. It seems that he's the neighborhood hot-rodder. Drives up and down the street like a maniac. They warned him a couple of times that they were going to break his ass if he didn't slow down, and tonight was his night."

"You can't blame them, I guess," I say.

"Hell no," Benny replies. "If that was my kid I'd make sure I had a piece of him, especially after he was warned and everything."

We have backed into the firehouse, and are taking off our rubber gear at the rear of the apparatus floor when the bells start. Box 2596, again, Home and Simpson streets. In ten seconds we are out the door.

I had forgotten about the souped-up Chevy, but I can see it now completely engulfed in flames. In his haste to leave the scene, the driver forgot about it, and the police who are now questioning him evidently figured it would be safe double-parked on Home Street.

There is no crowd now in the middle of the street, except for a small group involved in a crap game at the corner. The car burns, and few watch as we pull the hose off and extinguish the fire. All the windows are broken, and all the tires are flat.

It was a good-looking car, deep violet, and well cared for. All the chrome was removed, in hot-rod fashion, and the rear end set lower than the front. It was probably the most valuable thing the driver ever owned, and now it is destroyed. As we roll up the hose, I think about how much longer this will hurt him than the beating he took tonight.

As we turn the corner at Simpson Street, the men playing dice stop to watch us pass. The man with the close eyes and the flowered wool jacket is there, and he waves to us, and smiles, in that ironic way that means he knows more than we do.

It is now after 10:00 P.M. as we back again into the firehouse. The men of Engine 85 and Ladder 31 have already eaten the Irish footballs, and are now washing their dishes and cleaning up. Billy-o sees us coming and begins to cut the meat for us. McCartty already has a big pot on the table, and he is forking cabbage quarters onto each plate.

I have taken only one bite of tenderloin when the bells come in again: two—seven—three—seven. That's a lucky break for us. The housewatchman yells, "Get out, Engine 85 and Ladder 712. Chief goes too. Vyse Avenue and 172nd Street."

The Chief was sitting behind me, and he walks past with a paper napkin to his lips, saying, "It never fails, never fails." I once kept a running account of how many meals I could eat in the firehouse without interruption. It went for three and a half months, and in that time I never ate one uninterrupted meal.

I am eating now as fast as I can, but the bells come in. At least I have finished half—enough to satisfy me anyway. The housewatchman yells, "Two, Seven, Nine, Three, Boston and 169. Get out 82 and 31." Forty seconds later we are racing up 169th Street, past Stebbins Avenue, past Prospect Avenue, past Union Avenue. Benny Carroll leans to the side of the apparatus and looks up the street. He looks at us now—me and the other men working tonight: Vinny Royce, Ed Montaign, and Carmine Belli. We are huddled on the back step of the fire engine, gripping the crossbar. He says, "Looks like this is our night for accidents. There's a guy up there just knocked down the traffic signal."

The pumper stops in the middle of Boston Road, a broad, main thoroughfare in the Bronx. There was once a traffic stanchion standing in the middle of the road. It is now laying flat on the ground, partly covered by a new Continental. The car evidently climbed five feet up the pole before the pole came crashing down.

There are six people in the car. Four are unconscious, and one, a woman, is dazed, and muttering incoherently. The driver has the steering post through his chest and looks dead.

Herbert and McCartty come with Ladder 31's first-aid box. They begin unraveling bandages and applying them to head wounds. The two other women begin to come to, and one starts screaming, "Rufus, Rufus, Rufus." She is hysterical, and Herbert and O'Mann lift her out of the car and lay her on the ground. The conscious woman gets out of the car and sits down next to her. The third woman is moaning, and bleeding badly from the mouth. All her front teeth have been knocked out. I climb into the back seat and sit next to her. I put my arm around her, and her head falls onto my shoulder. I begin to clean her with a gauze sponge.

A lanky youth, about nineteen or twenty, leans in the car, with his hands on the floor. "What do you want?" I ask.

"It's okay," he replies. "I'm the man, man."

"Well you go be the man somewhere else," I tell him.

There is a crowd around the car, and people keep poking their heads in the rear. I keep telling them to keep back, until Carmine comes over and stands guard by the door.

Chief Niebrock responds from the other alarm—it was an MFA (malicious false alarm). He holds his portable lamp close to the driver. "Better take him out," he says to Ken Lierly, Ladder 31's lieutenant.

The man is obviously the worst off of the six, and the only way to give first aid is to remove him from the car. He is a heavy man, and it takes four firemen to lift him. He may be dead, but only a doctor can say that for sure, so Bill Finch, the

[24]

Chief's aide, applies the resuscitator to him. The other two men in the front seat have hit the windshield, and their foreheads are wide open. McCartty and Herbert have more room to work on them now.

Two police cars are at the scene, one from the Forty-first Precinct, and the other from the Forty-eighth. The boundary between the two precincts is Boston Road, and the car has crashed dead in the middle of it. There is some disagreement as to which car will take the accident. All those forms and reports that have to be filled out means one of the cars will be a loser, and the other a winner. They finally decide. The two men in the car from the Forty-first will take it, and the other car drives off.

After twenty-five minutes or so, two ambulances arrive. The men are quickly stretchered and driven away. The two seriously hurt women are put in the other ambulance. The third woman is walking around the car crying, "Has anybody seen my pocketbook? Please give it back. You can have the money. I need my keys and my cards. Please, oh God, please, PLEASE give me back my pocketbook!"

The crowd looks wonderingly at her, and the cops and the firemen search in, under, and around the car. A cop goes back to the ambulance, and returns saying that the other two women don't have their pocketbooks either. The crying woman falls to the ground amid broken glass and drying blood. "I am not leaving until I have my pocketbook!" she screams. Herbert and I gently lift her to her feet, and she becomes passive. We lead her to the ambulance, and sit her in the corner seat. The yearning cries, "Rufus, Rufus!" will occupy her mind until they reach the hospital.

We are about to return to the firehouse, but I ask Bill to drive past the squad car, where the two cops are recording the information in their logbooks. "Hey, Officer," I yell. "Which one was Rufus?"

"The driver," he replied.

[25]

Bill directs the pumper toward the firehouse, stopping for the red lights along the way. We are about to turn onto Intervale Avenue when the apparatus begins to go faster, and the siren begins to penetrate the air. The Captain has received an alarm over the department radio.

We turn down Hoe Avenue. There is a small crowd of about thirty people waving to us. Bill stops the pumper next to the crowd, and as we push through them Benny Carroll says, to no one in particular, "Looks like an O.D."

There is a boy, about fifteen years old, lying on the hood of a car. His eyes are closed and his arms spread out, like he was crucified on the '69 Oldsmobile. The car is white, and the boy's black face seems darker against the solid white background.

I get to him first, and as I check his arms, I can hear Captain Albergray asking "Does anybody know him?" There is no reply from the crowd. The boy's friends are probably there, but if they are, they are high, and know they can't get involved.

The boy's wrists and forearms are covered with holes, and round, purple scars. I raise his eyelids and see that his eyes haven't rolled back yet. They stare straight out as if belonging to a catatonic.

"Someone go get some ice for us!" Benny yells to the crowd. A man turns to a woman, talks to her in Spanish, and she runs into one of the tenements.

The boy is breathing, but his breath is dangerously slow. An overdose of heroin slows up the system until everything stops completely. We lift the boy up and begin to slap his face and shake him. He isn't conscious enough to walk around. If this boy lives it will be because his blood begins to circulate normally again.

The woman returns from her apartment with a small pot filled with ice. Benny takes it and thanks her. He puts a half dozen cubes into his handkerchief, and knots the top. "Pull his drawers down, Dennis," he says to me.

Ladder 31 and the Chief have pulled into the block now.

Billy-o comes over with a blanket, and he and Vinny Royce lift the boy up as I pull his dungarees and shorts to his knees. Carmine Belli has the blanket, and shoves it under him. Benny takes the ice pack and places it under the scrotum. He covers his arm and the boy's legs with the blanket ends.

The crowd looks on with interest. There is no yelling or pushing, only the fast syllables of conversational Spanish. A man once told me that he was told by an immigration officer in Puerto Rico to call the Fire Department if he ever needed emergency help in New York City. The people in the South Bronx know that when the corner alarm box is pulled the firemen always come. If you pick up a telephone receiver in this town you may, or may not, get a dial tone. If you get on a subway you may, or may not, get stuck in a tunnel for an hour. The wall socket in your apartment may, or may not, contain electricity. The city's air may, or may not, be killing you. The only real sure thing in this town is that the firemen come when you pull the handle on that red box.

Billy-o is rapidly squeezing the boy's cheeks. Bill Finch has the resuscitator turned to the inhalator position, and puts the face piece an inch from the boy's mouth. The boy finally begins to moan and move slightly. The crisis is over for him, at least until the next time he squats in a vacant building, wraps a belt around his arm, and puts a match under a bottle cap filled with white powder.

"Put in another call for an ambulance," Chief Niebrock says to Captain Albergray. It is now near 11:30 P.M., and I make a mental note to pick up a container of milk and a piece of cake on the way back to the firehouse. I have lost any hope of being satisfied with dried-out Irish football.

We have been here a half hour when the ambulance arrives. We are able now to walk the boy to the ambulance, although he still cannot support his own weight. The nurse in the ambulance looks at me and says, "What a night!" I know what she means.

Some nights our job has little to do with fire. Since the O.D. case on Hoe Avenue, we have responded to eleven alarms. One was a water leak—a guy's bathtub overflowed at four in the morning. Another was a fallen street wire, which required the emergency crew of Con Edison. And the other nine were false alarms—one each hour from midnight to eight.

It is a little after 8:00 A.M. now, and I am sitting in the kitchen having coffee and a roll. The men working the day tour begin to arrive, but I'm too tired to say much more than "Good morning." Instead of driving the sixty miles to where I live, I think that I'll take the subway to my mother's apartment in Manhattan. At least there I'll be able to get six solid hours of sleep in. I'll have to get up at four, because I'm due in again tonight at six.

3

I can hear a vague voice calling, "Dennis, Dennis." I don't want to get up, but I realize I have no choice. I was dreaming, but I can't remember what about. It must have been pleasant though, because I feel relaxed, relieved. "Dennis, Dennis," my mother calls. Her words sound apprehensive. They lack conviction, like she doesn't want to say them, but knows she has to. "Dennis, Dennis," the words soak through my body, and I make an effort to rise. Then the words suddenly change in my mind, and I am hearing "Rufus, Rufus," and I rest my head back again. I wonder what that woman is doing now. Before I left work this morning, I heard that Rufus was D.O.A. at the hospital, and now all I can think of is the yearning, pleading sound of his wife's voice.

"Dennis."

"All right, Mom. All right. I'm up."

"Do you want some bacon and eggs?"

I look at the clock on the kitchen wall. "No thanks, I don't have time." It is four-thirty. I like to be in the firehouse before five, but now I won't make it there until five-thirty.

"How about a cup of coffee, or tea?"

"Yes. Tea. Fine. Thanks." I get up from the living room couch, and look for my socks on the floor. I get on my knees and look under the couch. There they are. Now my pants. I left them on the chair, but I don't see them. "Hey Mom, did you see my pants?"

"I put them on a hanger. Somebody has to take care of your clothes. They're hanging in my closet."

O.K. Now where is my shirt? "Hey Mom, did you see what happened to my shirt?"

"It's here in the kitchen. I just pressed it."

I walk to the kitchen and kiss her cheek. "Thanks. It looks fine." I sit at the table and spoon sugar into my tea. My mother puts two pieces of toast in front of me and goes to the refrigerator for a jar of jelly.

"You know, Mom," I say, "you should have been named Goldberg. I'm surprised you don't give me some chicken soup."

"Well," she says, "I was born a Hogan, and I married a Smith, but a name doesn't make any difference to a mother. A mother is supposed to mother, and that means to take care of her children." She sits down opposite me. "And while I'm at it," she continues, "maybe I shouldn't mention this, but you really aren't getting enough rest lately. I don't know why you don't transfer out of that place you work in. You've been there over five years now, in that rotten neighborhood, with all those fires. Can't you get a job working in the Mayor's office or something?"

My mother thinks that having a city job should entitle me to have a say in its government, that the job should be a sinecure, and I'm not supposed to do any actual work. Many people in New York, like my mother, remember the old Democratic clubs, and the dying days of Tammany Hall patronage, but they never realized that the system died.

"Listen Mom," I say as forcefully as possible, "there are a lot of hard-working people in that rotten neighborhood, but because they are black, or because they speak Spanish, they can't live in midtown Manhattan, even in a tenement like this. Even the people who could work, but don't, are entitled to city services. That's what I do. I provide a service—an emergency service. And that's what I like to do for a living. When the day comes that I'm not happy doing what I do, then I'll transfer, but until then I don't want to talk about it."

"Yeah, I guess you're right. I guess you know best, but I still think you're crazy to work there when you could go downtown and work in a nice clean office."

"Thanks for the tea, Mom. I'll call you in a few days." I learned a long time ago that one explanation a day, regarding anything, is enough. If I had to explain everything I did, I'd never get a chance to do anything.

I'm on the Lexington Avenue subway, on the way to the Bronx. The seats are filled with Saturday shoppers returning from a day downtown, and there are a few people standing. Sitting across from me is a dark-haired Puerto Rican girl, about twenty-five years old. I don't want to stare at her, but the smoothness of her olive skin, the perfect symmetry of her lips, and the brightness of her dark brown eyes have attracted me beyond control. Her synthetic fur car coat is opened, showing a soft blue pleated skirt, which sits above the middle of her thigh. Tucked tightly into her skirt is a white nylon blouse, her full rounded breasts pushing against it. The muscles in her legs slope gently, and the underside of her thighs sit flat on the hard plastic seat. Her whole body moves in small, graceful motions as the train starts and stops at the stations.

Thank God that she has not been victimized by the Seventh Avenue mid-calf skirt. But even if she were, if her legs were completely covered, if I couldn't see the shadowed triangle where her skirt falls over her thighs, if the nuances of movement were hidden beneath the modern style as she crosses and uncrosses her legs, even then, I would still have her face to look at.

She is made uneasy by my staring, and pretends to read the advertisements plastered all over the car. She is probably wishing she had a book, a newspaper, or anything to focus her eyes on. I've taken possession of her beautiful face, and if I had pencil and paper I could sketch her perfectly, even though I know nothing about drawing. Her eyes meet mine occasionally, but she turns quickly away, making a little movement with her lips. I can see as she turns, the soft, almost invisible down at the side of her cheek reflected in the light. How I would like to run the back of my fingers over it in an easy up and down way.

I am trying to look at her now in a different way. She is a human being, I say to myself, with friends, perhaps a husband she loves dearly, children, a life-pattern with ordinary or even extraordinary ambitions, jubilations, and miseries. She probably knows a lot about something, and enough about everything, to make her interesting in ways other than sexual. The train stops, and a man sitting next to her gets off. Maybe I should sit next to her now. The train begins with a jolt, and she has to uncross her leg to regain her balance. She settles in the rhythm again, and recrosses it, generating in my body a return to passionate perception. Stop it. Stop it. Go sit next to her and say, "Hello, my name is Dennis, and I've been trying not to look at you in a dehumanizing symbolic way, but as a real person, with feelings and intelligence, opinions and a point of view. I don't care about the tightly tucked blouse, or the shadowed triangle. I want to know what you think, and why you think it. Do you think Spiro Agnew will be President? Will cybernetics ruin us? How are you handling future-shock? Are you a Consciousness III person?"

The train stops again, and I look out of the window. Simpson Street. Freeman Street will be here next, and I'll have to get off. The train starts and I try to think of something else to say to her, but I can't. I wonder what kind of a night we'll have. A Saturday night in the South Bronx is always hectic, and there is no reason to think this will be any different. I get up without taking a "good-bye-I-loved-you" glance, and stand with my back to her by the train door. The doors spring open, and I step into the cold of the Freeman Street Station. I don't look back. It never makes any sense to look back, especially on the Lexington Avenue express.

It's five-thirty as I walk toward the firehouse on Intervale Avenue. In the summer time Intervale Avenue is a concrete swamp. The constant running of open hydrants makes the street dank, and muddy. But now it's just dirty. I can hear the choir practicing as I pass Mother Wall's Baptist Church, and the high, quick sounds of the gospel music remind me in a curious way of a siren.

The firehouse is empty. As I walk up the stairs to the locker room I hear the sirens and the air horns coming down 169th Street. They pass the firehouse, and the sounds fade. They are coming from one alarm and going to another. I change clothes. There is blood on the sweatshirt I wore last night, so I fumble through my laundry bag for a clean one. Even with three small boys to care for, my wife always makes certain to have a clean change of clothes in my laundry bag. On the left side of the sweatshirt there is a six-inch maltese cross. In the circle of the cross, in bold letters, it reads: "ENGINE 82"—a mark of identification in one way, and a boast in another.

It is 5:45 P.M. now, and Ladder 31 and Engine 82 are backing into quarters. Engine 85 is still out somewhere, along with Ladder 712 and the Chief. I see Ed Kells and ask him how the day went. He says, "Same old crap—about ten runs, most of them rubbish. Engine 85 caught a good 'all hands' this morning on Hoe Avenue." (An "all hands" is a serious fire, but not serious enough to call for a second alarm.) "Don Butts got a kid out," Ed continued, "and they're gonna write him up."

"Lot of fire?" I ask.

"Yeah, a frame building fully involved. Don got the kid out a rear window with a portable ladder. It was a great job."

"How's the kid?"

"He's in the hospital with second degree burns, but he's O.K."

The boy really isn't O.K. What Ed means is that he will live. The Fire Department does not like to give medals for saving people who die, and since the boy is still living Don Butts has a better chance of getting a medal.

I go to the company journal to check that my name has been entered by the housewatchman. It has, and I'm officially on duty. I go to the rack on the side of the apparatus floor and get my rubber coat, my boots, and my helmet. I make sure I have a pair of gloves and a flashlight in my coat pocket. I put my gear on the pumper and go to the kitchen for a cup of coffee. Jerry Herbert is sitting in the corner. I'm ready for one of his inevitable wisecracks. He spots me and says, "I see you finally took that sweatshirt home for an oil change."

"No Jerry," I return, "I took it out to your house and your old lady did it for a dime. If you gave her some money once in a while she wouldn't have to work on the side."

"Ahhh, so that's what kind of a night it's gonna be," Jerry says to the eight guys sitting around the kitchen. "Dennis must have ate a tough pill, and thinks he can hit flies with the big guys. Well, lemme tell ya pal," he says, directing the words to me now, "you better go upstairs and eat about ten more of those pills 'cause I'm gonna eat you up." He emphasizes the "up," and everybody laughs. I know now that the joke is over so I pinch him on the cheek and say, "What we need around here, Jerry, is more love." He makes a dirty gesture, everybody laughs again, and he continues the conversation that was going on before I entered.

Jerry is the oldest member of Ladder 31. He is thirty-eight, the chauffeur of the truck, and the senior man. He is called the "first whip," a term which has survived from the days when horses pulled the fire engines. He is also the union delegate of Ladder 31, and he is talking now about a cousin of his who is a waiter in a fancy restaurant in Manhattan.

He says, "I'm tellin' ya, the guy makes at least three grand more than me each year. I know. My other cousin does our taxes. The people of New York are willin' to pay a guy who does nothin' but bring them food a damn good salary—20 percent tips on everything. But, do they support the firemen when we demand a livin' wage? Damn right they . . . "

The bells start coming in. Everybody stops what they are doing. I stop putting sugar in my coffee. Jerry stops talking. Two bells. Seven. Four. Then three. We know that box well—2743—Charlotte Street and 170th. We go to that intersection more often than any other. It is usually a false alarm, but there is no such thing as "crying wolf" in this business.

As we hustle toward the kitchen door, the housewatchman yells out, "82 and 31 goes." I kick my shoes off by the pumper and shove my feet into my rubber boots. Jim Stack slides the pole from the second floor. He is the senior man in Engine 82 —the first whip—and I always feel good when I work with him. He's thirty-nine, and in great shape because he loads soda trucks on the side. Like most of us, he has a wife and a few kids, and a house in the suburbs. If he didn't work that extra job he would be still living in the Bronx. He is the most experienced engine man in the house, and when he is with me on the nozzle I could fight my way into the core of the earth.

As I put on my rubber coat I see Vinny Royce standing next to me on the back step of the pumper. He is a quiet, sincere guy, and the Fire Department is his whole life. He used to work in Harlem, but he transferred to Engine 82 when we became the busiest company in the city. There is enough action in Harlem to keep any fireman running, but Vinny wanted that little extra that made him part of the busiest.

The pumper starts to roll out and I lean down to help Carmine Belli up to the back step. Carmine is an exercise buff. He runs three to five miles each day. He's also an excellent folk

[35]

guitarist. Like Royce, he doesn't say much, but he is quick to laugh at the jokes that fly so often through the firehouse air.

As we roll up Intervale Avenue, I see Benny Carroll riding on the side step of the pumper. Along with Carmine and me, this is his second night of duty. He looks a little tired—like he didn't get any rest today. He is studying hard for the coming lieutenant's test, maybe four or five hours a day. Hundreds of facts about building laws, chemical formulas, personnel management, fire intensity, and department regulations were floating through his head as I slept calmly on my mother's couch. He is a handsome guy with perfect white teeth, and when he smiles I always think of a toothpaste commercial.

We are now going up Wilkens Avenue. I remember going up this street one night recently. I was riding on the side step where Benny is now. A kid threw a rock, and everything turned black. I was hit in the middle of the eye, and my knees buckled. My grip on the handrail tightened, as it tightens now. Some little kid who was never taught any better threw a rock, and I remember now how lucky I was to have had a grip on the handrail.

The pumper turns up 170th Street. Ladder 31 is right behind us, and the sirens and air horns are wailing. Few people even turn to watch us go by. Screaming fire engines and police cars are part of life in the South Bronx, just sounds to which people have adjusted.

There are three men sitting on milk boxes near the alarm box drinking from cans of beer wrapped in small brown paper bags. Jim Stack and I walk up either side of Charlotte Street looking for smoke or waving people. We have done this a thousand other times, and it seems now to be a dumb ritual.

The three men are disinterested, and talk among themselves. Captain Albergray looks around and goes to rewind the alarm box. I walk over and ask the men if they saw anyone pull the box. One man, without looking at me, said, "Yeah, a kid. He went up the street."

"I guess you didn't think of grabbing him," I said.

"That's not my job, man," he said.

I would like to tell this guy about Mike Carr, and about the letter the President sent to his widow. But I know that he doesn't care. He doesn't want to hear it.

Bill Valenzio yells from the driver's seat of the pumper, "Hey, we got another run."

The siren and air horn begin to wail again as the pumper turns down 170th Street. I can see the radio at Captain Albergray's ear. We don't know where we are going, but we know that a box has been pulled somewhere.

The pumper turns up Freeman Street and we can see a lot of smoke on Stebbins Avenue. It is an abandoned Pontiac convertible, about a year old. The flames are shooting ten feet above the car. We don't have to hook up to a water hydrant because the pumper has a 275-gallon water tank for small fires like this. I pull off the small, one-inch booster hose that is already connected to the tank. The water spurts and I direct the stream behind the rear wheel. The gas tank must be cooled off to keep it from blowing. I've only seen one gas tank blow since I have been a fireman, and that one sent a guy to the hospital. As I extinguish the rest of the fire, the men of Ladder 31 open the doors, the hood, and the trunk. The trunk is empty. The block and the radiator are all that is left under the hood. The car is sitting on wooden crates, the tires and rims gone. There are no license plates. The guy who owned it will never find out what happened to it. It must have given someone a few hours of joy riding, and whoever got the tires must be twenty dollars richer. We extinguish four or five of these fires every day.

It is 6:30 P.M. as the pumper backs into quarters. As I walk to the kitchen to attempt another cup of coffee, Bill Valenzio pulls a hose to refill the booster tank. It means a lot of extra work for us if that tank is empty. I remember the times we had to stretch six or more 50-foot lengths of hose to put out a simple car fire, or a garbage fire. When the fire was extin-

[37]

guished the hose had to be uncoupled, each length drained, and then reloaded onto the pumper. You can see why Bill makes sure the tank is full at all times.

In the kitchen, Billy-o and Jerry are making a shopping list for tonight's meal. One of the younger guys, or "johnnies," will go to the store.

"What's on the menu, Billy-o?" I ask.

"Dennis pal," he replies, "everything will be just the way you like it." This is a phrase Billy-o uses often. He continues, "To begin with, a little tomato juice for an appetizer, breaded pork chops topped with a baked peach for the entree, and Jerry is gonna make his great potatoes with sour cream sauce. And for dessert," he adds with a twinkle in his eye, "the cabinet is filled with Alka-Seltzer."

I laugh and ask, "What about the vegetable?"

"Me and Jerry were just thinking about that. Any suggestions?"

"Asparagus with wine vinegar."

Billy-o smiles his usual half-smile, and says, "Dennis pal, that's an excellent suggestion." He turns to Herbert, and says, "Make it string beans, Jerry."

"I knew I could help you, Billy-o," I say.

There are eighteen firemen in the kitchen now. Engine 85 and Ladder 712 have returned from the fire they were working. It was a small job, two rooms in a vacant building. A few men are playing gin at the corner table. Four guys from Engine 85 have started a Scrabble game at the next one. Matt Tunney carefully makes the first word: "ANUS." The other players laugh. I look down at his rack and ask him why he didn't use the other A to pick up an extra point. He says, "You mean sauna. I thought of that, but nobody would've laughed."

The bells start sounding again—Box 2508—Hoe Avenue and Aldus Street. Engine 85 and Ladder 712 are assigned there. I sip my coffee easily as I watch the men hustle through the kitchen door. The room is quiet now, and I can understand

[38]

what the news reporter is saying on the TV. The phone rings. It's an alarm for Ladder 31. Three more guys run to the kitchen door. Jim, Vinny, and I watch the news.

One hundred and twenty people have been arrested at an anti-war rally. Jim says, "You know, the way I figure it, it's just that times have changed. I would have been madder than hell if they had protested the Korean War the way they do this one. And we were fightin' for the same thing. Right? Most of these protesters are in college just to keep out of the Army, anyway. And they talk about democracy and equality. If they took away the college deferment, and made the draft equal, then they would have a reason to protest. But you never hear them yelling about that."

The department telephone rings—three distinct rings in quick succession. We know from the signal that it won't be a false alarm. Someone has called the department, and they are relaying the information. Vinny chalks on the blackboard: "1284 Fox, apt. 30." The pumper is in the street in less than thirty seconds. It is only two blocks up Intervale Avenue to the address, and on the way I suddenly remember hearing that Jim has a Bronze Star and a Purple Heart, but I never heard him mention either of them.

We can smell burning wood and plaster in the air. We all know that Ladder 31 and Ladder 712 are at other alarms, and it will take a few minutes for another ladder company to get here.

As we turn the corner we see smoke coming from two windows on the third floor. Vinny says, "I'll take the ax and a claw tool," then yells to Benny, "Take the hook and water can." Benny nods as he puts on his gloves. Luckily, the fire is only on the third floor. Jim, Carmine, and I can handle the hose work while Benny and Vinny do what a ladder company is supposed to.

The pumper stops in front of the building. Captain Albergray yells out, "Five lengths, inch-and-a-half," and then runs into the building. Benny and Vinny follow right behind. Jim

[39]

takes the nozzle in his left hand, and puts his right hand through three folds of inch-and-a-half hose, one fifty-foot length. I take a length as Jim steps down, and Carmine takes another length. Carmine lays his folds on the ground, and pulls off two more lengths of hose. Jim yells to Bill, "Take off," and the pumper moves to the hydrant, the coupled hose dropping off behind it.

The stairs are crowded with excited people. We tell them to watch the hose as they go down. We reach the third floor with two lengths to spare. Carmine flakes it out down a long hall. We pull our boots up to our thighs. Captain Albergray comes out of the apartment, and the smoke billows out with him. "We met the lady who lives here on the way up," he says. "She had two kids with her and said the place was empty. Benny and Vinny are in there searchin' anyhow."

Vinny comes out with mucus running from his nose. He wipes it off with his glove, and says, "Listen Jim, the fire is at the end of a long hall. Make a left at the end, and it's the first two rooms."

We are all bending low now because the smoke is starting to bank down. Benny comes out of the apartment on all fours. He asks, "Did a truck company get here yet?"

"No," Captain Albergray says. "You better go up and get the roof." As Benny leaves to ventilate the smoke and heat at the top of the building we can hear the water running through the hose.

The fire has already broken the glass in the front two rooms. The heat will be able to escape, but Captain Albergray tells Carmine to get a mask, just in case. We have to put the fire out fast, before it extends to the floor above. We are on our hands and knees as we hump the hose forward. We keep our heads as close to the floor as possible. It is sooty as hell, and the smoke has filled the hall. It's tough pushing in, but we get to the end of the hall and see the vague red glow to the left. The heat hits us full for the first time.

Captain Albergray's walkie-talkie is blaring. The Chief has

ordered Engine 94 to stretch a second line to the floor above, but they won't need it. We're in now. The smoke is lifting and we are sitting on our heels. Jim keeps the nozzle moving in a circular motion. The water is bouncing off the ceilings and walls, and hits us in the face as steam. Every ten seconds Jim yells, "Gimme three more feet," and we hump the hose in.

Ladder 31 is here now, and Allen Siebeck is in the room pulling at the ceiling with a six-foot hook. "Where the hell ya been, Allen?" I yell to him.

"We stopped for dinner at Delmonico's, you dumb ass. Where else would we go?" Allen would normally have a lot more to say, but it's his job to check for fire extension, and he ignores me.

"Just a few more feet and we got it," Jim yells.

"Beautiful, beautiful," Captain Albergray keeps saying.

Benny is back now, and he helps me with the hose. Jim makes the far room.

The fire is out now and Chief Niebrock is checking for extension, but the fire never got beyond these two rooms. Jim and I go over to a window. The air tastes good. I look at Jim and at the mucus running over his mouth. He takes his glove off and blows his nose into his hand. He coughs up a large glob of stuff from his diaphragm and spits it on the wall. It hits solidly—black with occasional veins of gray.

Ladder 31 and Ladder 19 start tearing the walls and ceilings down. Everything in both rooms is burnt—a bedroom set, a couch, a couple of stuffed chairs, a television console. A cop leads a woman into the room. She looks around and screams hysterically. She didn't have much, and now she has nothing. She collapses, and Benny helps the cop carry her into a neighbor's apartment.

Before leaving, we give the rooms a heavy bath. Our underclothes are sticking to us, and the brisk breeze sweeping through the ventilated apartment chills us. I think of those men on Charlotte Street, and wonder how people can drink beer on street corners in weather like this.

The kitchen clock reads eight o'clock as I put fifteen cents in the soda machine. Matt Tunney looks up and says, "They took Nick Riso to the hospital."

"What happened?" Vinny Royce asks.

"We were coming back from Hoe and Aldus and some guy threw a brick and hit Nick in the chest. Not a half brick. A full fuckin' brick. The pumper was going about twenty-five miles an hour, and if it would've hit him in the face, it would've killed him."

"Is he hurt bad?" I ask.

"Well, they're lettin' him outta the hospital, so it can't be too bad."

Matt looks up, and a smile appears on his face. Riso is standing at the door.

"How ya feel?" ask Matt and Vinny at the same time.

"A little weak," Nick answers. "A lot of blood vessels in my chest are broke." He opens his shirt and shows us the redness on his chest. "If I didn't have my rubber coat on, the impact would have knocked me right off the pumper. It absorbed the impact, ya know. The Doctor says I need a lotta rest."

The bells start sounding again—Box 2402—and the guys of Engine 85 and Ladder 712 hustle out of the door. Nick goes upstairs to change clothes. He'll be on sick leave for a few weeks. We call it "R & R (Rest and Recuperation)."

I follow Nick up the stairs. In my locker somewhere there is an old battered book of Yeats's poems. I search through the pile of dirty laundry, the paperback mysteries, the worn copies of *Playboy* and the *Saturday Review*. Ahh, there it is. The red cover is coming apart, and some pages have loosened, but it's still complete. I remember reading a poem where Yeats talked about wise men becoming tense with a kind of violence before they can accomplish fate, and I finger the pages looking for it. It is this kind of violence I am feeling now, as Nick Riso slowly changes his clothes across from me. What can be done with people who throw bricks at the very men who are most com-

[42]

mitted to protecting the lives of the brick throwers? I feel empty and helpless, because I know that nothing can be done. And I feel violent, because I know that this insanity will continue until the brick throwers are educated, until they find decent jobs, and until they have better places to live in.

I come to "Under Ben Bulben," and start to read, but three short rings of the telephone interrupt me. A voice from downstairs yells, "82 and 31, get out." Benny Carroll closes a fire protection manual, and runs to the pole hole. Nick says, "So long, guys," as I wrap my arms and legs around the top of the long brass pole.

As I slide the pole the bells come in—Box 4746—Prospect Avenue and Crotona Park East. It's a job. The telephone alarm and the location give me a feeling that we'll have a worker. It's like a sixth sense.

It is 8:20 P.M. As we turn up Prospect Avenue we can smell the smoke. There is only one smell like this: burning paint, plaster, and wood. We can see the smoke banking down on the avenue before us, but we can't see the fire yet. Ladder 31 is right behind us, so we know we will get the ventilation we need.

As we turn the corner at Crotona Park we can see the fire. Flames are licking out of eight windows on the third and fourth floors of a six-story tenement. There must have been a delayed alarm, and I imagine people alerting other people—alerting everyone but the Fire Department. There is a crowd of people on the sidewalk. Some are in nightclothes. Some are barefoot. Many are simply interested passersby. People are still rushing out of the building, crying, sobbing, or just sullen.

We have to take the heavy two-and-a-half-inch hose for a body of fire like this. Jim Stack takes the nozzle again, and the first length, I take the second, and Carroll the third. Vinny and Carmine head for the mask compartment. *"Take off!"*

People are screaming that there are people trapped on the fifth floor. They are angry and confused because we are not paying any attention to them. They haven't seen Ladder 31 go into the building. But we know if there is a rescue to be made, Ladder 31 will make it.

As we start to hump the hose into the building I notice that Jerry Herbert has already raised the aerial ladder to a fifth-floor window. Richie Rittman and Billy-o are climbing up it.

The lights in the building have blown, and Captain Albergray guides us up the stairs with his portable lamp. He tells us that Chief Niebrock has ordered a second alarm. We'll need the extra help.

We reach the second floor and flake out the hose. We go to the top of the stairs at the third-floor landing. The whole front half of the building is on fire. The flames are in the hallway and shooting up the stairs to the fourth floor.

We have to wait now for the water to come through the hose. It's getting hotter, and Captain Albergray tells us to back halfway down the stairs.

Jim turns to me and Benny, and says, "When we get water we'll hit the hallway and then make a left into the first apartment. It's going to be a hard bend, so keep the hose low. I don't know how far we'll be able to go, but we'll try."

Captain Albergray says, "All right Jim, but don't push too fast. The goddam fire must be through the roof by now, so we'll be here for hours anyway."

We can hear the water gushing through the line. As it reaches the nozzle, Jim says, "Let's go," and he moves up the stairs with us humping the hose behind. I can see Engine 45 moving up the stairs below us with another line. I tell them to move in on the second apartment as soon as they get water, but my words are unnecessary. They'll be there.

It is starting to get smoky now that the water is on the fire. The fire in the hallway goes out quickly. We are putting 250 gallons of water per minute on it. Jim makes the landing, and fights with the hose as he makes the bend. Captain Albergray is next to him. "Beautiful. Easy now. Keep low. Beautiful," he is saying. Carroll and I are behind pulling on the hose to take the strain off Jim's arms. The heat in the walls is radiating out, and my body is dripping and my clothes are saturated with perspiration.

I put my mouth to the floor in an attempt to breathe cool air, and suddenly my throat hurts, like it does after a two-day drunk and a thousand cigarettes. I must have taken in some super-heated air. I forgot about the second apartment. The fire lapping out of it has lit up the hallway again.

"Hey Jim," I shout, "you better turn the line, or else we're going to get caught between it."

Jim struggles to turn the line again, and he hits the fire in the hall. He moves a foot or so into the apartment.

Captain Albergray says, coolly, "The ceiling is down, Jim, and the floor upstairs is beginning to go. Watch it, 'cause it'll come down in pieces."

"Well, let's try to move in just a little more," says Jim. "Then maybe I can hit that room on the left." We push the line in a few feet, and Jim yells, "Ahh, ahh, your mother's ass. . . ." Part of the floor above has given way.

Jim is on his knees, and he wants desperately to get out of the apartment, but he knows better than to shut the nozzle down in a fire like this. The water is our only protection. So I crawl up fast, and take the nozzle from Jim. Vinny and Carmine are down on the floor now. Their masks will make it easier to fight this fire. Vinny takes the nozzle, and I back downstairs to get a mask. Jim is already in the street breathing the clear air heavily. He has multiple burns on the ears, neck, and shoulders. I put my arm around his waist, and say, "You did a beautiful job Jim—like always."

Jim attempts a weak smile, and replies, "It couldn't have been too beautiful, the fire's not out yet, is it?" I laugh a little, and run to the pumper for the masks. I pass a leaking hose connection, and bend low for a drink of water, but I can't swallow. I spit the water out. Valenzio has taken out two masks for me. I put mine on, and throw the other over my shoulder for Captain Albergray.

The second alarm companies are in now. Hose lines—spaghetti—are all over the street, up the adjoining building, up the fire escapes, up the aerial ladder. Some are bulging with water, and some haven't yet been charged.

As I return to my company I pass Carroll on the stairs. "What's up, Benny?" I ask.

"I got a goddam cinder down my glove. The back of my hand is all blistered, so I'll have to take up for a while." He sounds defeated.

"Take care of yourself," I murmur as I continue up the stairs. I feel sorry for Benny, because I know he wouldn't leave the action for a burned hand, not unless Captain Albergray ordered him down.

I meet the company on the third-floor landing. They were pushed back. Captain Albergray backs down the stairs a little to put his mask on. Carmine is on the nozzle now, and I ask him how they were pushed out of the apartment. He tells me that Engine 45 had water pressure trouble, and they had to shut down their line. The fire then got into the hall again, and my company was caught between the two fires. A fundamental rule in this business is never to let the fire get behind you, so 82 had to fight their way back to the hall stairs.

I take the nozzle, and tell Carmine to "take a blow." The nob is heavy, and the back pressure makes my arms strain. I know I won't lose control of it though, because Vinny has a firm grip on the hose behind me. We are now keeping the fire inside the two apartments. At least it hasn't crossed the hall.

Engine 45 gets pressure in its line again, and returns to the landing. The fire is now spreading throughout both floors above us.

We yell to Engine 45 to take the second apartment again, and Engine 73 passes us as it humps its hose to the fourth floor. It is still ash hot, but the masks make it a lot easier to

[46]

breathe. We are now at the door of the first apartment, and Engine 45 is at the second. We move in a little, and 45 moves in. Captain Albergray is next to me, and I say, "The only way to put this fire out is to move in on it. Otherwise, we'll be here all night."

"We're gonna be here all night anyway, so take it slow," he answers.

Vinny moves up and takes the nozzle, and Carmine moves behind Vinny. Deputy Chief Kelsen is on the scene now. He calls the Captain on the walkie-talkie and Albergray tells him our position and progress. Chief Kelsen tells him to hold the position, and not to take any unnecessary risks. We have advanced five feet into the apartment. The fire is burning freely overhead in front of us, and we watch it closely, as closely as anyone would want to watch a fire. We have killed a good part of it in the room on the left, but we can't get it all unless we move up a few feet. But we can't move up because of the fire overhead. We don't want to get directly underneath it. God knows what will fall.

Suddenly, the fire starts pushing in at us. It's coming hard, and our line can't hold it back. We know what it is. A company has opened a line from the front fire escape, and they are pushing the fire toward us. We have to retreat to the hall again. Captain Albergray calls the Chief on the walkie-talkie, and asks him to have that line shut down. In a minute the order is given, and the fire lets up. We can move in once more.

Carmine takes the nozzle from Vinny, and I move behind Carmine. We know now that we'll have to drown this fire, not attack it, and we try to get in the most comfortable position possible. Carmine sits on his heels, and I kneel on both knees.

We start to get sprayed with rebounding water. Engine 73 is above us, and trying to move in. Carmine leans over, puts one hand on top of his helmet, and starts shaking his head. He doesn't say anything, but his head still shakes.

"What's wrong, Carmine?" I ask.

"I think I got burned."

"Where?"

"On the neck."

I ask Captain Albergray for his lamp. Carmine is still moving the nozzle back and forth. I move his helmet up, and pull back his coat. "You did get burned, Carmine. It's all blistered already, about three inches long. It must have been an ember."

Carmine moves out, and Vinny takes the nob. I try to think of something funny to say to Captain Albergray. I can tell that he doesn't feel too happy. "Your company is slowly diminishing, Cap," I say. "Pretty soon there won't be any more Engine 82."

He smiles resignedly, and says, "It's just one of those things. Look at the great job we did earlier. No one got hurt there. This is just one of those fires. They happen from time to time, that's all."

The fire has darkened down. Chief Kelsen calls on the walkie-talkie: "Engine 82, I'm sending Engine 88 to relieve you. Report to me in front of the fire building."

We don't mind giving the line to Engine 88, because it's only a question of holding the position now, and keeping water on the fire. We did our job. The pressure is off and we walk down the stairs to a well-needed break.

Vinny Royce, Captain Albergray, and I report to the Chief. He is a big man, handsome in that disciplined military way. His eyes are bright and alert, and as I look at them I can sense intelligence and concern. "You did a good job in there, Cap," he says to Albergray. "Take your men now and rest for a while." He looks at Vinny and me, "Nice job, 82."

We walk to the pumper where Benny, Jim, and Carmine are sitting, waiting for an ambulance to take them to the hospital. I am about to ask them how they feel, but Benny speaks first. "Did you hear about Richie Rittman?"

"What?" Vinny asks.

"He broke his ankle—at least they think it's broke, but he made a good rescue. He got two kids and their mother out

[48]

from up above. They were huddled in a bathroom. And as he was carrying a kid down the aerial he missed the last rung and went over on his foot. They took him to Bronx Hospital, so I guess we'll see him there."

I go to get a drink of water from a kind of spigot Bill has set up at the hydrant. My mouth is very dry, but that happens after every fire. As I swallow the water, a strange feeling makes me bend over and spit out what is left in my mouth. It feels like the water has been pressed through a pinhole. The throat passage isn't working right, and I tell Captain Albergray that I can't swallow normally. He sends me to the Chief.

The Chief takes my name and tells me to wait with the others for the ambulance. Besides the guys from Engine 82 there is a man from Engine 45 who tripped over a hose in the hall. He has a gash across his forehead, and he holds a handkerchief to it.

The ambulance finally comes. It looks like a converted bread wagon, but it's warm, and I feel relaxed as I sink into the soft mattress of the stretcher.

"C'mon, get up and make room for the rest of us," orders Benny. "What the hell ya think this is, a hotel?"

It's almost ten-thirty as we walk into the emergency room. There is a doctor and two nurses waiting for us. The doctor ministers to the man with the cut forehead, and the nurses go about cleaning the burns. One of the nurses, a large black woman, makes small talk as she works on Jim Stack. "You firemen are always in here. I don't know why they don't make a special room for you, with a big sign at the door: 'FIREMEN ONLY.' This hospital is busy enough, but you firemen make us twice as busy. What is it that you do that you can't do without getting hurt? Lord knows the fires have to be put out, but can't you find a better way?"

The other nurse quietly washes Carmine's neck. She is slender and pretty, and reminds me of the girl on the subway. Smooth olive skin, and long black hair pinned up beneath her starched cap. She moves in quick, determined motions, with an air of professionalism that attracts me. She leans her elbow on the back of Carmine's lowered head, applies the bandage, and then confidently lifts his chin with her fingers. "Would you sit over there, please," she says. It is not a request, but a pleasant command. She looks at Benny. "Are you next?"

Benny sits on the stool, and she holds his hand. He has a burn the size of a silver dollar behind his right thumb, and he winces as she wipes it with soapy gauze. But he is enjoying the attention, and I silently wish I could trade places with him.

The doctor comes to me armed with a flashlight and a tongue depressor. He chokes me in the gentle, easy way all doctors choke people when they look at throats. "You'll be O.K.," he says, "but don't smoke for a week, or use your voice too much. The throat is irritated, but it's not burned, luckily." He writes a prescription for a syrup, and tells me to take it three times a day.

The telephone rings. It is the Fire Department Medical Officer, and he wants to talk to the attending physician. The doctor talks into the receiver in the matter-of-fact way doctors talk to each other. The conversation is brief, and he turns to me, and says, "The Department doctor wants to talk to one of you."

"This is Fireman Smith speaking."

"Listen Smith, are the other men with you? Carroll, Stack, Belli, and McDowell?"

"McDowell?"

"Yes, the man from Engine Company 45."

"Oh, yes, everyone is here." I had forgotten about that guy.

"Well, tell them that you are all to report to the medical office a week from Monday. We won't have to worry about Rittman, because he has a broken leg. Do you have the message?"

"Yes sir, a week from Monday, thank you, good-bye."

4

I live in a small town called Washingtonville. It is a pretty town located sixty miles north of the city, and the only objection I have to it is the length of its name. The surrounding countryside is filled with the soft, rambling hills of pasture land, and it is only in the past decade that the dairy farmers have begun to sell pieces of their farms to developers. People were, and still are, moving from the city in droves, buying their little piece of America. Cops, firemen, construction workers, school teachers, engineers, and auto mechanics—all abandoning the place that provides them a livelihood. And why not? After living in tenements all my life, I want to give my three sons a little more space than I had, a place where they can ride a bicycle and breathe clean air.

My piece of America is a four-bedroom house on a half acre of ground. The house is built on top of a hill, overlooking distant mountains and my neighbor's backyard. It is peaceful and plain. I can't enjoy the solitude Thoreau talked about, not with the kids playing noisily in the yard, or the roar of a neighbor's lawnmower or snowblower, but I can plant a bean row if I want to.

A little old lady died a few years ago in Boise, Idaho. She left no will, and her property was divided among unknown relatives. My wife's uncle, a poor blind man living in Ireland, was made rich by Irish standards, and a wealthy cousin was made richer. My wife was given several thousand dollars, enough for a down payment on the house. We could never have saved that money on a fireman's salary. That is what life is all about—living in a three-room apartment with three kids until a strange lady, a thousand miles away, dies.

Washingtonville is a bastion of Goldwater Republicans. The people are not unfriendly, but neither are they friendly. It's a mind-your-own-business kind of town, and as long as the law is obeyed, the high school students are orderly, and the taxes are kept low, the townspeople remain passive. But if, as happened recently, a student bewildered by the shootings at Kent State paints a picture of the American flag rimmed with question marks, and the school's art teacher hangs the painting in the main corridor, the local chapter of the John Birch Society can be counted on to protect American ideals by demanding that the teacher be fired. It was the most exciting series of events since I've lived here. The Birchers made headlines in the local paper for three days, but finally they succeeded only in making a lot of noise. The painting remained hanging and the teacher kept his job—facts that instill confidence in my Irish-Catholic-Democratic heart.

The town was a stopping place of the underground railroad, which provided freedom for so many Negroes prior to the Civil War. As a result, there is a large black population in Washingtonville. But even the blacks are insulated from the problems faced by residents of bigger towns. There is no real poverty or deprivation here. Very few people are on the county welfare rolls. There is no black section of town, but there are black and white sections. A black family lives down the street from us. A young black couple just moved in two houses away. Nobody got excited, and that's what I like about Washington-ville. It's unfortunate, though, that I had to travel sixty miles away from New York City to find it.

Like most firemen who have moved from the city, my children are my first consideration. I want them to be able to go to school without being held up by a fifth-grader for their lunch money. They can ride their bicycles through the neighborhood with a feeling of freedom. They can park their bikes and go rambling through the woods, knowing that the bikes will be there on their return. They can learn to defend themselves, and to stick up for what they think is right by arguing with the kids next door. They won't have to fight their way through a band of marauding youths. There aren't any. They have a good chance of reaching adolescence unscarred.

Of course, things change, and people change from day to day. The day may come to gather family and possessions and move on. It's my job as head of the family to watch for changes that will alter our relation to our society. Right now we feel secure. Tomorrow, perhaps, we may have to move on. It's not like running away, but rather like keeping one step ahead of insanity.

New York City is simply too big. I have lived in it too long to hate it, but I know it too well to love it. I am still a part of it, yet I feel removed, like a broken jockey who grooms horses. I earn my living caring for it, but I feel helpless because I know that I can't train it, or ride it, or make it win. New York's leaders are aristocrats who have never labored, or political hacks who have conned and schemed their way up. I have never been convinced that aristocrats really care about the problems of the poor or the ignorant, about the vermin-infested, broken-walled coops that people are forced to huddle in and call home. Rather, they have developed through their private educational system and their Parke-Bernet preview-showing kind of society a patronizing benevolence that sounds good in campaign speeches, and looks good in print. But they never knew there was a drug problem in this country until their own children began to get arrested. They find easy moral arguments against the war in Asia because it isn't their own who are coming home in rectangular boxes, and they don't have to rationalize the significance of death.

I have more respect for the old-style machine politicians. They, at least, had the perception to recognize an ugly system, and to learn how to operate within it. They paid their dues in city government. They didn't buy it. They learned how to fold their napkins after dinner, push their way to the front when photographers were shooting, and say the right thing when asked questions. They never ordered cops around, but spoke quietly to the Captain in a side room. They understood their power, and utilized it without making waves. In their own way they got things done.

But things aren't getting done in New York City anymore. The city is dying. City tax dollars flow to Albany and little is returned. The finances of the richest city in the world are controlled by men who represent farmers in the State Legislature. It makes no sense.

The last real hope for New York City was when Norman Mailer and Jimmy Breslin ran for Mayor and City Council President. Mailer wanted to make the city the fifty-first state, and divide the city into a lot of small towns, any one of which would have had a population larger than the state of Vermont. And Breslin is one of the few human beings in this world who realizes that what the guys are saying at the corner table of the steamfitters ball has some validity. But both men were defeated in the not-too-close race. The wheel of democracy turns slowly, and when it revolves again to the next mayoral election I won't have my say. I'm going to miss that. Like the jockey, I have an affection for the horse, and I am just a little bitter because I don't have a part of the action.

Yes, New York City is too big for me—too big for anyone really. There are too many people, too many schools, too many officials, too many people in jails, too many Cadillacs, too many people on welfare, too many banks, too many abandoned buildings, too much misery. But we would still be there—the five of us in a three-room walk-up—were it not for an old lady who forgot to make out a will.

I am sitting in my kitchen now, waiting for my wife Pat to finish cooking a mushroom omelette. She is standing with her back to me, and her whole body is vibrating as she beats the eggs in the frying pan. It is three o'clock. The children are outdoors. I wish I had time to hold her softly, and tell her I love her, and more. But I have to go to work, and only have time for an omelette and tea.

I have been on medical leave for the last two weeks. My throat doesn't hurt anymore, and I'm anxious to return to the firehouse. It's boring just resting. A man has to do things with his hands and body. I have read a lot of magazines and newspapers during the past weeks, but it is not enough to exercise the mind. Like a drunk without a drink, I feel a little "mokus," the need to get back to what I like. Fires are burning in the South Bronx, and I get paid to fight them.

Pat places the steaming omelette in front of me. She leans toward me. Her lips touch mine, and she begins the game we call love metaphor. I can feel her soft, moist lips moving as she asks, "How much?"

"This much," I say, extending my arms as far as possible.

She looks both ways to make sure both hands are open, and the fingertips stretched. "In money?" she asks.

"The Pope's treasury."

"In minerals?"

"A flawless diamond."

"In animals?"

"Big as an elephant."

"In mountains?"

"Mount Everest, of course, and Rolls Royce in cars, and New York in cities, and *On the Waterfront* in movies."

I wrap my arms around her and end the game. She laughs lightly, as she laughed eight years ago when I first held her in my arms. I think how little our relationship has changed in all those years. Our feelings for each other have grown stronger, and we've learned to adapt to each other's strengths and weaknesses, but we still play the same games, laugh the same laughs, and kiss the same kisses.

Her slender frame wriggles in my arms, and finally she escapes.

"Your eggs will get cold," she says.

"I always leave hungry when I leave without you, baby," I say.

"Well, eat your eggs, and at least your stomach won't bother you," she retorts.

God, is there anything in this world that time doesn't cheat you out of at least once? How many times have I wished for another hour, or even thirty minutes? And how many fires have I fought in freezing cold or exhausting heat, wishing each minute that another hour would pass?

"It's three-fifteen," Pat says. "You'd better hurry if you want to get to the firehouse by five."

She pours a cup of tea, and sits across from me. She looks at me with her sharp, sensitive eyes, and bites the inside of her lower lip, a habit she has when there is something on her mind. Her gaze is fixed on me as I start the omelette, but she says nothing. I continue to eat, and still nothing. Finally, I finish the eggs, and put some sugar in my tea. As I stir the tea, I say, "All right, Patricia Ann, stop biting the lip and let it out."

"What do you mean?" she asks.

Every time there is something important for us to talk about, Pat insists that it is not really important.

"You know what I mean," I answer. "When you look at me, and bite your lip, there is always something to say."

"I wasn't thinking of anything in particular, really. I was just wondering if you feel all right, if you should really go back to work."

"I feel fine, sweetheart. Cross my heart. If I had known you were concerned I would have brought you a note from the doctor."

"Don't be funny, Dennis. I was talking to your mother the other day . . ."

"So that's it!" I interrupt her.

"Yes that's it, and she's right! How many years are you going to work in the South Bronx? I never worried half as much when you used to work in Queens, at least then you came home to me with some life in your body. But, now you come home dead tired—if you come home at all, if you're not tied up at some hospital getting stitched, or X-rayed, or burns patched. Even in Viet Nam they send the soldiers home after a year, but you've been in Engine 82 over five years."

I can see that she is genuinely upset, and her concern surprises me because she has never mentioned it before. Every fireman's wife worries about her husband, but up until now Pat had her anxiety under control. Her face begins to contract, and it looks as though years of suppressed worry are about to surface. I have to reassure her, comfort her. I realize, however, that there is little I can say to her that will calm her fears. How many years? I have never thought about it. Is it time to transfer to a clean-upper-middle-class-white neighborhood, where the only false alarms transmitted are those caused by European visitors mistaking the alarm box for a mail box? Where there are no abandoned buildings or abandoned cars to ignite? How many years? Am I working in the South Bronx because of some abstract moral commitment, a belief that poor people must have professional protection from fire and that it's my obligation to protect them? Like crime and disease, fire victimizes the poor most. Am I crusading? Or am I just doing a job?

I reach over the table and grasp her hand. "Listen baby," I say, "I wish you wouldn't worry about it. I've told you before that if a fireman is going to get hurt, or even killed, it happens just as easily, just as quickly, in Queens or Staten Island as it does in the South Bronx. Okay, so I come home tired once in a while, but I'm still a young guy. I can take it. Have you ever heard me complain about the work?"

"That's not what I mean, Dennis," she says imploringly. "I just don't know why you want to work down there when you could get a job at the local high school, five minutes away from home. You could work from nine until three. You would be home for Christmas for a change, and you could have the whole summer off every year. Not only that, but you would make more money teaching. I don't even care that much about the money. It just doesn't make any sense to me!"

I feel defenseless, stripped naked, because I realize I don't know how to justify my job except to say that I like doing it. I put my empty tea cup into the sink, walk to where Pat is sitting, and hold her pretty face between my hands. "Just think, Pat," I say in a near whisper, "in twelve short years I'll be able to retire at half pay. I'll only be forty-two years old, and we can move to a quiet academic town somewhere in the New England hills, to Ireland, back to New York City, or anywhere we please. Life will be easy, relaxed. The children will be grown. We can travel or not travel, but at least we'll have the choice. Right now though, I like what I'm doing. I'm pleased as a worker and as a man. I have something to contribute."

The telephone rings. It's for me. Artie Merritt who lives ten miles below me wants a lift to work. His car broke down. It is three-thirty, and time to leave for the firehouse. I kiss Pat good-bye. I can tell she is not happy with my explanation, but the wisdom of her eyes prevails, and the question of working in Engine 82 is left floating in the air.

Brendan is off somewhere riding his bicycle, but the two younger boys come running from a neighbor's yard where they

[58]

have been playing. Neither can ride a two-wheeler yet, and they stay close to the house, always ready to say hello or good-bye to their father.

"Good-bye Dennis. Good-bye Sean. Say good-bye to Brendan for me."

Both heads nod, and little hands blow kisses as I back down the drive. Pat is on the porch, her arms folded below her breast, and her long hair blowing in the cold wind. She waves.

"Good-bye baby. Love ya."

Artie Merritt is waiting for me at the bottom of a steep hill. He rents a house at the top of the hill because he says living up there is one of the few ways a man can feel on top of the world. He lived until recently in a Greenwich Village apartment. He moved when he realized that he could live on top of a hill for the same rent—away from traffic noise, crowded subways, teenage beggars, urine-stenched hallways, and away from people walking aimlessly, hopelessly, on cracked sidewalks, guided by the wide, unmoving, catatonic eyes of the chemically possessed.

Artie has been a fireman for over ten years. But he is different in many ways from other firemen. He has a beard, a master's degree in sociology, and a way of speaking that is hardly funny, but always convincing. His eyes are small, and glare out above the full Brahms-like beard, following, studying reactions as he speaks. His voice is low-keyed, but each word is carefully pronounced and fully thought out.

He used to work in another company in the South Bronx, but transferred to Ladder 31 because he was having some trouble with a Battalion Chief who didn't like the idea of a fireman having a full beard. Rather than put up with the Chief's subtle harassments—you don't fight a Battalion Chief—Artie asked to be transferred to Ladder 31. His differences don't bother the men on Intervale Avenue. Artie is a tough firefighter, and that's what counts.

Artie and I don't speak much as we drive down the Palisades

Parkway; he is reading a book of Malcolm X's speeches, and I have to focus my attention on driving. A light drizzle begins to fall. It's a dismal day. It reminds me of a thousand afternoons I spent standing on the stoop of a midtown tenement, wishing with friends that there were something to do. The sky would be overcast, as it is now, and the buildings down the block would become vague images, quiet and lonely. Soon, the occupants of my stoop would trudge off to their buildings for want of something to do, and I would sit on the wrought iron handrail alone, not wanting to climb the stairs to the still lonelier confines of a four-room railroad flat. Cars would pass, and the strange sound of tires riding over wet pavement would excite me. "Whisshh," they would go. "WhisSSHHH." Each sound taking people places.

I listen now to the tires of my own foreign economy car. The sound is steady, "sshhh," with no beginning and no ending, and the "polop, polop" of the windshield wipers completes the monotony.

"It's too bad," Artie says, breaking into my thoughts.

"What's too bad?" I ask with interest.

"That Malcolm was zapped," he says, closing the book, and throwing it on the back seat. "You know," he continues, "I bet our times get named. Just like the Age of Reason, the Enlightenment, and the Great Awakening. Our life-time is going to be known as the Great Zap. You know, historians will look back and say 'It's too bad about those people in the twentieth century. You know. It could have been an age of peace and harmony, but they let their leaders get zapped.' "

Artie has a habit of saying "you know," but he never says it questioningly. It is a declarative statement, and seems to reinforce what he says. The rain beats harder on the Palisades now, and it is more difficult to drive.

I laugh a little, and say, "Listen Artie, the day is depressing enough."

"Yeah, you're right," he says. "There must be something we can say to bring a little sunshine into this car. You know. We

[60]

can talk about the Miss America contest, or some other equally important American venture. Like, you know, television quiz games or the vice-presidency."

"I know, Artie," I say. "There is a consistency of metaphor there somewhere."

"At least you're laughing," he says.

I can see the vertical beams of the George Washington Bridge. We will be at the firehouse in fifteen minutes. The rain has slowed to a drizzle again, but it is icing on the windshield. It is going to be cold riding on the back of the fire engine.

It is five minutes after five as we enter the firehouse. Engine 82 and both Ladder 31 and 712 are out. Engine 85's pumper is parked in the corner of the apparatus floor, and the Chief's car sits in the middle. Bob Beatty and Marty Hannon—two of the senior men in Engine 85—are playing gin rummy in the kitchen.

"Hey Beast," I yell over the screaming unwatched television, "where are all the troops?"

Beatty throws his cards on the table, kicks his chair over, and hollers, "Ya doesn't hafta call me Beast. Ya can call me Robert if ya want, but ya doesn't hafta call me Beast." Hannon doubles over in laughter. Beatty picks his chair up, sits down, and regroups his cards. He ignores us. Beatty is a tall, thin man who sports a handlebar mustache. He is a hard-drinking, good-looking unmarried fireman, and a good man with his fists when the time comes. He is also the firehouse mimic.

"Bob is having one of his attacks," Artie says. Beatty twitches a small smile, but concentrates on ignoring us. He must have waited in the kitchen, silently practicing the routine, until we arrived.

"Let me try again," I say. "Marty, would you happen to know where the other companies, and the firefighters assigned to those companies, are?"

Marty Hannon has one of those fresh, rose-colored faces that makes him look like he just stepped off the boat from County

Meath. As he speaks his sullen Irish eyes smack of sincerity. "No, I'm sorry Dennis, I don't. But the Beast probably does."

Beatty again kicks his chair over. "Ya doesn't hafta call me Beast. . . ."

As we walk out of the kitchen, Artie says, "You should have known better."

"Yeah."

As we walk up the stairs to the locker room, the man on housewatch begins to pull the heavy chains of the overhead door. The companies have returned from wherever they were. I am halfway up the flight of twenty-three stairs, but I turn and walk down again. Engine 82 backs into its spot, and I take my gear from the rack. With boots, helmet, and rubber coat in place I can now change into my work clothes without having to worry about looking for them if an alarm comes in.

Benny Carroll's locker is next to mine on the second floor. I am happy to see him, and we ask simultaneously, "How are ya feeling?" and then laugh. I ask about his hand, and he shows me the silver-dollar scab, hard, and chocolate brown. He could have taken another week of medical leave, but he was as anxious as I to get back to the firehouse. The burn still hurts him if he stretches the skin, if he makes a fist, but he faked it at the medical office, and got a full-duty slip.

The bells ring as I change my pants, but it's for Engine 85 and Ladder 712. As Benny and I are walking down the stairs, the bells sound again. This time it's for us. Box 2597. The house-watchman yells, "Union Avenue and 165. Eighty-two and Thirty-one goes. Chief goes." Men are sliding the poles, running from the kitchen, and from the cellar. Benny is looking for his gear at the rack. John Horn takes his gear from the back of the pumper as Benny steps up on the back step. "Take up, John, you're relieved." Vinny Royce steps up muttering that it's about time we came back to work. Kelsey and Knipps, who are always together, are riding the side step. The firehouse clock reads five-thirty.

[62]

The pumper tears screaming up Home street, down Prospect, over 165th Street to Union. Nobody there. We start to
walk up the street, then run back to the pumper. There are
people waving down the block. The pumper stops in front of
a three-story wooden frame house. There is a little smoke seeping from a window on the second floor. The men of Ladder 31
run into the building, O'Mann, McCartty, and Siebeck. Artie
Merritt runs into the adjoining building to check the rear and
the roof. John Milsaw stands in front. The Chief's aide walks
into the house, followed by Chief Niebrock. A group of children come running up the street to investigate the excitement.

It smells like food on the stove. Even the wind can't hide
the deep, putrid smell of burnt food. The rain has stopped, and
the streets are drying. The wind passes, but it is mild, and the
temperature almost pleasant. Only light smoke leaves my mouth
as I open it, but the mist hanging beneath the street light tells
me that the smoke will get heavier as the night grows. The
mass of cold air has broken, and the break is moving through
the South Bronx. The colder half will soon follow.

Chief Niebrock comes out of the building. Benny has his arm
through the hose folds just in case. "Food on the stove, Chief?"
The Chief nods. We are waiting now for our Lieutenant, Tom
Welch, who is inside with the ruined dinner.

Lieutenant Welch is forty-three, but looks much younger. He
is a hip-looking guy, with long hair. When he is off duty he
wears western clothes, and, occasionally, small beads around
his neck. He plays the guitar even better than Carmine Belli,
but because his guitar is so expensive he doesn't take it to the
firehouse much. Things get stolen on Intervale Avenue. I get
the feeling that all things in his life come second to the Fire
Department. He has worked in the South Bronx for over fifteen
years, and he has a reputation for getting in and putting the
fire out no matter what the conditions. It's good having him work
with us. If the fire can be reached, Tom Welch will reach it.

I open my rubber coat and take the pack of cigarettes from

my shirt pocket. Benny and Vinny Royce each take one. As I strike the match I can hear a series of shouts coming from across the street. Some children have gathered there by the street light, and have begun to chant. There are seven of them. Seven black youthful faces peering at us. The oldest of them can't be more than ten years old. At first their chant is disjointed, then finding harmony it fills the street. "Pig white motherfucker. Pig white. . . ." It repeats, and repeats.

There is no discernible hatred in their faces. No wickedness. Seven young boys, as young as unweaned calves, yet filled with words beyond their understanding. Like carolers they are grouped in a semicircle, but unlike carolers they are poised to run if a fireman makes a quick move.

As youthful and spirited as colts, their voices are high and carry easily through the mist. I wonder what motivates them to chant such an ugly phrase so naturally. Benny Carroll says, "What they need is a good kick in the ass." Vinny agrees. But I'm not so sure. Somebody needs a good kick in the ass, but not these boys. Chanting sin without being sinful, they need to be talked to by someone who loves them, or by someone who finds value in loving. Father forgive them for they know not what they say. But, that's not important, for they haven't sinned, they have no malice. So young, I think. So young. Who is the sinner? Who teaches? His ass is the one to be kicked.

Tom Welch comes from the building and climbs into the pumper. John Milsaw makes a quick move, and the kids run down the street. Everyone laughs, and John shakes his head.

The pumper moves, and the chant is forgotten. Benny and Vinny plan the evening's meal. Broiled half chickens, they say. French-fried potatoes. Salad. Creamed corn. I can hear what they are saying but all I can think of is pig, white, guinea, spic, hebe, motherfucker, nigger, donkey, mick, fishhead. Each word brings with it a flash of remembrance. The final solution sounded like a funny thing on the streets of the east Fifties when I was a kid. Any guy who didn't look Irish was a wop to us. And

[64]

nigger was a thing we caught by the toe before we played stick-ball. If someone called one of us a donkey he'd get his lumps if he wasn't too big, and if he was too big three or four of us would lay for him.

Funny, isn't it, I think. And who's to blame for the way we thought as kids? Our neighbors, our teachers, our parents? It's too late. But it wasn't too late for me. I got my ass kicked when I was sixteen. I quit school, and started reading books. In that order. I have a lot of bruises. The milk bottle filled with black ink in the Baltimore Catechism No. 2 belonged to me. That was the one where the ink stood for mortal sins. But if I'm still around as my own boys grow up they will be sure to learn that people don't hate other people. It is only when other people are dehumanized that they can become hateful. The Jews in Poland, Hungary, and Germany were never people, but an abstraction called "final solution." Slave ships were filled with niggers, not people. Nobody would buy people. Guineas couldn't join Irish-dominated trade unions, but people could. If Brendan, Dennis, and Sean can understand that, then maybe the empty milk bottle in the Baltimore Catechism No. 2 will belong to them. But those kids back on Union Avenue, they'll have to work it out by themselves. The truly sad thing about it is that I do realize how much easier it is if you're white.

We have just come from a rubbish fire. It's two-thirty in the morning. There have been eleven alarms for us since we were at Union Avenue. Our meal was interrupted by two false alarms, but it didn't matter. Chicken is as good cold as it is hot, and I didn't mind doing without the creamed corn.

I take my coat off, and throw it on the rig. My legs are beginning to tire so I climb the stairs to the second floor. One-half of the huge room is taken up by our lockers, and the other half is filled with eighteen beds, spaced about twelve inches apart. Theoretically, we can sleep here until we are relieved at 9:00 A.M., but like many theories, it never works

[65]

out in reality. I don't take off any clothes before I lie down, because I know I won't be here long. I fall asleep quickly.

As I awaken, the lights are on, and the bells are tolling. The housewatchman is yelling "85 and 31 goes." Good, it's not for me! I lie back. But the housewatchman yells "82 goes too. Get out 82." I look down as I slide the brass pole, and make sure of my footing as I hit the floor. Benny slides the pole behind me. Kelsey, Knipps, and Royce come from the kitchen. The clock reads three-thirty.

Engine 85 and Ladder 31 are going to Southern Boulevard and Jennings Street. We have been special called to Hoe Avenue and 172nd Street, and we follow them up Southern Boulevard. Suddenly, the pumper screeches to a stop. Ladder 31 has stopped before us. But we have to go up to 172nd Street. As we pull around the Ladder truck we see that it has crashed into the back of Engine 85. Bob Beatty is lying in the street, blood gushing from his forehead. The pumper stops momentarily, and then races toward 172nd Street. Evidently Lieutenant Welch ordered the chauffeur to keep going. We all want to stop, to help Bob, but we know that we have to get to the box on Hoe Avenue and 172nd Street. Every second will count if there is a fire.

There is a man at the corner of Hoe Avenue waving to us. He runs into a tenement house, and we follow closely behind. "What's the matter?" yells Lieutenant Welch. "Is there a fire?" But the man doesn't speak English "Meda, meda," he keeps saying. Come, come. Here, here.

Lieutenant Welch and I follow up the stairs. The others wait below in case a hose line has to be stretched. The man leads us into a bedroom on the fourth floor. A woman, I guess his wife, is lying under a sheet on the bed. She is sweating, and breathing irregularly. The room is wet with heat, and the radiator is steaming. The place is stuffy, like the back of a saloon.

"We'll have to wait until a Chief gets here with a resuscitator," the Lieutenant says. "It looks like she may have asthma, or it could be an emotional attack."

That's true, I think. I have seen many Spanish women gasping for air, only to be quickly revived when an ambulance attendant puts smelling salts under their noses.

"Let's get her to a window," Lieutenant Welch says. "This place is like an oven." He puts a chair in front of the window, and motions to the man that we want her to sit on it. The husband understands, and pulls the sheet from her. She is naked, but for a pair of panties.

Lieutenant Welch and I lift her to the chair, and her husband wraps her in a blanket. She is a young girl, about twenty-five, and her breasts are full and erect. The blanket is draped over her shoulders, and opened at the front. I pull one end over her bared breasts, and across her arm. How strange that the first rule of administering first aid to women is to cover them up, because no matter what their injury might be, no matter how severe, they may worry more about their modesty.

Lieutenant Welch opens the window, as I wipe her forehead with a towel. The night air hits her, and she begins to understand where she is. It looks like she's all right, but that's not for us to determine. I wish the hell we could get out of here. I wonder how Bob is. Is he hurt bad? Will he live? Will I get to see him before he dies? Why do we always think of the worst when a friend is involved?

The Chief of the Eighteenth Battalion arrives. He sends his aide down for the resuscitator. Lieutenant Welch and I carry the woman back to the bed. She doesn't speak English either, but it seems as if she is telling us that she feels all right.

The Chief asks her, "Do you need an ambulance? Do you want to go to the hospital?"

"No! No!" she says. "No ambulancia." She understands that. The Chief says that our job is done here. The woman lies back on her pillow, and is breathing quite regularly now. "Gracia," she says. "Gracia, gracia," her husband says.

We race back to the scene of the accident. Chief Niebrock has already taken Bob to the hospital in the Chief's car. John Milsaw is sitting on the curb. He is shaken. Charlie McCartty finds himself in a role he has played before. He'll be O.K., John. Don't worry.

Marty Hannon tells us the story. Matt Tunney was driving Engine 85's rig. They were going to Jennings Street, but they saw a man waving wildly one block before, at 170th Street. Matt jammed on the brakes, but Ladder 31 didn't have enough time to stop behind them. John Milsaw tried to avoid the guys standing on the back step, but couldn't. Beatty tried to jump out of the way, but got caught between the back rail of the pumper, and the front of the truck. It was just his arm and leg though. If his chest had been hit, it would have killed him sure. The alarm at Jennings Street and Southern Boulevard was false.

"What about the guy waving?" I ask.

"Drunk," Marty says sadly. He spreads his hands, and says, "What can you do?" His Irish face looks like it is going to be wet with tears.

It is now seven-thirty, and daylight is shining on the South Bronx. We are all sitting in the kitchen awaiting news of Bob. I have had five cups of coffee in the past three and a half hours. We've all sat here since the accident, except for the two false alarms and the one rubbish fire.

Bob limps slowly into quarters, being held up by the Bronx Borough Trustee of our union. It is the trustee's job to look after all seriously injured firemen, or their next of kin. It's a rotten job.

The trustee says that Beatty refused to be admitted to the hospital. He wanted to go home. He doesn't like hospitals. The doctors were furious, but there was nothing they could do to detain him. The trustee says that Bob made a lot of noise at the hospital.

The Beast looks dead. There is dried blood all over his clothes, his head is bandaged, his arm is in a sling, and the side of his face is completely scraped. He must have hit the ground hard.

[68]

I can tell that he is still in great pain. He gives Marty Hannon the keys to his locker. "Just get my clothes, Marty. All I wanna do is go home." Everyone wonders why his leg isn't broken.

The trustee says that the X-rays showed no breaks. He tells us again how mad the doctors were. Marty comes down the stairs with the Beast's clothes, and he puts them in the trustee's car. It takes great effort for Bob to get into the car. He shouldn't have gotten out of it to begin with. He grimaces as he bends his leg to put it in the car.

"So long guys."

"So long Bob."

"All I want to do is go home. The trustee will drive me home."

I'm anxious to get off duty and to get home. I'm tired, and I need to sleep. I shouldn't have drunk all that coffee.

5

IT's 2:30 A.M. We're spraying 250 gallons of water a minute at the fire and it seems like the wind is driving each cold drop back into our faces. With each bitter gust I swear to God I won't stand another one. But, I do—another, and another. We've been here over an hour now. The fire is still burning freely. If we could only go inside the building and get close to the heat. The Chief says it is too dangerous—that the roof might collapse at any moment. I'm breathing through my mouth, because the cold has penetrated beyond the roof of my nose and my head aches. The wind picks up and now the water is hitting us like pellets shot against a plastic surface. Icicles have formed on the protective rim of my leather helmet, and they break off as I move to reinforce my grip on the fighting hose.

"Why don't we get some relief here?" I yell to the men supporting me from behind, the men of Engine Company 82.

"Do you want a blow on the line, Dennis?" Benny Carroll

yells over the wind and the noise of the fire. Benny was once a student at the Fort Schuyler Merchant Marine Academy, and I wonder as he approaches if he ever thought that his life with the sea would be realized by directing hundreds of gallons of water through a brass nozzle.

"Yeah, Benny, you take it for a while," I say, as he grasps the hose, "but what I really want is a bearskin rug in front of an open fireplace."

"Say no more," says Benny laughingly—an expression he always uses for agreement.

Kelsey, Knipps, and Vinny Royce will back Benny up on the line. It's my turn to get lost for a few minutes. Lieutenant Welch is standing nearby watching, waiting for the roof to cave in. I tell him that I'm going to look for a place to get warm. The water has frozen over his rubber coat, and it flares at the bottom like a ballerina's dress. Because he is an officer he has to stay with the men on the hose line at all times. He is jumping from foot to foot trying to get his blood to circulate. He looks at me and nods his head. He doesn't talk because he knows words don't mean anything at fires like this. He only cares about putting enough water on the fire. Tom Welch has been working in the South Bronx for over fifteen years, and he knows there is no challenge in this fire. If we were crawling down a hallway or fighting our way into a cellar, he would be talking all the time. He would be saying the words that give us the confidence to move into a building everyone has run out of. But now we are just standing in front of a building, pouring water on it. It's cold, and our bodies are being beaten, and Lieutenant Welch just nods.

As I walk down the street in search of a warm hallway I hear a soft but distinct crashing noise, like someone dropping a steel safe on a pile of thin balsa wood. As I turn I see a giant mushroom of fire surge toward the sky. Part of the roof has fallen, and the new oxygen overhead acts like a magnet for the fire.

The old, dying building is a three-story wooden structure

[71]

called a Queen Anne. It's the kind of gothic house that Edgar Allan Poe would have delighted in writing about. It has a series of peaked roofs and widow's walks, and many small rooms with spaces between the walls and between the ceilings and floors. This type of building is particularly difficult for firemen to work in. Fire spreads quickly in small enclosed spaces.

It was just a little over an hour ago that we were sitting in the firehouse kitchen. The radiators were hissing, and the coffee was steaming. We had already responded to twelve alarms since our tour of duty started at six o'clock, and, except for one, all had been small ventures into the night's cold. Two were mattress fires, one was a burning abandoned car, and the rest were garbage fires or false alarms. The exception was a midnight alarm for a burning couch. We saw the smoke coming from a window on the sixth floor of a tenement building on Charlotte Street. It seems that most of the fires we have are on the top floor. Each time I drag hose up five or six flights of stairs I curse the designer of the building, and I think how much easier the job would be had he taken firefighting into consideration. He could have put a standpipe in the building, or at least a well between the staircases so that the hose could go straight up instead of snaking around the bends.

We stretched four lengths of hose into the building, and five more lengths trailed behind to the fire hydrant. Nine lengths of hose for a rotten couch fire that could have been extinguished with a glassful of water five minutes earlier. The guy who lived in the apartment was sitting on the stairs in the hall, smoking a cigarette, and saying that he didn't know how the fire started. He looked and sounded drunk, but who knows? And when you think about it, who cares?

The weather got to us on Charlotte Street. When we tried to uncouple the hose connections we found them frozen solid. Each of the five lengths laying in the street were bound together by the cold, the cold that now prevents my fingers from moving. We had to lift each 71-pound length of hose over the standing exhaust pipe of the fire engine to warm the connections. This kind of extra work is frustrating because there is no one to blame but nature.

Kelsey and Knipps had involved almost everyone in the kitchen in a plan to beam the ceilings in Knipps' house. Plans were being worked on, and a scale drawing was put on the blackboard. Knipps had asked Kelsey if he knew anything about installing overhead beams. Kelsey asked everyone else. And what had begun as a simple inquiry turned out to be a full-scale project where beam designs were being created for all his rooms. Firemen are like that. The slightest problem or question invites full participation.

That is what we were doing a little over an hour ago when a second alarm was sounded for Box 2317, Forest Avenue and 158th Street. Plans, drawings, coffee, and hissing radiators were left behind as we hustled our way to the fire.

Three engine companies were assigned on the first alarm, and two ladder companies. When the Battalion Chief saw the large body of fire he ordered a second alarm. Engine 82 was assigned on the second. We could see the red glare in the sky as we left our firehouse, which is about a mile away. As we turned the corner on Forest Avenue we saw that Engine 73 and Engine 41 were backing their lines out of the building. We knew then that we would be here for some time, because the faster you can get close to a fire, the faster it will be extinguished. But because of the imminent danger of a roof collapse it was impossible to get close.

Now I'm standing across the street from a burning building, and I'm hoping for its quick destruction. If the rest of the roof would only come down, then we could go in and put the fire out.

I can hear the firehouse radiators hissing as I walk down the street searching for a warm hallway. Except for the burning building's, the hallways on the block are cold. I try each door, but as I enter I find each colder than the one before. I return to the building directly across from the fire. Several firemen from other companies have the same idea as I, and are standing around the lobby. They are walking back and forth, or jumping up and down. It is too cold to sit on the floor and relax. I take a cigarette out, and heavy smoke pours from my mouth as I ask for a light. Three men search their pockets before a dry pack of matches is found.

Jim Gintel from Squad 2 lights my cigarette. Jim is an old friend of mine. We played the bagpipes together in the Emerald Society band.

"Bad night, Dennis, bad night!" he says as he takes his rubber coat off. Like all of our coats, his coat is frozen, and it stands by itself against the wall. The lobby light is reflected by the ice and the coat appears jeweled. Jim laughs, "Now if we were only Pigmies we'd have a ready-made tepee." Everyone laughs at Jim's joke, but nobody adds to it. It's too cold to be funny.

I can't help thinking that in another place, another city perhaps, where fires are uncommon and exciting, apartments up and down the street would be opened, and residents would be serving coffee and biscuits and offering the warmth of their homes to the firemen and to the victims of the fire. I think of Dylan Thomas' Miss Prothero asking if I would like something to read. But we are in New York City where neighbors traditionally don't bother to find out each other's names, where people live their lives within the walls of their apartments, where a raging fire across the street burns unwatched.

There are six doors around the lobby, but it is almost three o'clock in the morning, so I erase the thought of knocking on any one of them from my mind. I remind myself that people have to go to work in the morning. Anyway, this is what I am paid for—fighting fires all the time, not just on pleasant spring afternoons.

Jim Gintel, who was pacing, jumping, and rubbing his arms, has found a seventh door.

"Hey man, anyone got a claw tool?" he asks, his words echoing through the hall. He is a medium-sized man with graying hair, and he wears an ever present smile. Even in the worst situations Jim has something funny to say. We were once trapped above a fire along with Lieutenant Nandre, Kelsey, and Knipps. The burning building was a two-story factory, and we had thought that the fire below us was completely extinguished. Jim was helping us advance the hose on the second floor. We were making slow but sure progress when we realized the floor beneath us was burning. We tried to back down the stairs, but they were completely engulfed in flames. There was too much fire for our one hose line to control, and there was no way out. We had to make a choice between sticking it out and hoping that other lines would appear quickly to help us out, or jumping out of the window. Fire is fast and deadly, so we didn't have much time to decide. I was for making it out the window, since it was only about a twenty foot drop. Kelsey and Knipps were for sticking it out, since they were sure Engine 50 would have another line there in a minute or two. Lieutenant Nandre had gone to the window to look things over. We looked at Jim Gintel, and through the thick smoke we could see him sitting back on his haunches. We were all choking and coughing, but Jim put a cigarette in his mouth, smiled, and said, "Anyone got a match?" Fortunately, the Chief realized where we were, and had a ladder placed to the window before I had to think about lighting Jim's cigarette, or keeping the fire from lighting it for him.

Looking around the lobby I can see that no one has tools with them. "No claw tools around here Jim," I reply. "What do you want one for?"

"The furnace room is under the stairs," he says, "but it's locked up. All we need is a claw tool to break the hasp. The way I feel now all I want to do is open the furnace doors and crawl in with the coals. Somebody go get a claw, or a hook, or a halligan —anything."

Big Van, a huge man from Ladder 42, leaves us to look for a tool. There are now seven firemen in the lobby, including Jim and me, and we all gather around the furnace room door. Jim is the only man who has ventured to take his coat off. The rest of us know that there is no sense taking our coats off until there is some possibility of getting warm. Jimmy McClure, from the Squad, has a screwdriver, and begins to turn the screws in the hasp. Good, now the superintendent of the building won't be as mad as he would be if we broke the hasp off altogether.

Jim Gintel asks, "Anybody stop to think that this is breaking and entering?"

"A small crime committed in the name of humanity," I say, rather proudly.

"Humanity, hell!" Jim retorts, "I'm only thinking about us here. There won't be enough room in there for the rest of humanity."

Big Van returns with a halligan tool, a steel bar with a claw on one end and an adz and a pick on the other. "Shove it," Jim says, "McClure's almost got it now."

McClure removes the last screw, and the hasp swings freely on its hinges. I have carefully positioned myself on McClure's left, so that I'll be the first one in as the door is opened. As the door begins to swing out I can feel the moisture and the warm air escaping. I am the first one in the room. There are two concrete steps leading down to the boiler pit. I don't want to go any further unless I can see where I am going.

"Someone turn on the light," I say. Hands go up on either side of the doorway, and they slide the walls. The switch is found and the room is lighted. I look around and begin to shake. I can feel my stomach turning, and the relief of the room's warm air just brings sweat to my forehead. The walls are covered with cockroaches and water bugs scurrying in every direction. Some are as long as three inches, and as they scamper, the smaller ones drop from the walls. The light has surprised and confused them. I look up at the ceiling, and it, too, is a moving black mass. Roaches are falling all around us, and as they hit the floor they shoot in the direction of the coal pile as if propelled by a twisted rubber band.

There is a concrete ledge around the boiler pit, just high enough to sit on. McClure throws his coat against the wall. It hits, then falls on the ledge. He walks down the two steps, picks up his coat and begins to swing it against the wall. The roaches are fleeing from this madman, and he continues until a portion of the wall is cleared. He sits down, and the other men begin to sit or stand around him. I don't want to appear alarmed in front of the other firemen, but I know I have to get out of this room, out of this building. I've been nervous about roaches since I was a kid.

I grew up on the East Side of Manhattan, in the shadows of Sutton and Beekman Places. I lived in a tenement much like this one, and each Sunday my aunts, uncles, and cousins would climb the five flights of gum-stained marble stairs to our apartment. They would bring beer, and soda, and food for the weekly visit. At the end of the day, after all the Irish songs were sung and after a fist fight with a cousin or two was won or lost, the empty bottles would be gathered up and stored beneath the bath tub, which was prominent in our kitchen. The following morning the bottles would be put in a large brown paper bag. It was my job to take them to the store for the deposit, which my mother would share with me.

One sunny Monday morning I noticed as I was carrying the bag down the stairs that there was a half inch of beer remaining in one of the bottles. I put the bag down, and put the bottle to my lips. Since children don't sip things, I put the lip of the bottle wholly into my mouth. The bottle was emptied, and as I was about to swallow I felt something moving within the liquid. I spit the beer out, and with it came a long, thin brown roach. I was nine years old then; it happened more than twenty years ago, but I still can't forget it.

Jim Gintel is running back and forth in the small space in front of the furnace. He is demonstrating how to masturbate an elephant, and as he runs toward me both of his hands are about a foot apart and above his left shoulder. He stops, puts both hands above his right shoulder, and runs back. The men are laughing wildly. I leave the room unnoticed.

In the lobby I see that Jim's coat is still standing. I take my own coat off, and hold it at arm's length. The cold quickly penetrates my arms and chest. I inspect the coat carefully for roaches, and then put it back on. I take my heavy canvas gloves from the pocket, and push my hands into them. They are frozen, and I have to apply strength to move the fingers. I pull the metal door open, and return to the fire.

In the street, I can hear the man in charge of the fire, Chief Marks, yelling, and his voice reminds me of a high G on a saxophone. Some Chiefs direct fire operations the way NASA Control directs moon shots—calmly, and with great self-assurance. Others, like Chief Marks, lead their men like Leonard Bernstein conducts the New York Philharmonic in a Stravinsky symphony—with frenzy, and great excitement. While a competent man, he is known by firemen to be a "screamer," not a very complimentary title in our business. Instead of controlling overall operations with dignity and expertise, he runs helter-skelter at a fire, overseeing each operation, each hose line, each ladder placing. I once saw him yell at a respected New York photographer for standing around, and ordered him to place a ladder at the side of a burning building. The photographer, who was taking shots on assignment, simply walked away. I guess the Chief took him for a fireman, because he was wearing a rubber coat that he had borrowed—evidently he missed the wide Cardin tie, and gleaming Gucci shoes.

Chief Marks holds the rank of Deputy Assistant Chief of Department, which in the military structure is roughly equivalent to a bird colonel. When he yells he expects people to react as an Army Private would to a General. He is now yelling at Lieutenant Welch, "Keep that line directed at the roof, Lieutenant. What the hell is the matter with ya? Keep the line where I tell ya."

Tom Welch has been around for a long time, and even before he was promoted to Lieutenant he didn't think of himself as a Private. He was a fireman who knew what he was doing, a professional.

The wind is gusting heavily now as I stand behind Vinny Royce, but I can hear my Lieutenant yell over the noise, "Listen Chief, I'm freezing my ass off, and I want to put the fire out as much as you do."

"What did you say?" the Chief asks, the anger bulging out of his Irish face.

Lieutenant Welch realizes the futility of a confrontation with a Chief at a fire. There is no such thing as being a Jacksonian democrat in the Fire Department.

"Yeah, Chief," he replies, "at the roof, I know." Years of experience show in his resignation.

Benny Carroll has the stream directed at the fallen roof. The icicles hanging from his helmet look like tassels on a party hat, but there is no indication that the wearer is having fun. His face muscles are strained, and the veins in his neck are raised. The wind is howling fiercely now, and the water comes back like a sand blast. It seems like small particles of glass are being wedged into my skin. I think momentarily of the small pleasure of heat in the furnace room across the street. Benny is calling for relief, and Willy Knipps moves up to take the nozzle. I take my place behind Kelsey and Royce, grasp the two-and-a-half-inch hose with all my strength, and push forward to relieve the back pressure.

Lieutenant Welch is standing next to us, and I say, "That Chief has a big pair yelling like that, especially on a night like this. All he has to do is walk around with a walkie-talkie for a little while, and then he gets into a heated Chief's car and forgets about us."

"Yeah," Lieutenant Welch says, "but at least you know what to expect from him. He yells a lot, and he's a ball breaker, but he'll never hurt ya."

I'm a little surprised that he's defending the man who just harassed him, but I know what he means. Some Chiefs never yell, but if a fireman is a minute late for work, if he has white socks on instead of black, or if he is found smoking on the apparatus floor of the firehouse, they will not hesitate to write Department charges against the man. The Fire Department is run as a semi-military organization, and we have a *Book of Rules and Regulations*. These rules are inviolable. If a man is charged with an infraction of these rules and regulations, then, as in the case of a military court-martial, he is required to stand trial before Department administrators. Very few firemen are found innocent at these trials, and when found guilty a man can be fined as much as thirty days pay or even be discharged. So when a fireman says a Chief will never hurt ya, it is a very high tribute.

The fire in front of us has darkened down some, the flames have disappeared into the building. Hundreds of thousands of gallons of water have been poured into it, and it won't be much longer before it is a smoldering, rickety ash-heap. Tomorrow the cold will sweep through its charred rooms, and its dispossessed tenants will sift silently through the ashes looking for something to save. But there won't be much left. And they will leave the building forever with half-empty shopping bags.

Lieutenant Welch is next to me, and he is jumping from foot to foot again. His arms are crossed, and he is squeezing himself. "It's getting to you, Lou, huh?" I say.

"Yeah," he replies. "When we first got here, I forgot to pull my boots up, and I have about two inches of water in them. My feet are freezing, but I don't want to pour the water out, you know, because what's in there is acting like insulation. I think I'd give a week's pay and two of my children for dry boots and a pair of socks."

He smiles and I laugh. My own boots are up to my thighs, and my feet are dry, and I feel a little guilty that he's suffering more than I am.

There is a loud cracking noise, and the sky before us is again filled with fire. The rest of the roof has come down, and the fire is let loose from its confinement, but it won't last long. All the lines around the building are directed at the roof. The fire darkens quickly, and we know it will be over soon. The cold has beaten us, but we won't have to outlast it.

Chief Marks comes toward us, and in his excited manner yells, "Lieutenant, get an inch-and-a-half line, and take your men to the top floor." He doesn't wait for Lieutenant Welch to respond, but passes us to scream his orders to another company.

Bill Kelsey doesn't wait for Lieutenant Welch's instructions, and leaves us to get the smaller hose. The fire has suddenly become a challenge, and I can see the enthusiasm in the Lieutenant's face. He calls to Royce, in a voice loud enough for all of us to hear, "We won't need masks. The place is vented enough. With the inch-and-a-half we'll have this fire out in ten minutes." The smaller hose is much easier to work with.

Kelsey returns with a fifty-foot length of inch-and-a-half hose, and he couples it onto the two-and-a-half-inch nozzle. Carroll makes a motion to take the hose, but Kelsey says, "Up yours, Benny. I went to get it and I get to take it in."

Carroll laughs, and says, "Well, it was worth a try." I can see that Benny is disappointed. The real work, the real challenge in firefighting, lies with the man controlling the nozzle.

Kelsey follows Lieutenant Welch into the building. We are right behind them pulling on the big hose, which trails behind the smaller length. Engine 73 is already in the building dousing the small pockets of fire on the first floor. Engine 50 is doing the same on the second floor, and Ladder 42 and Ladder 19 are pulling at the ceilings and walls with hooks and halligan tools.

The smoke is light, but irritating. My eyes are tearing. My head still aches from the cold, but I don't think about it as the warmth of the fire sinks into my body. We pass the companies working on the second floor, and pull the hose to the third. There is still a lot of fire here, but it is buried beneath the fallen roof and ceilings. The fire burns a deep orange, duller than if it were burning in the open air.

There is a long hall at the top of the stairs. The bearing wall which once separated the hall from the apartments is now a crumpled mass of plaster and metal lathe. I can see the rear wheel and the sprocket of a bicycle protruding from the debris. It's a sad part of this business to see the ruins of what must once have been a child's most valued possession. But I'm glad it's only the bike. It's much sadder when we have to dig the little owner of that valued possession out from under a mess like this. Fortunately, the occupants of this building all made it to safety, but each foot of the building will be searched nonetheless. I can remember finding the body of a man who died from heat exposure in a fire. We had been told that the man had moved out of the place, that he was living with his daughter. We found him in his pajamas, lying dead on the bathroom floor.

The smoke is heavy now, but it is broken by the wind pushing through the caved roof, and it is lifting. Our noses are running, even with the inconstant smoke, and we have to keep our heads low. Heat and smoke rise, so a fireman usually stays as close to the floor as possible.

Kelsey is on his stomach, and crawling through what was once a doorway on his left. Lieutenant Welch is beside him, directing the beam of his portable lamp before them. The nozzle is opened, and Kelsey is swinging it wildly, but with confidence. He pushes into the apartment rooms, slowly but progressively, killing the fire as he goes. Suddenly, he jerks up to his knees. He closes the nozzle, shoves it down his right boot, and reopens it. The water spills over the boot top.

"What's the matter, Bill?" Knipps asks.

"I don't know," Kelsey answers. "I must have gotten something down my boot."

"Did it burn ya?"

"I don't know, but it hurts like hell."

"Lemme take the line," Knipps says, as he moves up.

"No, it's all right. Let me make the next room."

"C'mon take a blow. We have the whole goddam floor to go yet," Knipps says, almost pulling the nozzle from Kelsey's hands.

"Yeah, go take a blow Bill," Lieutenant Welch says. "See how bad it's burned."

Kelsey has no choice now. He moves out, and I take my place behind Knipps. "Give me some more line," Knipps yells. Carroll and Royce struggle to hump the hose in. We pass through what is remaining of the last two rooms. The bulk of the fire is extinguished, but there is still smoke coming from behind the walls by the window frames. A ladder company will have to rip holes in the wall so that we can get to the source of the smoke.

We can back out of these rooms for the time being. There is still fire in the other apartments. Knipps hands the nozzle back, and I hand it to Carroll. "It's about time," he smiles, and his teeth are emphasized against his smoke-darkened face. The floor is burned through in places, and Lieutenant Welch cautions Benny and Royce to be careful.

Vinny Royce is saying "That's it, Benny, that's it. Move in, move in," but Benny is a seasoned firefighter, and needs no words of encouragement. He moves quickly in and out of rooms, over and under arched beams laying across their path, moving the nozzle in a circular motion as he goes.

Vinny, Lieutenant Welch, and Benny return to the hall, and are about to enter the last set of rooms. "I'll take it now Ben," I say.

"No, that's okay. I can manage," Benny replies. Benny is one of my closest friends, but he wouldn't give the nozzle over to his mother if it meant a free trip to Ireland.

There is only one tactic for me to employ, and if it fails I'll be boxed out of any action at this fire completely. "Listen Lou," I say to Lieutenant Welch, "the easiest way to do this, probably, is to relieve each other on the nob."

Lieutenant Welch smiles, and I can see he knows what's going on. It doesn't matter to him who has the nozzle, because he is next to the man all the time, and anyone in Engine 82 can do the job. "Dennis is right, Benny," he says. "Let's not knock ourselves out."

"Say no more." Benny says, as I take the nob. This is a game we play among ourselves, called "steal the nob," and Benny understands. We can play it at a fire like this, because we are not having great difficulty in breathing, and the job is relatively easy. But, it is not a game we can play often.

The rooms before me are hotter than I anticipated. I am on

my knees, and sitting on my heels. Lieutenant Welch is beside me in the same position, and Knipps is behind feeding the line to us. We advance slowly, moving our knees forward, inch by inch, as if we were on a holy pilgrimage. We can't see the sky in this apartment, and the smoke has nowhere to go. We have extinguished the remaining fire in three rooms, and there is only one more room to go. It is in a corner of the building, and the fallen roof gives the impression of a cathedral ceiling. We have to creep along on our stomachs. The room has lit up completely, and the fire is reaching out towards us. It seems to be dancing, and as it moves it makes me think of an animated film of the sun I saw recently at a science fair—all about a moving fire, one hundred and ten times larger than the earth, holding our solar system together. The room before me is only ten by twelve feet, but it's the closest any of us will get to the heat of the sun.

I have my head down now, and the nozzle is directed at the ceiling. I don't have to look up. I know the fire is cooling because the smoke is banking down. Lieutenant Welch is next to me, saying, "Beautiful, Dennis, beautiful. Keep the stream on the ceiling, we've got it made. It's a cup of tea. Let's move in another foot."

The fire is out now, but the smoke is still heavy. There must still be fire in the walls, or caught between the ceiling and the roof. We will need a truckman here fast, before it lights up again.

"Hey, get a Ladder company up here to pull the ceilings," Lieutenant Welch yells back to no one in particular.

The room is still hot, but we are kneeling again. The water from the nozzle is cooling the walls, and spraying back at us. My body is wet with perspiration, and the spray feels good.

"Shut down the line. I'm comin' in, and I don't wanna get wet," comes a voice from behind.

"It's too damn cold out to get wet."

I had forgotten about the cold. Big Van from Ladder 42 has come with a six-foot hook. The long wooden handle with its spiked end looks like a broom handle next to Big Van. He is two heads taller than I, and when he reached 260 pounds he quit drinking beer. He drinks scotch now, by the glassful, like we would drink beer, or a Frenchman his wine.

"What's the problem here? Whadda ya want me to do?" he asks in that sincere way peculiar to big men. The smoke doesn't seem to affect him at all.

"Pull the ceilings Van," Lieutenant Welch says. "See where all that smoke is coming from at the corner."

Van pushes his hook up at the ceiling, and it goes through the plaster and lathe like a pin through a sponge. He pulls the ceiling down in huge chunks, and we can see the fire. He backs out of the room so I can hit the fire, and when he returns to pull more of the ceiling he complains about the drops of water falling on him.

Our job in this apartment is finished. The ceilings and walls are opened. The fire is out. We return to the other rooms to let loose a final bath. Big Van works with his hook, and Vinny Royce, who has usurped the nob, takes care not to get him wet.

Chief Marks thunders into the room. He directs his portable lamp around the corners, and carefully checks for signs of living fire. "How are you due here, Lieutenant?" he roars.

Lieutenant Welch answers quickly, "Second due on the second alarm, Chief."

Since we are the second engine company assigned on the second alarm, Lieutenant Welch knows that there is not much left for us to do here, and he waits for the order that relieves us. The first alarm companies will give the building a final wash down.

Chief Marks moves from room to room, apartment to apartment, looking at every cranny and corner, fallen beam and ceiling. He moves past us, and without looking in our direction, says, "Take up, 82." Those are the words we want to hear. We will be back in the firehouse soon, and with dry clothing on we will sip coffee in the warmth and security of the kitchen.

Again in the street, the cold attacks me. The wet clothes stick to me. Chills run up and down my back. There is still a lot of work to be done here, but it's not our work this time. The wind and the cold won't bother us any longer. The first alarm companies will have to fight it out. We're going home.

Chief Marks' aide is standing in front of the burned-out building, a walkie-talkie strapped over his shoulders. The thing is blaring out the Chief's orders, and Carroll has to yell over the high screeching sound, "Hey, what happened to Bill Kelsey?"

"Who's Bill Kelsey?" the aide yells back.

"The guy from Engine 82 who got something down his boot."

"Oh, him," the aide returns. "They brought him to Fulton Hospital in the Chief's car. He's got a nasty burn on his thigh, you know?"

"Anybody else hurt?" Carroll asks.

"Yeah, a guy from Engine 50 fell through the floor—a guy named Roberti, or Roberto, or something like that."

It's all very impersonal. When a guy gets hurt at a fire, it's easier to remember the injury than the man's name. There are many names, but the injuries are all about the same—a guy got burned, he fell through the roof or a floor, he got cut by falling glass, the ceiling or a wall fell on him, or he was overcome by heat or smoke. These injuries can't be prevented, not as long as the best way to put out a fire is to get close to it.

The hose couplings are frozen, and we have to hoist them over the exhaust pipe again. Billy Valenzio, the company chauffeur, leans down from the top of the engine, grabs the hose with one hand, and lifts it over the steaming pipe. I can see the strain in his handsome Italian face, and say, "I'd help you, Billy, but I know that a good-looking guy with muscles like yours can handle the job by himself."

"Yeah," Benny Carroll says, "if I had arms like you Bill, I'd pick the hose up two by two."

"Anyway," Royce interrupts, "you'd probably get mad at us if we tried to help ya. Every time ya pick the hose up ya say to yourself 'Man, this is good for my arms. I can just feel the muscles gettin' bigger and bigger.'"

[86]

"C'mon guys, what did I do?" Valenzio laughs. "Just because God gifted me with strength and beauty is no reason to take this abuse from guys like you."

Billy, in fact, has large muscular arms, that go with his large muscular chest, and he has every reason to be vain. But he isn't. It is because he is such a humble guy that we give him the business every once in a while. "You're all jealous," he says, as he strains with the next coupling.

"I'm not jealous," Knipps says, climbing up the side of the apparatus. He helps Billy with the hose until the coupling thaws, and loosens. "I figure if I do what you do, maybe some day I'll have arms like you."

The laughing is over, and the hose is laid on the bed of the apparatus. The wind blows even harder as the apparatus moves down the street toward the firehouse. It's almost 5:30 AM. as the truck backs into the firehouse. The stillness of the early morning hour is broken by the harsh sound of a siren as a police car speeds down Intervale Avenue, but we don't pay any attention to it. All we care about is sitting in the warm kitchen and relaxing for a while.

I am changing into a dry pair of pants as the bells come in. "Damn it, give me a break," I think as I slide down the pole from the second floor to the apparatus floor. Fortunately, the box that has been pulled is only five blocks away, on Boston Road. It is a false alarm. In ten minutes we have responded, made a search of the neighborhood, and returned to the firehouse. We have two more false alarms before the day crew begins arriving at eight o'clock. It is nine o'clock before I start the sixty-mile drive home to a good day's sleep.

6

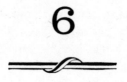

THE night is balmy, unlike anything I remember of past March nights. There is an easy wind blowing over the South Bronx from the Hunts Point Bay, bringing with it a peculiar garbage-smell of spring. The doors of the firehouse are open, and standing about in the front of our quarters we watch a small pack of boys ride their bicycles aimlessly up and down Home Street, stopping occasionally in front of Pete's Bodega to talk with a group of girls gathered there. The bicycle rims shine in the twilight, and foxtails hang casually from rear fenders. I count the circling boys and their bicycles. There are eight in the pack, dungareed and polo-shirted, healthy black or tan faces smiling, satisfied and happy on the first warm night of the year. Five of them ride sleek English racers, their backs arched over as they control the low half-moon handle bars, and the click-clicking sounds of sprockets are heard intermittently through the din of traffic as they coast down the street. The other three ride the heavier-type American bike—like the formidable Schwinn I dreamed about as a boy, but never owned. How hard their fathers must have worked to buy these bicycles, and how their mothers must have saved, for there is never an excess of money for people who live on Home Street.

As I watch the boys ride down the darkening street, I remember begging Bobby Walsh for a ride on his bicycle. "C'mon Bob, just a little ride, down to Jasper's candy store and back. C'mon Bob." How different this poverty of today is from the poverty of my childhood. Kids ride new, gleaming, expensive bicycles, mothers watch television between telephone calls, and fathers drive automobiles. Yet, the poverty is just as real, just as hurting, and the ignominy of being without money—being poor in a country where there is gold mixed with the street's concrete—is as obvious to the people of Home Street as it was to me on East Fifty-sixth Street twenty years ago.

I was twelve years old when our first television set was given to us. My uncle was working for the railroad, and his track boss bought a new set. He gave the old one to my uncle, and my uncle gave it to us. It had a ten inch screen encased in a wooden cabinet. I don't remember the cabinet style, or the shape of the control knobs, just that the reception was never very clear. My uncle delivered the set on a summer weekend, and I remember that my mother worried about how she would hide it from the welfare investigator. Television sets weren't allowed then, nor were telephones. I never understood that. Why should we hide a television set that was given to us? It was the rules. If one welfare family had a television set, even if it were given to them, then everybody on the dole would expect one. The set was covered with an old bedspread. It sat in the corner of our living room looking like a square box covered with an old bedspread. My mother would occasionally put a vase on top of it to make it appear that it had a purpose, but it still looked like a square box covered with an old bedspread. In the afternoon, the bedspread could be removed, because the welfare investigator only visited in the mornings. Either the afternoons were his own, or he spent the time in his office writing reports about suspicious-looking objects covered with old bedspreads. I don't know. But, that was during the McCarthy era, and everyone and everything was suspect.

One morning the investigator came. I was sitting at the kitchen table, which my mother had covered with the left-over linoleum from the kitchen floor. I was eating cereal, and my older brother was across the room from me, bathing in the kitchen tub. My mother was sitting in the living room reading a magazine—she always read a lot—when the knock on the kitchen door came. My brother left his bath quickly, because you don't lie lazily and relax when the bathtub is in the kitchen, and my mother adjusted the television bedspread before going to answer the door. She put her hand on the painted doorknob, then paused for a moment as if she remembered something. She turned, and looked briefly into the medicine-cabinet mirror hanging above the kitchen sink, turning her head from side to side and patting her hairdo. She adjusted her housecoat, and opened the door. There, standing in the unlighted hall was the welfare investigator. His face was black.

What's he doing in this neighborhood? Suppose someone saw him knocking at this door. What would they think? They would find out that we were on welfare. The news would get around, and my friends would do a job on me. I would be ridiculed, and I would have to fight my way out of any dirty remark. Why did they have to send this guy? What happened to Mr. Feeney, the regular investigator?

My brother dressed, and left the house. I went into our room, squeezed past the chest-of-drawers, and climbed up to the top bunk bed to read my collection of *Hot Rod* magazines. I tried to listen to the conversation that was flowing over the kitchen table, but the voices were low, and I couldn't hear. Instead, I looked at pictures of bullnosed '49 Fords.

After a short while, the investigator left, and I jumped down from the top bunk. My mother told me his name was Mr. Fogey, which I thought a strange name for someone who wasn't Irish. She said he was a much nicer man than Mr. Feeney. He was recommending extra money for us so that we could buy coats for the coming winter, and he didn't even bother to look through the rooms.

The boys of Home Street have disappeared with their bicycles, and twilight has become the dark of night. It is seven-thirty, and we have had only one run, a false alarm, since I started work at five-thirty. I am glad that it is slow—surprisingly slow for such warm weather—because today is the day after Saint Patrick's Day, a day of recuperation for many New Yorkers. Yesterday I played the bagpipes with the Fire Department Emerald Society Pipe Band, my kilt swaying in the wind as we marched up Fifth Avenue. After the parade we went bar-hopping down Lexington Avenue. The bars were overcrowded and turning people away, but always ready to receive a bagpiper and his friends on March 17th. Give the firemen a drink on me, a hundred voices would say, and ask the piper to play "Scotland the Brave."

"Not on Saint Patrick's Day. I won't play that, but I'll play the Garry Owen for yas," I say, "and O'Donnel Abu."

We talked to girls named Jablonski and Bluestein, their hair dyed green for the day, and to a Hawaiian bartender who wore a Kiss-Me-I'm-Irish button. A pretty black copy-writer explained to me how things would have been different in Ireland had Wolfe Tone been able to muster the soldiers in France for the '98 rebellion. It was a day of surprises and free booze. A young girl in a Forty-seventh Street bar lifted my kilt when I refused to tell her what I was wearing under it. I let it go, but a few minutes later when I lifted her skirt to her shoulders she took great offense.

"What's good for the goose . . . ," I told her. "Go ask Women's Lib."

[91]

By midnight I was exhausted and hiccoughing, and I took a cab to my mother's apartment for a night's rest.

Captain Albergray walks down the stairs from the second floor. "Everybody in the kitchen for company drill," he says.

Benny Carroll has suppered on aspirins and Alka-Seltzers, still suffering from "It's-a-great-day-for-the-Irish." He holds his hands to his head, and says, "Listen, Captain, let's not do anything too strenuous, if we can avoid it."

"Ya can't expect to wallow with the pigs one day, and soar with the eagles the next," Captain Albergray says. Benny laughs, and we walk to the kitchen for the hour drill period.

The members of Ladder 712 and Ladder 31 are sitting around a kitchen table, their attention focused on Billy O'Mann who has just announced that he has something interesting to say. He has a newspaper clipping in one hand, and a cup of coffee in the other.

"Listen to this," he says, waving the oblong piece of paper. "Yesterday, while all the brothers were enjoying themselves at the parade, Engine 82 had four rubbish fires, one right after another, up in Crotona Park. Each time they would put the fire out, and each time they left, the kids would light up another trash can. Lieutenant Nandre was working, ya know, and he was really pissed when they left here for the fourth time. So he gets to the park and sees the cans on fire. There were fifty kids around, but of course nobody knew who lit the fire. The guys in the engine stretch the booster line, and Lieutenant Nandre gets on the radio to report the fire. Get this. He says, Eighty-two Engine to the Bronx. We have another rubbish fire here at 2745, and one engine company is sufficient. Additional information: Upon arrival, he says, we found a squirrel overcome with smoke. One of the members revived the squirrel and it's now running around Crotona Park playing with its nuts."

There is a lot of chuckling, but Jerry Herbert doesn't believe it.

"C'mon, Bill," he says.

"So help me Christ," Billy says, "that's what he said." Billy-o holds up the newspaper clipping and waves it in front of everyone. "And a reporter must have been monitoring the fire calls, because the story is right here, out of one of the biggest newspapers in the world." I walk over to take a closer look at the clipping, and the headline reads, sure enough, BRONX FIREMAN REVIVES DYING SQUIRREL.

Captain Albergray interrupts the laughter, and the story, by yelling, "Hey Jerry, shut the television off, will ya. It's drill time."

As Jerry turns the switch, Lieutenant Lierly enters the kitchen, and says quietly, for the noise has toned down, "Ladder 31, on the apparatus floor."

Jerry, Billy-o, Dulland, McCartty, and Tom Leary head for the door. Ordinarily, we would drill together, but Lieutenant Lierly wants to train with the new power saw that was recently issued to Ladder 31.

Engine 85 is operating at a deep-seated rubbish fire out at Hunts Point—an East Bronx industrial area, filled with junk yards and automobile graveyards. The trash is piled high in Hunts Point. Small contractors pay someone, although no one knows who, to drop their truckloads of refuse in the vacant streets by the bay. Or they drop their loads without prearrangement, but they're always ready to part with a fifty-dollar bill if caught—small-scale graft that ends inevitably in hard work for firefighters. We know that Engine 85 will be out there for a few hours, pouring water on heaps of smoldering garbage, hoping the water will sink through and extinguish the fire.

Captain Albergray opens his worn, three-ring binder of training bulletins on the kitchen table. Lieutenant Coughlin of Ladder 712 sits beside him at the table, and we gather around them in a semicircle, sitting on armless chairs, or tables. Captain Albergray speaks.

"All the companies of the 27th Battalion are due for evaluation in the next few weeks. Now, the officers from the Bureau of Training are tough, and very little gets by them. You either know the stuff, or you don't. We, as firefighters, know that we are responsible for a lot more than extinguishing fire, and the evaluation officer can pick questions from reams of technical information. We don't know what they will ask, but I'm confident that we will have the right answers. In any case, we will review as much as we can during our drill periods for the next few weeks."

The men are uneasy in their chairs. They, as I, would rather drill on fire tactics or rescue procedures—and the interesting, exciting stories that invariably arise. But, the department requires that we know as much about a hose or a rope as a soldier knows about his rifle. A two-and-a-half-inch cotton jacketed fifty-foot length of hose weighs 71 pounds, and when filled with water weighs 178 pounds. The roof-rope we use in rescues is 150 feet, weighs 40 pounds, and is made by turning South American hemp fibers into yarn, twisting the yarn into strands, and braiding three strands into rope thirteen-sixteenths of an inch in diameter. Yes, it is going to be a boring drill period.

"We'll talk about the Scott Air-Pac first," Captain Albergray says. "We use this mask daily, and we should know its specifications."

"I use my car daily, and I don't know its specifications," I say to Benny, low enough not to be overheard.

"Cosmo, how much air does the cylinder contain?"

"In pounds or in cubic feet?" Cosmo asks.

"Both."

"There are 1980 pounds air pressure, or forty point three cubic feet."

"Okay. Benny, what is the cylinder tested at?"

"At 3000 pounds air pressure." Benny is studying chemical reactions, and this answer seems simple for him.

"Okay. Royce, what does the Air-Pac weigh?"

"Thirty pounds," Vinny answers.

"All we should know about that is," I can't help saying, "that the thing is too damn heavy and cumbersome, and the department has the responsibility to buy a better one."

"That may be right, Dennis," Captain Albergray says, slightly annoyed, "but the evaluation officer would call it a wrong answer."

The arm on the wall bell begins to move. The box sounds out: 2544. Saved by the bell. Everyone moves out, through the kitchen door, past the members of Ladder 31 sitting on their heels around a power saw, and climbs on fire engines while throwing shoes to the side of the apparatus floor. Willy Knipps is on housewatch, and yelling, "Kelly Street and one six seven," as he runs to the pumper.

The pumper stops at the corner of Kelly Street. A small boy says something to Captain Albergray and runs ahead. We follow him into an alleyway between two six-story tenements. At the end of the alley, in the backyard of one of the tenements, is a two-story frame building. The house is ramshackle, paint peeling from its splitting wooden sideboards, a step missing from its porch stairs. Caught in a circle of towering dwellings, the house is a reminder of the Bronx past, when the land was zoned for two-story multiple dwellings.

Inside, a mother is surrounded by the young boy and four smaller children. Their clothes are stained, and torn, and remind me of an illustration from a book of Dickens' stories my mother used to read to me. The mother does not speak English, and she points with some confusion to the interior of the apartment.

"She means the bathroom," the boy says.

There is a bedspring and a mattress in the living room, and a television set sits on the floor. That's all—a makeshift couch, striped and buttoned, and a T.V.

We pass the bedroom. In it there are three beds, all without head- or footboards. There is no other furniture, only a large carton filled with clothes, pushed between a bed and the wall. "THIS SIDE UP" it says on the side of the carton, with an arrow pointing to the ceiling. It would be called Pop Art in a rich man's home.

The kitchen is large, the walls patched with old, unpainted plaster. In the middle of the room there is a square wooden table, only slightly larger than a card table, painted white. Standing on either side of it is a straight-back chair, with carved legs unlike the legs of the table. The only two chairs in the apartment.

The kitchen floor is covered with large puddles of water. The tenant in the apartment above must have left the bathtub water running, and dozed off, or left the house, because the water is falling heavily from the bathroom ceiling and the pipe recesses. Lieutenant Coughlin sends two men from Ladder 712 to check out the apartment upstairs. Chief Niebrock, a gentleman always, excuses himself past the firemen gathered in the kitchen and looks about the bathroom. He studies the condition of the ceiling, and the light fixture. There is no hazard—only a mass of water that will certainly buckle the linoleum on the bathroom and kitchen floors.

The boy is standing next to me. He is wearing rubber shower clogs, and the water flows above the thin bottoms to wash his feet.

"How long have you been living here?" I ask him. He looks down at his feet, instead of up at me, and I am sorry I asked the question.

"Since Christmas," he answers, his voice low and unsure.

The men of Ladder 712 return from the floor above. They report to the Chief. The apartment upstairs was empty, but the door was open. The tub was running full force above the safety drain. They locked the door on the way out. The Chief gives the order to "Take up." Going through the rooms again I notice that there is not a single thing, no picture, mirror, or calendar, on the walls. It is all so desperately bare.

It is eight o'clock, and the space on the apparatus floor reserved for Engine 85 is still empty. The men of Ladder 31 are still examining the intricacies of the power saw—the nuances of engineering that they understand better than I.

There is still time for a half-hour drill, and we sit around the table again. Captain Albergray takes his place beside Lieutenant Coughlin.

"We'll try it again," he says. "Dennis, explain the procedure to be used if the regulator of the Air-Pac malfunctions."

I am about to answer, but I am conditioned to be quiet as the bells come in. Box 2738. The men of Ladder 712 respond, but we are safe. That is Engine 85's box. I begin to answer again, but stop when the telephone sounds three short rings.

"Take it in Eighty-two," Willy Knipps yells. In less than thirty seconds we are responding to 2738, Southern Boulevard and 172nd Street. Dammit, I knew that answer cold too. If you don't get enough air into the face piece, turn the bypass valve away from the body. The red valve. Then turn the knurled nut of the regulator. And the regulator valve. The yellow one. I wish I had known the answer that cold when we were in the cellar of that plastics factory. The smoke was gravy-thick, and we couldn't find the fire. We kept pushing in through the deadly atmosphere. Suddenly, I couldn't draw air, only an odd sucking sound. I started to rip my face piece off, but remembered where I was. I could make out all right in an ordinary fire, in ordinary smoke, but this plastic stuff is hard to take for more than twenty seconds. I remember thinking, red valve first? Yellow first? Like I was taking an exam. I dropped the hose, and turned both simultaneously.

Ladder 31 is behind us as we rush up Southern Boulevard. They must have been special-called too. The traffic is backed up, and we turn into the oncoming lane, forcing cars to the curb. We reach the intersection, and the pumper turns up 172nd Street, and stops opposite the alarm box. This is the box that Mike Carr never made it to, and as I picture the letter President Nixon sent to his widow I wonder if the President read the text before he signed it.

I stop thinking about Mike Carr and the President. Standing on the back step of the fire engine, I look at a wild scene before me, in the middle of the intersection. Ladder 712 and Ladder 31 are stopped side by side on Southern Boulevard, and Engine 45 is facing them having come from the opposite direction. Between the companies there is a naked man, his eyes flaming torture, his writhing body dancing in insane lament, and his mouth bellowing scornful, mad sounds in Spanish. In his hand he holds a whip, and like a Central Park carriage driver he swings it savagely.

Some Saturday mornings we would buy "guinea-heros," and walk the nine blocks from East 56th Street to Central Park. Salami and Swiss, with lettuce and mayonnaise, for a quarter. Put it on the bill, my mother said it's O.K. Our sandwiches were secured to our belts with old string as we climbed imaginary rugged mountains. It was Texas. Bobby Benson is being held on the other side of the hill, but the B BAR B boys will save him. At noon, we found a niche safe from strollers, and bit into the soggy, melting bread. Satisfied, but thirsty, we searched for a jumping-water fountain. Found it, and saw the Victorias rolling by, and the bobbing heads of tired mares. Run fast. Stay low. Grab the spring, the strong curved metal bar, and pull up. There is a crossbar to hold the ass. The driver sees us. The knotted whip end flies backward, and we take Spango, his eye bleeding, to the hospital.

The handle is four feet long, wrapped in black leather, and the whip is as long. Chief Niebrock tells Lieutenant Lierly that the man has to be restrained, but the whip swings dangerously on target for all who approach. A crowd has gathered. It yells taunts with great amusement, while impatient motorists lined up and down along the boulevard honk their car horns.

"Better surround and rush him," says the Chief. Benny and I move wide on the periphery to get behind him, but he watches us, and realizes what we are going to do. He runs to the front of Ladder 31's truck to ensure that no one will get behind him. McCartty gets a hospital blanket from the Chief's car, and opens it wide. He will hold it in front of him as a shield, and then wrap the guy up.

The man is not more than thirty, and filled with great energy that is made even stronger, I suppose, by his insanity. He takes the thin, tapered end of the handle, and swings the heavy end at the truck. It hits forcefully, and cracks run quickly from the point of impact along Ladder 31's windshield. Lieutenant Lierly, thinking of the damaged property report, yells "Goddammit," and Charlie McCartty, the blanket held at eye level, yells "Now." Seven firemen run towards the pathetic figure, and the whip swings frantically, but not fast enough. Charlie has the blanket around him, and the man is on the ground before I reach them.

"Pick him up, and carry him into a hallway until the ambulance comes," Chief Niebrock orders. The man is a wriggling mass, but I manage to grab his legs as Charlie lifts his shoulders. Somehow, the man frees his arms from the confines of the blanket, and lashes out, his nails digging into Charlie's cheeks. Both sides of his face are scratched, and slightly bleeding, but Charlie doesn't drop his end. "Get his arms!" he yells, but not before Billy-o and Tom Leary have grasped them. The man never stops squirming, and it is a continuous struggle to carry him.

In the hall, we lie the man face-down on the floor. The building is one of many old brick tenements lining the boulevard, and the hall reeks with strange odors. It looks like the floor has not felt the soft surface of a mop for months. Cagey Dulland enters with another blanket, and puts it under the man's face. At least he won't be able to smash his head against the hard marble floor.

"We can handle him," Charlie says. He and Billy-o have a firm grip on the restraining blanket, and Leary is holding the man's shoulders to the ground.

Benny and I, knowing that our part of the job is done, return to the street. There a man is saying to the Chief, "I know him. His name is Juan. We were together."

He talks in rapid, hard-to-understand, broken English. In

[99]

small, sharp phrases, he relates what has happened to his friend Juan.

"Juan and me drink together across the street in the Blue Velvet. Juan say something to a girl. The girl's boyfriend was there. An argument. Then a fight. Other men join in. Juan is on the floor. I run out of the bar, and stay across the street. For five minutes maybe. Then Juan is thrown out from the Blue Velvet by men who take off his clothes."

"Where did he pick up the whip?" asks Chief Niebrock.

But, the man doesn't answer. He shrugs his shoulders. Nobody knows.

"Did the cops get here yet?"

"Not yet, Chief."

"Well, stay with this man until the cops get here. He'll have to tell this story to them."

As we return to quarters I am thinking about the events that drove Juan from the edge of sanity. Time, it seems, is a circling tower. The action is always the same, only the actors change. It was only last week that Benny and I were sitting at a bar in the North Bronx. We had worked a tough day tour—more hours of the tour were spent inside of burning buildings than not—and decided to go for a few beers after work. We needed the relaxation that is easily found hopping from bar to bar. The hours passed quickly, and it was almost ten o'clock as we entered a small place on East Tremont Avenue. The joint was nearly empty. There was no one at the bar—only a group of four men sitting at a table in the rear.

"Two beers," Benny said, laying a five dollar bill on the bar. I threw up three singles, and some change. The bartender looked at us coldly, with a suspicious glance, pulled the stick for the two steins, and took one of my dollars. He rang it up, walked to the other end of the bar, picked up the *Daily News,* and ignored us. "Friendly, huh?" I said to Benny.

"Say no more," he replied.

We were going to drink the beer and leave. Any joint where

the man behind the bar is reading the newspaper isn't worth staying in.

Benny and I were talking about the day's fires when our attention was redirected by a loud slam. The door of the ladies room at the rear of the place snapped shut. A young girl, about twenty, walked past the men at the table, and approached us. She was not bad looking. She was built nicely, but her mouth was shaped in a peculiarly repugnant way, which implied that her favorite words were "Go screw yourself!"

She walked directly to me, as if she had planned the move. "You're sittin' on my stool," she said.

I looked down the bar, empty but for Benny and me. The bartender's nose was between the pages of the newspaper, and the men at the table were talking amongst themselves. I didn't know what this girl was up to, but I had drunk enough beer not to care. "Listen sweetheart," I said, "there are twenty empty stools in the place, but this particular one is yours, right?"

"That's right," she answered, moving her body so that one shoulder was lower than the other.

"C'mon, give me a break," I said to her with a forced disinterest, and looked away.

"That's my stool, and I want it," she said.

"Well, you're not going to get it," I said.

She turned in a huff, and walked to where the men were sitting. She said a few words to them. All four men got up. Three took their drinks to the middle of the bar. The fourth walked to my side. He smiled slightly, but in that ironic way that told me that he knew more about something than I. And God was he big. Bigger even than Charlie McCartty. "I can vouch for the girl," he said. "She was sitting right there."

"Look," I said, wishing that Charlie was with us, and Billy-o, and Herbert, "it's really not that important. If the girl wants the stool so bad I'll give it to her." The girl smiled, and approached us. Benny moved to the stool at the corner of the bar. I moved over one. The girl sat, still smiling.

"Ya know, you're a real snotty guy," he said to me, both hands on the bar. It was going to be hard to avoid a confrontation. I remember laughing inwardly at that understatement.

I tried to ignore him. "We're in trouble," I said to Benny.

"I can see that," he replied. "I really don't wanta leave my teeth laying on the floor here, but I don't think we'll have much choice."

The man spoke again. "I think I'm gonna break your ass just for laughs. Just as soon as you make the wrong move." The three others, poised and confident, chuckled. The bartender put the paper down, and became interested.

I looked at Benny as he played pensively with a book of matches. "Listen Ben," I said, "you don't have to get involved in this, but I'm going to have to make a move."

"I'll be right behind you. Say no more."

Just then the front door opened. A small-framed man walked in. "Benny Carroll," he sings. "How are you? Haven't seen ya in years."

"Hey," Benny forgot his name. "How are ya? What are you doing here?"

"I own the place. Bought it about six months ago." The bartender walked up to the front end of the bar, and listened to the order. "Buy my friend, and his friend, a drink!"

It was over. The God of my grammar school days watches over me. He who lived in the tabernacle on Fifty-fifth Street and First Avenue protects me still. I am safe in fires, sober and frightened, and in bars, drunk and unafraid. My enemy took the girl by her elbow to the table in the rear, making room for our redeemer, the lost friend—the owner.

Yes, life seems to make recurrent statements. I don't fully understand karma, the three gunas, or the Blessed Trinity, but I know they exist. They operate differently, but their meaning is the same. They control. They lead me up a winding staircase, assuming that with each step I'll be able to see farther. But I never do. The horizon is the same, and I can only compare it with what I saw at lower steps. It has no profound implications. I only know that I would have been lucky to leave that bar naked—or at all.

Yes, time, if studied, is cyclical. Only at death does it become linear.

It is a little after nine when we return to the firehouse kitchen. The ambulance came for Juan, and the police came to talk to his friend. It will all be recorded officially—the police report, the fire report (no fire, assisted distraught civilian), the ambulance report, the hospital report. And Juan will end up in Bellevue for a few days if luck is on his side, or in a state hospital for the rest of his life, forgotten by all but a few close relatives.

Engine 85 is back from Hunts Point, tired and disgusted. They had to stretch two full blocks for a rotten garbage fire. Wasted time, wasted effort, all because the laws are meaningless when a few dollars are available. They tell how the men of Ladder 48 wore themselves out overhauling the mountains of trash. Pulling with their hooks, their halligan tools, their hands at car bumpers, fenders, refrigerators, mattresses, metal boxes, wooden boxes, bedsprings, car seats, tires, and hundreds of brown paper bags filled with American waste.

Cagey Dulland is cooking the night's meal. The kitchen is crowded, as it usually is before the meal. Men pass the stove, excited by the cooking smells, looking for a little knosh, a small indicator of the meal to come. Willy Knipps begins to cut the meat. Thick slices of sirloin, cut on the bias, hot juice spilling over the cutting board, mushrooms falling to either side of the meat. He cuts into the burned edges of the steak, through the reddening center, and again through the crisp edges. Each time he feels the cutting board he flicks his wrist, and the meat falls uniformly into a chrome serving pan, carried there by a slight movement of the arm and a turning knife. Fourteen, fifteen slices, and Willy comes to the end, the lonely tapered end not worthy of slicing. He cuts it bruskly into three parts. He puts one in his mouth as he knifes another and offers it to me. Cagey, watching the progress closely, reaches past me for the third. My mouth waters, and the meat dissolves like a communion wafer, the juices leaving a desire for more.

There are two more cuts waiting to be sliced, and Willy raps the knife quickly against the long thin metal of the knife sharpener. I walk onto the apparatus floor, counting the minutes until the bell rings signaling mealtime, and leaving the space behind Willy for another to watch him slice down to the knosh end.

It is a quarter to ten as Billy-o pulls the hammer of the bell on the Chief's car. The price written on the blackboard is "$1.35." I take the money from my pocket and put it into the collection bowl sitting on a shelf next to the blackboard.

"Just to show you how much confidence I have in you Cagey, I'm going to pay for the meal before I taste it."

Cagey grins as he walks by me, plate in hand. There is a running joke in the firehouse that the meal does not have to be paid for if it is not absolutely satisfying. I run my finger across my chalked name on the blackboard, and take a place between Billy-o and Tom Leary.

On the plate before me there are two pieces of meat, and a large baked potato. Next to the plate there is a side dish of salad: lettuce, tomatoes, cucumbers, red onions, scallions, stripped carrot. There is a bowl of french dressing, and a bowl of sour cream and chives on each of the four tables. Tom is telling Billy-o about the months of skin grafting he underwent. Skin from his belly to his leg and foot. Micro-thin layer over layer. He was working, making a search, in the apartment above a fire. The floor gave way. Tom's leg went down. He couldn't get loose. His leg jutting into a roaring inferno, he screamed, and screamed. His boot was gone when they pulled him out, but parts of it were stuck to the bone of his leg.

"Jesus," I say, "can't we find a more pleasant topic to talk about? Please pass the salt and pepper."

"We're professionals, Dennis," Billy-o says, passing the two shakers. "We should be able to talk about anything when we eat, and not be so involved with it. Like doctors, ya see. We've got a job where we see a lot of ugly things, and what happened to Tom shouldn't bother you. At least he lived. How many people have you seen with all their skin burnt right off their bodies?"

As he talks, Billy cuts another piece of meat. "Pass the salad dressing, will ya," I say, disregarding his question.

"Don't want to talk about it, huh?" Billy-o says.

"No," I reply, taking the bowl of dressing from him, "but, you go ahead. I'll just listen." Billy-o and Tom laugh, and Tom continues to explain his operations.

The steak is the best I've eaten in a long time, and I decide to ignore the conversation and enjoy it. I have cut and chewed two small pieces when the dreaded bells begin to chime. Box 2743. Charlotte and 170th Street. It figures.

Going up Wilkens Avenue I think about Tom Leary. I have never been caught above a fire, except for that one time when Gintel asked me if I had a match. I'd rather be in a fire, or in front of it, than above. But that is a truckman's job. He must make a search above the fire, because that is where the hazard is. That is where people get trapped. No, going above the fire is not what I like to do. I like to have that nozzle in my hands. I like to fight the fire, not gamble with it. All firefighters take risks, but being above the fire is the greatest of all. Tom got caught, and he ended up in a hospital bed for three months. Yet, that is what he likes doing. It's part of the job. Anyway, the doctors worked a miracle on his leg. He doesn't even limp. It doesn't hurt him anymore either. It just looks ugly.

The pumper stops at Charlotte Street. It looks like a false alarm, but we make the search. Up and down the street. Thumbs down—*the signal ten ninety-two is transmitted for Box 2743.* I wish the city would look at the records, the statistics, and take this alarm box away from this location. They should post a policeman at the corner, with a walkie-talkie. In the long run it

would be less expensive. And maybe I would get to finish a
meal now and then.

As the pumper begins to back into quarters the dispatcher
orders us to respond to Box 2744. Stebbins Avenue and 170th
Street. That is two blocks up from Charlotte Street. We head up
Wilkens Avenue again, but this time I think about the evaporat-
ing juices on my plate in the kitchen. It is another false alarm.
Probably the same guy who pulled the box at Charlotte. He was
probably walking home, or to a party, or even to work. But,
that's only conjecture.

As we return to the firehouse, there is a row of garbage cans
burning on Wilkens Avenue. Someone must have seen us head-
ing toward 170th Street, and became inspired. But, that's conjecture, too. We stop to extinguish the fire. Ladder 712 stops to
help, but Captain Albergray waves them on. There is no sense
keeping two companies from their meal when we can operate
with one.

Benny pulls the booster hose off. I sit on the back step, and
watch Knipps and Royce turn the cans over. I can feel anger
building within me, and I don't like the feeling. I am hungry,
and the meat will certainly be cold and dried out when we return. Why do people set these fires? It had to be set. Flame
doesn't jump from can to can. Why? Especially when I am hungry. Goddam lawless bunch of bastards. Who? I don't know. I'm
annoyed with myself. I know I'm complaining because there's
a meal waiting for me. But there are plenty of people around
here who have never had a meal as good, hot or cold. Stop
complaining. You get paid to serve the people. When the alarm
comes in, you go out. When you see a fire, you stop and extinguish it. So someone pours gasoline on a bunch of garbage cans,
or someone pulls a false alarm. So what? Your meat gets cold,
and the potatoes. So what? There are people with serious problems in this town.

I feel a little better as we return to the firehouse, but I am
still hungry. Mayonnaise. That's it. A couple of pieces of bread,

a little mayo, and the meal is saved. Potatoes are fattening anyway.

It is three-thirty in the morning now. Ladder 712 went off duty three hours ago. Ladder 31 was special-called to an "all-hands" down on 149th Street, and while they were gone Engine 85 caught a job in an occupied building on Hoe Avenue. Chief Niebrock is going to recommend them for a unit citation, because they operated there without a ladder company in the initial stages of the fire. They rescued seven people huddled above the fire. We had a few more false alarms since meal time, a couple of rubbish fires, and a small, inconsequential, one-room job in an abandoned building.

The night is still warm, and the doors of the firehouse are wide open. There is a slight breeze, and pieces of paper flutter along the cobblestones of Intervale Avenue. Some of the men have gone upstairs to lie down, some are in the kitchen watching the *Late, Late Show*, and four of us are standing under one of the open overhead doors. Harry Maye is in Engine 85, and he is telling Benny, Billy-o, and me about the fire they had on Hoe Avenue. Suddenly, two shots ring through the air. There is only one sound like the cracking of a pistol, and we all jump toward the street to see where it came from.

A young man is running down Home Street. He is across the street, passing Mother Wall's Church, and another shot is let off. The man is directly across from the firehouse. He turns north and runs up Intervale Avenue. We can see now why he is running. There is a cop chasing him, and there are about thirty yards between them. The man crosses Intervale Avenue to our side of the street, but the cop continues his chase on the other side. A squad car careens down Home Street, its red light blinking.

"They'll get the guy now," Harry Maye says. The car turns up Intervale Avenue, but the driver doesn't see the fugitive on our side of the street or the cop on the other side. The car passes both men, and speeds up to the corner of Chisholm Street. It stops. The man sees that he cannot continue up Intervale without running into the squad car, so he turns and runs south on Intervale. The cop on the other side lets off another shot, and starts to cross the Avenue.

We are standing outside of the firehouse now. I am against the building, next to a community bulletin board that protrudes three inches from the firehouse wall. The man is running toward us now. Another shot zips through the air. None of us say anything, but we are all thinking the same thoughts. Should we tackle the guy as he runs past? The man is coming, straining with effort as he runs. He is a young man, powerfully built. I can see the desperation in his face as he approaches. Then another shot bursts, and our minds are decided. It has only been seconds since we saw the man running down Home Street, and five shots have been fired. We run into the firehouse for cover. The man passes, and I look to see if he has a gun in his hand. He doesn't. The cop passes, and falls from exhaustion as the man runs into the building next to the firehouse. He is a young cop. He can't be more than twenty-two or twenty-three. I feel very sorry for him as he falls, and a little guilty that I didn't put my life on the line and stop the fugitive. I rush out of the firehouse to help him, but he is on his feet again as I approach.

Ed Shoal of Engine 85 is on housewatch, and he has called for additional assistance. He used to be a cop before he came to our job, and he called as soon as he heard the first two shots. He knows the danger. He knows that there is trouble when triggers are pulled.

The squad car has turned around, and is speeding down Intervale. The cop has followed the man into the tenement, and we wave the squad car down.

"They went in there," we say, pointing to the building.

An older, bigger cop gets out of the squad car, pistol drawn, and runs into the building.

Sirens are wailing through the neighborhood, and soon there are six patrol cars on Intervale Avenue. Cops go into the building, into the cellar, into the adjoining building. A cop and a Sergeant stand guard at the front of the tenement. I move to where they are standing, and I recognize the cop's face. It is Knipps' brother-in-law, and an old friend of mine.

"How ya doing, Whitey," I say, my voice serious and concerned.

"Oh, hello Dennis," he replies happily. He has worked in this precinct for a good seven years, and nothing shakes this man up anymore.

Two policemen come out of the building, the fugitive braced between them. The young cop is right behind them. He talks to the Sergeant and Whitey as the fugitive is placed into the back seat of a squad car. The Sergeant is still writing in his logbook as the young cop gets into the car next to his prisoner.

Other firemen have joined me in leaning on a parked car. Whitey comes over to pass the time of day, for he knows most of us on Intervale Avenue.

"That cop did a nice job in catching that guy," I say. "What did they want him for?"

"Well," Whitey says, his eyes sparkling, and his mouth grinning, "it started out as a domestic squabble. The guy's wife threw him out of the house, and he tried to get back in through the fire-escape window. The sector car got there, and they tried to settle the dispute. We get these things all the time—four or five a night. Anyway, the guy took a rap at the cop, and ran away."

"Is that all?" Ed Shoal asks, "and there were five discharges?"

Whitey laughs, and starts to walk away. The Sergeant is ready to leave. "What can I tell ya?" he says. "It was a young cop. He'll learn."

"We'll see ya, Whitey," I say.

"Yeah, so long guys. Say hello to my little brother-in-law for me, will ya."

"He's in the kitchen watching television. Want me to get him?"

"No, I don't have time. Tell him I'll see him Sunday."

"Okay. S'long."

The excitement is over, and we walk back into the firehouse. Billy-o is standing by the door, and he notices the bulletin board. "Hey, look at this," he says.

We walk over to investigate. He has his finger in a hole in the side of the steel encasement. "Is this a bullet hole?" he questions.

"Let me see," Shoal says, looking over Billy-o's shoulder. "It sure looks like it. Sure it is. Look. The bullet is in there. I'll be damned. The bulletin board was just put up there two weeks ago, and it has a bullet hole in it already."

"Jesus, and we were standing right here too," Billy-o says.

I take a look. I put my pinkie in the hole, and feel the bullet. It is caught between the outer and inner casing. "Man, and I was standing right next to the thing." And I felt sorry for that cop, too. Well, he's a young cop. As Whitey said, he'll learn. But he almost killed me. Well, he didn't though, did he? Almost doesn't count in anything. I learned that early.

The bells interrupt my thoughts. 2743. Charlotte Street. "Get out Eighty-two and Thirty-one. Chief goes too."

Again, going up Wilkens Avenue. It's probably another false alarm. I hope it's a fire. I don't want anybody hurt, and I don't want to see anyone's property destroyed, but I need something to occupy my mind. But, it is another false alarm.

On the way back to the firehouse I think: If time is cyclical, I wonder what my next experience with a bullet will be?

7

Tomorrow is Easter. I have the day off, and will be at home with Pat and the boys. My brother and his family will come up, and my mother. My brother will talk about the mentally disturbed children he teaches to read and write, and we will scold our own children for making too much noise. I'll talk about fires and firefighters, and my mother will relate the successes and failures of the guys I grew up with. We'll laugh, and sing songs with the children. The youngest of them will grab at the strings of my guitar and the songs will be interrupted. We will eat heartily, and afterwards the children will ask me to play the bagpipes, and I will tell them I am too tired, and too full. When the table is cleared, the half-devoured ham wrapped securely in plastic, the dishwasher belching its ugly sound, we will sit by the fireplace, joined by the women, and sip brandy and crack nuts, throwing the shells into the fire. It will be a fine day.

It is now eight o'clock, and I have just crossed the George

Washington Bridge. The traffic on the Cross-Bronx Expressway moves slowly. It is a cold day, and I can see the exhaust of the cars before me rise up to the morning sky, adding mist to the already heavy air.

As I drive down Home Street I can see that one of the overhead apparatus doors is still broken, still in that open position. The door has been out of order for two weeks now, as the repair requisition moves from one department to another. The radio newscaster just said it is one of the coldest April days in history, and the firehouse door is only partially covered with a thin piece of canvas. I park the car, and think about organizing a sit-down strike, as I walk to the firehouse. I have called the union, and the officers have followed the requisition with phone calls, but we get the same stock answer from both the administration and the union: "We're working on it." Yes, they work on it while we freeze our butts off. I would like to organize a strike until we get a firm commitment from the city. A good union would not settle for "We're working on it," and would demand that the workers be relocated to a warm building. Don't make waves, I tell myself, or you'll find yourself working in the ass end of Staten Island. The order can come down, *"Fireman First Grade Dennis E. Smith, from Engine Company 82, to Engine Company 400,"* and it would take me three hours to drive to work. No, don't make waves. Put another sweater on.

It is twenty after nine as I enter the kitchen for a cup of coffee. Charlie McCartty, as usual, is the center of attention. He is telling a story about bouncing around last night on Westchester Avenue. The men are sitting, or standing, coffee cups in hand as Charlie talks.

"So I end up in this joint there by 174th Street. There's a beauty behind the bar, almost naked, big boobs, but she had pasties on. A cheater, ya know. So I had a drink, and looked the place over. There were a lot of good-lookin' Puerto Rican girls, but they were all with guys, so I figured I'd have a few and look at the chick behind the bar. Then in came these three guys, and you could tell they were cops, sports jackets on, shined shoes, and all. This one guy stood at the bar, and cased the joint like he was gonna buy it. He pushed his jacket back, and put his hand on his hip, so that his gun was showing, and I don't know why, but I thought that was a shitty thing to do. So, I said to myself, screw him, and I didn't even ask him to dance."

The guys chuckle, but nobody is floored with laughter. Billy-o throws his newspaper on the table, and says, "Is that all there is to that story, Charlie?" Charlie backs against the wall, as if ready for an attack.

"I don't know," Charlie replies. "I left my notes up in my locker."

"Well ya better go and reread them, 'cause that was not a very funny story."

"Listen to Billy-o, the Don Rickles of Intervale," Charlie retorts.

"I may not be the funniest guy in the world," Billy-o says, "but I know you long enough to rate your stories, and you get a zero on that one. Zip."

"That's how much you know, Billy. You wouldn't know a funny story if you were locked in a room with it. Anyway, it's nine-thirty, so you can take your *New York Times* upstairs and sweep the floor with it."

The nine-thirty test signal comes over the bell system. Eleven bells, and eleven bells. It is time for committee work. We all agree to do an extra thorough housecleaning job, so that the firehouse will be clean for those who eat their Easter meal here tomorrow. Also, if we do a good job today, there won't be much for tomorrow's crew to do. You can't ask a guy to mop floors on Easter Sunday.

The members start splitting up, each knowing their assigned duties. Billy-o heads for the locker room, and I grab a broom and go towards the cellar stairs. As I leave the kitchen, I can hear Charlie say, as he puts the chairs on top of the tables, "No wonder he can't tell what a funny story is. Nobody who reads *The New York Times* has a sense of humor." I laugh to myself as I walk down the stairs.

[113]

In the firehouse cellar there is a full-sized pool table, a small bumper-pool table, and a ping-pong table. We paid for them, but we don't get to use them very much. At least, I don't. Every time I start to play a game of pool or ping-pong the bells ring, and by the time I get back I've lost interest. Some of the men, though, are not as easily frustrated as I, and they spend most of the time between fires in the damp, dingy cellar. I spend most of my time in the kitchen, reading magazines, or watching the television, or just talking with the guys on the apparatus floor.

I am standing in the middle of the cellar floor. There is a big oil burner, and an oil tank that takes up a good part of the room, a table, a few wooden benches that were liberated from a school, and about three dozen standing jacks that were recently put there to support the aged apparatus floor above. The oil-stained concrete floor around the pool tables is covered with squashed cigarette butts. I start to push the broom around the floor. As I near the oil burner I notice the grating cover of the sump pump is moved to one side, leaving a gaping hole in the floor. Some of the men urinate here instead of walking upstairs to the bathroom. I stop pushing the broom. I take the hose connected to the oil burner water system, and hose the floor around the sump pump. I kick the cover over the hole, and hose that down. It looks a little cleaner now.

The cellar swept, I return to the kitchen. Billy-o is there tacking a notice on the bulletin board. He tells me that Chief Lany, the Chief who works opposite Chief Niebrock and us, has come down with hepatitis.

"I don't know for sure, but I bet he got it here," Billy-o says, "and there is only one way to make sure it doesn't spread. Read this."

The message, typed in bold letters, reads:

TO ALL MEMBERS OF THE BIG HOUSE

Due to the recent discovery of a case of hepatitis to one of the members, the second such case in a year, a consensus was taken from the members on ways to improve the sanitary conditions in the kitchen, and elsewhere in the house. One C.D. [cave or cellar dweller] suggested a bidet to be put over the sump pump. Another suggested a delousing machine, or a personal flit gun for everyone so they could spray themselves and their old lady before and after work. But, the serious-minded among us prevailed, and the consensus was to purchase a dishwashing machine or two. This costs money, so one dollar per payday will be collected until we have $700.00 (7 pay days). This, of course, is voluntary, but the alternative is leprosy, syphilis, gonorrhea, common cold, etc.

Thank you,
Billy O'Mann

"It'll never work Bill," I say. "I like the way you presented your case, but as long as there are probies around here to wash dishes you'll never get the guys to part with seven bucks."

"That's the point. As long as the probies wash the dishes, the dishes never get done right. They don't have their heart in the work."

Billy-o is right. The dishes and the silverware in the firehouse are always greasy, and we do need a dishwasher, but we just went for three hundred for a meat slicing machine, and few firefighters will be willing to cough up the dough for a machine that is not absolutely necessary. Inflation is hurting all of us.

It is a quarter after ten as the bells signal Box 2743. First run of the day. Charlotte and 170th streets. A day never passes that 2743 does not come in.

I can feel the cold penetrate my feet as I kick my shoes off and climb into my boots. Marty Hannon of Engine 85 is on housewatch, wearing his heavy rubber coat, and a scarf wrapped around his neck. He pulls back the canvas, and the pumper turns up Intervale Avenue.

There is a young girl waiting in the cold for us. She is about twenty-one or two, thin and sickly. She wears fur fringed slippers, and her cotton housecoat flaps in the wind. "My husband," she says, "he took an O.D."

"What's the address?" Captain Albergray asks.

"811 Seabury Place, Apartment 6," she answers.

The pumper takes off, leaving her to walk the short block to Seabury Place. We reach 811. Someone has painted a sign on the marble wall of the vestibule: "NO JUNKIES ALLOWED—ENTER AT YOUR OWN RISK." How ironic. We climb the stairs to the second floor. Captain Albergray and I, followed by Danny Gainful, Billy-o, and the other members of Ladder 31. The door of Apartment 6 is open, and there is a young man and a girl standing over the sprawled body of a handsome Puerto Rican. He is lying on the kitchen floor.

"Get us some ice," Danny says to the girl. She is high, and doesn't seem to comprehend what is happening. "ICE," Danny yells, but the girl still stares at him.

The young man moves to the refrigerator. Danny and I kneel at either side of the strapping hulk on the floor. Danny has a handful of ice in his hand, and places it under the guy's testicles. I take some ice and place it on the back of his neck. Danny slaps and pinches his cheeks, as I shake his shoulders as hard as I can. Chief Niebrock enters and orders Lieutenant Lierly to send one of the men from Ladder 31 down for the resuscitator, but Billy-o has already gone for it.

"What's his name?" Danny says to the girl.

She understands, and responds, "Peter."

I check his pupils—not dilated yet. The pulse is very weak. "C'mon Peter, wake up. Get up. Talk to me. Tell me how you feel. The dope is gonna kill ya if you don't wake up. C'mon."

Billy-o enters with the resuscitator, checks to make sure it is on the inhalator position, and puts the facepiece over the guy's nose and mouth. The pure oxygen helps. His wife is there now, and whimpering, "He's not a junky, he's not."

Danny asks, "Then why did you turn him on?"

"He turned himself on—he took too much," she cries.

Danny looks at me. "Yeah, he turned himself on. He almost turned himself off."

I know what he means. Danny has a look of disgust on his face. He understands the misery—the guy on the floor, his nodding friends, his helpless wife—caused by drugs, but he has seen so much he is convinced that nothing can be done about it. The ambulance attendant comes with a rolling chair, and the men carry the guy out. As we leave the apartment, Danny says, "This is some shithouse." I take a quick look around, and nod in agreement. "A shame," he says.

As we walk down the stairs I think of the muckraking novels of the beginning of this century. Things were bad then. Jews without money were ill-used, the Irish and Germans and Serbs and Italians were without money and ill-used. But that was fifty and seventy years ago. The people of the South Bronx are without money, and they aren't used at all. They are left to pine in lethargy while their children put needles in their arms.

In the kitchen again. It is eleven o'clock. Billy-o and Jerry Herbert are cooking lunch. Two two-foot pans are on the chrome counter, and Billy-o is filling them with sausage—the long, thin breakfast type. Jerry is cutting green peppers to mix with the already cut onions. Fourteen loaves of Italian bread wait slicing in the corner of the counter, enough for twenty-eight sandwiches. It will be a good lunch for sixty cents.

Three short rings on the department phone interrupt the business of the cooks. The housewatchman yells, "Eighty-two and Thirty-one. 1335 Simpson Street. Third floor." He yells it again, and adds, "Chief goes too." The pumper leaves quarters, followed by the truck and Chief's car. Up 169th Street. To Simpson. There is smoke seeping through the frame of a third floor window.

"Stretch three lengths," Captain Albergray says as he hurries by. We drop three lengths, and the pumper takes off to a hydrant, leaving a tail of hose in the street as it moves away.

Vinny Royce has the nozzle, and he enters the building. Willy Knipps and I follow, dragging the folds of empty hose.

The stairway is filled with exiting Puerto Ricans—old men trying to walk faster than they should, young girls with babies in their arms screaming back to still more young girls, old ladies being guided by pretty teenagers. There is much confusion as the parade moves by. An old man trips, a woman sobs uncontrollably, a toddler is lost by a hysterical mother. The rapid sound of Spanish seems even quicker in the excitement, and higher in the echoing halls. Sharp series of shrill noises bounce from the walls, making the exodus seem even more desperate than it is. On the third floor, three teenage boys squeeze past us. Two are carrying either ends of a television set, the other carries a portable phonograph. There is fire in the building, and the poor try to protect their most expensive possessions.

We wait in the hall for Bill to connect the pumper to the hydrant, and open the discharge gate. The men of Ladder 31 have made a search of the apartment. It is vacant and unoccupied. Richie Rittman is on his knees, his face stained, his nose flowing. "It's only one room," he says to Royce, "nothing to it— a cup 'a tea."

The water comes, and Royce braces himself for the hardening of the hose.

"Let's go, Vinny," Captain Albergray says.

They crawl into the apartment, and I hump the hose behind. It's a long hall—a snotty hall. Vinny reaches the end room, and opens the nozzle. At the ceiling. All around. In circles. One hundred and fifty gallons per minute. The fire is out in a minute. Sixty seconds of water, and the building is saved. A perfect job. Minimum water damage. The apartments below will not have to be vacated because of waterlogged and fallen ceilings.

Knipps takes the nozzle as Vinny goes for a blow to an open window and clean air. We wait for the smoke to lift. Chief Niebrock takes a thorough look, and leaves for the floor above where he will check for fire extension. McCartty and Billy-o are in the room, hooking down the charred and blistered ceiling.

The minutes pass quickly. We give the room a slight and final bath. Take up. The job's done.

There is a commotion in the hall. A woman screams. "I've been robbed. I've been robbed." Two small boys huddle at her side. "My television set. My phonograph. They are gone."

I look at the boys. Two pre-schoolers, handsome in their little pea-coats. But their faces are dull. The adventure of the fire next door to them is gone. Dull, and unhappy, as if they realize that there will be no more Saturday morning cartoons for a while. No more *Sesame Street*, or *Mister Rogers*.

Chief Niebrock investigates. Writes the name and the apartment number in his notebook for the fire report. The police will come to investigate also.

I can remember Sister Mary Jean telling us that it was a much more serious sin to steal from our neighbors than it was to steal from a place like Macy's. I was in the fifth grade then, and I believed it. I still believe it.

My childhood home was on East Fifty-sixth Street one block west of Sutton Place. One block. A black and white contrast I'll always remember. Even then, Sutton Place was reserved only for millionaires. Winter-tanned boys in camel's-hair coats would wait on the corner for a taxi, or for their school car. They had plenty of money in their pockets, lunch money at least, but we never thought of roughing them up for it. They were people. Instead, we walked to Bloomingdale's. Three blocks up, and two over. Leather gloves, baseball mits, pocket knives, shirts, ties, cuff links—we took anything we could sell. Bloomingdale's wasn't people. We never stole from people.

"Do ya think those guys set the place up to create the confusion?" Vinny asks, looking back as he drags the limp hose down the stairs.

"Probably," I answer. It doesn't make sense to say any more about it. "We were lucky," I continue, "that we got here as fast as we did. A few more minutes and we would have had a second alarm on our hands."

"Yeah," Vinny replies. "Lucky."

We are back in the firehouse, and it is twelve-thirty. The sausages are popping in the oven, the peppers and onions sizzle in a frying pan. We are all dirty, faces blackened and greasy, mucus hardened under noses, ears filled with grimy dust. I head towards the bathroom to wash up. Billy-o climbs down from the back wheel—the tiller of the truck. He takes his glove off. His hand is covered with a bloodied handkerchief. Vinny, Knipps, and I take a look, joined by Rittman and McCartty.

"It's nothin'," Billy-o says, looking at the gash across the back of his thumb. "A piece of glass must have gone down my glove when I took the windows out."

"Nothin' hell," Rittman says, "I'll bet you need ten stitches."

"How much you wanna bet?" Vinny says looking at the thumb.

"Two dollars, for ten stitches," Richie says.

"I'll take two dollars for eight stitches," Vinny replies.

"I'll take two for seven stitches," Knipps says. "It doesn't look like it will take ten."

"Okay, nine stitches is open," Vinny says looking at me. "Do you want to take nine, Dennis?"

"I'll take nine," McCartty says, before I have a chance to answer.

"Holy Christ," Billy-o says, "I can't get you guys to give a dollar a payday for a dishwasher—"

"All right," I interrupt, "I'll take a deuce for six stitches. That's ten bucks all together, right?"

Everyone agrees. Billy-o leaves us to report the injury to Lieutenant Lierly, mumbling to himself as he walks. Vinny chalks the stitch projections on the kitchen blackboard, so there won't be any disagreement later.

His injury reported, Billy-o drives his car to the emergency room of Bronx Hospital. His name will now be incorporated into the average of 5,000 injuries N.Y.C. firefighters suffer in the line of duty each year.

"I hope he remembers to bring back some bandages," Lieutenant Lierly says as Billy-o drives away. "Our first-aid kit is getting low."

Jerry Herbert has served lunch. The sandwiches are great, but I have an unsettled feeling in my stomach. I am not sure if it is because of the fire we have just come from, or because with every bite I expect an alarm to come in.

We eat the meal without interruption.

I put sixty cents into the collection bowl, and then boil some water for tea. I make tea the Irish way—half tea, half milk. There is a magazine on the table. The television is noising the nonsense of an afternoon show that sends the winners on weekend dates to Europe. The bells come in, but they are not for me. Engine 85, only. They hustle, half skipping, half running, out of the kitchen. I pick up the magazine and start to read. The Park Avenue rich, it seems, have concerned themselves with raising money to get a group of Black Panthers out of jail. A splendiferous party is given high above the boulevard gardens of Park Avenue, and the Pucci-clad chic and the dashiki-clad Panthers are exposed to each other. The story annoys me because I keep thinking of those two kids who haven't a television set to watch any longer. Come away from Park Avenue. Stop dealing with abstractions—the philosophic-cultural-social implications of high bail for media exploiters. Look at the real world. Take Simpson Street for example.

"Ping. Ping." The bells are hammered. Box 2558. I throw my tea bag into the garbage can on the way out. Intervale Avenue and 165th Street. Captain Albergray presses hard on the siren. Thirty decibels over rock sound. Hard rock. In an empty auditorium. I can feel the wailing going through both ears, and meeting at the auditory nerve. I wonder what damage is being done.

Ladder 31 and the Chief are behind us, red lights flashing, sirens squealing, jerking and jumping over the rough cobblestone surface of Intervale Avenue. The cold is biting, and I pull the corduroy collar of my rubber coat closer to my neck.

The pumper stops in front of a three-story, wooden frame building. The top floor is on fire, and the heat has already blown out the windows. This is a job for the big, two-and-a-half-inch hose. I take the nozzle, and three folds of hose, and begin the stretch into the building. The men of Ladder 31 pass me. Willy Knipps is behind me, and Bill Kelsey behind him, all dragging hose. Vinny Royce takes a mask case from the side compartment of the apparatus, opens it, and starts to don the mask. Cosmo Posculo helps the chauffeur to hook into the hydrant.

Captain Albergray is waiting for us on the third floor. The smoke is heavy, almost viscous. Dark brown waves with nowhere to go until one of the truckmen cuts a hole in the roof. The hose starts to bulge as I reach Captain Albergray. I crack the nozzle a little. The air flows out, sounding like someone has opened a valve on an oxygen bottle. Then the water comes, hitting the floor in front of me.

"Ready?" Captain Albergray asks.

"Ready."

"Let's go."

The fire is in the front two rooms, and probably in the cockloft, the space between the ceiling of the rooms and the wood of the roof. We have to make a hard bend around the hallway banister rail. "Give us about ten more feet," I yell back to Knipps and Kelsey. They hump the hose as I advance the line to the threshold of the fire. I am on my stomach, Captain Albergray at my side. Knipps comes and supports the surging hose from behind. Fluid runs from our noses and mouths as we work. I am starting to cough a lot, but I keep the nozzle moving—up, down, and around. Royce climbs over Knipps and taps my shoulder. "I got it, Dennis," I can hear his muffled voice through the face piece of the mask. Cosmo also arrives with a mask, and Knipps and I bail out.

In the street again. Kelsey is donning a mask, and a mask for Captain Albergray lies on the sidewalk beside him. But he won't need it now. We look up at the third floor. The fire is extinguished, and only smoke from smoldering cinders comes from the windows. The members of Engine 73 and Engine 94 are standing in front of the building, waiting anxiously for an order to go to work. But they are told to stand fast. In a few minutes they will be told to take up.

I am sapped of any vitality as I sit next to Knipps on the back step of the pumper. I would smoke a cigarette if I thought my lungs would take it, but I know I couldn't hack it. Knipps and I don't speak. We just sit there limp and satisfied, knowing that we did our job.

Kelsey returns from the building, carrying the two masks. "We need a length of inch-and-a-half to wash down," he says. I feel a little recouped, so I go to the side compartment for a rolled up length of the smaller hose. Kelsey takes it from my hands. It only weighs forty pounds, but that's forty pounds I don't have to carry up the stairs.

Vinny and Cosmo have their masks off, and are resting in the hall. The men of Ladder 31 are overhauling, or ripping apart, the burnt rooms. Chief Niebrock keeps his eyes on the ceiling as the men hook down the plaster and lathe. The fire has not extended to the cockloft.

A young black man, about twenty-two, walks through the rooms, shaking his head. A mild looking man, small-framed, he appears shaken by what he sees. He is modishly dressed, with flared pants and a wet-look plastic jacket, and he is careful not to soil the bottoms of his pants as he steps over the debris on the floor.

"Do you live here?" Chief Niebrock asks him.

"Yeah, this is all mine, man. What's left of it."

The Chief writes his name down, and asks him if he knows how the fire started. The man replies that he doesn't know, that he was sitting in a bar down the street when he heard the fire engines come by.

Suddenly, a big woman steams past us in the hall. "Where is that sonovabitch!" she screams. "Where is that sonovabitch!" She has a two-foot machete in her hand. A machete. Her eyes wide, and violent. "Where is that sonovabitch!" Not a question. A statement. She knows who she is looking for, and that she will find him. A huge woman, but not fat. About 200 pounds. Appearing out of nowhere, like a wild woman from a sugar cane field.

[123]

The machete is high in the air as she lunges forward. "Look out Chief." The Chief turns just as McCartty grabs the woman. The knife is still free, and she swings it crazily, missing the Chief by inches.

"I'll kill you you sonovabitch," she cries, tears falling from her eyes. "I'll kill you."

The young man who was standing next to the Chief runs to the next room. The woman struggles, and it takes three fire-fighters to control her. McCartty finally gets her to loosen her grip on the knife, and he pulls it, throwing it to the floor. The woman collapses in hysterical sobbing.

The young man is yelling, "That woman's crazy. Get her outa here." He peers out at her, and sees that the violence is subdued. Feeling safer, he re-enters the room. A light mist of smoke is still rising from the burnt contents.

McCartty and Rittman, two big men, have a firm grip on her. She sees the young man, her anger rises, and she attempts to free herself. But Charlie and Richie are too powerful for her. She realizes now the futility of struggling, and calms herself. She looks directly at the young man, and says with vengeance, "You did this, and I'll kill you for this."

The man throws his hands up in despair, and turns away from her. He turns again, and says to her quietly, but nervously, his lips twitching, "I did this?"

The woman does not answer, but continues her deadly stare. The man asks the question again, but this time his voice is loud and angry. "I did this? Man, why would I do this to all my own stuff? Why would I burn my own place down?"

"Because you told my daughter you was gonna do it," the woman retorts. "You told her this morning when she threw you out that you was gonna do it." I can see the hatred building up in her, and the need to strike. She attempts again to lunge at the young man, and the young man runs into the adjoining room, fearful that the firefighters will lose their grip. The woman screams, "And I'm gonna kill you for it, you sonovabitch."

Chief Niebrock orders Charlie and Richie to lead the woman

out, and down the stairs. He speaks into his transistorized walkie-talkie, and orders his aide to radio for police assistance. "The police are already on the scene, Chief," the walkie-talkie blares.

Two policemen arrive on the floor. The Chief says a few words to them, and they go into the adjoining room to talk to the young man. Captain Albergray enters the room, and asks them if they would kindly move out to the hall, for we still have work to do. They leave, and Cosmo opens the nozzle for a final wash down. "You can take up when you're finished," the Chief says to our Captain. He also tells Lieutenant Lierly and the men of Ladder 31 to take up, but they will stick around to help us with the hose. They are always ready to give us a hand with the uncoupling, draining, and repacking.

The young man, the woman, and the police are not in sight when we return to the street. Charlie tells us that they have left in a police car. It seems to me that the man was genuinely affronted when accused of setting the fire, but making judgments about crimes is a cop's job.

The hose is repacked after some trouble with frozen connections. We work fast, because that is the best way to keep warm. On the way back to the firehouse I wonder if there is an engineer back in Illinois or somewhere working on a way to manufacture hose couplings that will not freeze. It would save us a lot of hard work.

Billy-o is in the kitchen. It is almost three o'clock. He is sitting at a table reading the afternoon *Post*. Billy-o reads more newspapers than anyone I know. His hand is gauzed and taped. "How ya feeling, Bill-o?" I ask.

"Not bad," he answers, "but just a little annoyed. Tomorrow is the first Easter I've had off in four years, but now I'm on medical leave. But do you think I would be on medical leave if I were scheduled to work tomorrow? No such luck."

I am laughing as McCartty and Royce burst into the kitchen. "Well, how many stitches?" they ask simultaneously.

"What do you mean, how many stitches?" Billy-o asks, feigning anger. "At least Dennis had the decency to ask me how I feel first."

"You're walkin' aren't ya?" Charlie says, "what difference does it make how ya feel? Tell us how many stitches—and the truth."

"You're not gonna believe this, Charlie," Billy-o says, laughingly. He points to the blackboard where Vinny chalked the bets, and says, "I see you have six to ten stitches covered. Well, you should've asked a few more guys to bet, because I got twelve."

"Twelve?" Charlie says in surprise.

"I don't believe it," Vinny says. "Take the bandage off and show us."

"Listen," Billy-o says, "you'll have to take my word for it. The doctor put twelve sutures in, and promised that it wouldn't leave a scar."

"Sutures!" Charlie exclaims. "Just because you read *The New York Times* ya gotta say sutures? Don't give us that crap. Just take the bandage off an' show us the stitches."

Billy-o laughs, folds the newspaper under his arm, and starts to leave the kitchen. "I give up on you guys," he says, "I'm going home." He pauses at the door, and adds, "I hope you catch a fourth alarm this afternoon." He smiles as he closes the door.

Charlie, though, will not let him get the last word. He goes to the door, and yells, "See ya, Billy-o. Have a nice accident on the way home." He closes the door, and returns laughing. He remembers something, and opens the door again. "Happy Easter, Bill," his voice echoes through the apparatus floor.

It is three o'clock as John Nixon backs Ladder 712's apparatus into quarters. Lieutenant Coughlin directs him through the too-narrow doorway, as the "super-probie" holds the makeshift canvas door back. The "super-probie" was so named because one night a few months ago he refused to help Engine 85 with their hose. The fire was out, and the other members of 712 helped with the long stretch of hose, but the "super-probie" said that he was a truckman, and if he wanted to work with hose he would transfer to an Engine company. It was a little presumptuous of him to say that, since he had been a firefighter for less than a year at the time. He learned quickly that veterans like John Nixon would not support his position. Now, he goes out of his way to help with the hose, to peel potatoes or onions, to wash the dishes or pots—anything to show he is part of the team.

"Ready for a long night?" I ask John Nixon.

He climbs down from the cab, slams the door, and says, "I'm ready if you are, Dennis."

"But I only work 'til six, and you hafta go until midnight."

"Well," he says, "I'll try my best to get along without you after six." He smiles, appreciating the banter. Like many of the men in the firehouse, John always has something pleasant to say, and his conversation is painted with humor or irony. When he says he'll try his best to get along without me, he really means that he is one of the senior men in the South Bronx, and he can manage in any situation.

John is studying for the coming Lieutenant's test. He has an armful of books as he walks up the stairs. On the third floor of the firehouse there is a small locker room, and a table surrounded by a few chairs. John will sit there and read the Department Regulations, the Department Training bulletins, the *Fire Chief's Handbook*, the New York City Building Codes, the National Fire Prevention Association bulletins, the three-thousand page *Handbook of Fire Protection*, textbooks on personnel management, grammar, chemical reactions, building construction, occupational safety, and hydraulics. The bells will come in, and John will slide the poles—from the third floor to the second, from the second to the apparatus floor. When he returns he will climb the forty steps, and pick up another book. He may do that fifteen or twenty times a night, but he doesn't waste a minute of his time between fires. There is so much to know, so many books and magazines and pamphlets to read. Yet, after all that effort it all depends on which hundred multiple-choice questions the examiner chooses to ask.

Arnold Toynbee said that before 1840 it was possible for one man to know all about all that was known. Today, however, it is impossible for one man to know all about any one given subject. A man simply cannot remember all the facts about fire-fighting, codes, construction, chemical formulas, hydraulic equations, and the rest. I wish John well. I hope the one hundred questions are about facts he remembers.

The bells ring. Box 2733. John must have had just enough time to lay his books on the third floor table. The housewatchman yells. "Eighty-five and Seven twelve—get out."

In the kitchen, I boil a pot of water for hot chocolate. Vinny Royce and Willy Knipps are playing chess, a game I learned to play as a teenager. I watch them for a few moments, but Willy has captured the queen and both bishops, and it doesn't look like much of a contest. Charlie McCartty and Richie Rittman are talking about football, and about super-star quarterbacks. I hear phrases like "he's got the world by the balls," and "that guy is so good he could ask for anything and get it." The conversation turns me off.

I try to sip the hot chocolate, but it is still scalding. There is a copy of *Playboy* magazine on the table. I thumb through the beginning section until I come to the interview. Playboy interviews Elliott Gould, the actor. It doesn't take much to shape opinion in this country. I start to read it, but once again I'm saved by the bells. Two, then nine, five, and six. Stebbins Avenue and Freeman Street. That's right around the corner. "Eighty-two and Thirty-one goes. Chief goes too." The housewatchman's voice doesn't seem as loud on the cold apparatus floor. He begins to yell again, but the department phone rings. He answers it, then yells. "Forget it Thirty-one. Seven-twelve will take it in."

We can see Ladder 712 racing up Intervale Avenue as we leave quarters. We are at the intersection of Stebbins and Freeman in less than thirty seconds. The corner building is on fire, but it appears to be only one room on the ground floor. The hydrant is right in front of the building, and we'll need just two lengths of hose. Piece of cake.

"Stretch the two-and-a-half," Captain Albergray orders.

We could fight this fire easily with the smaller hose, but the regulations call for two-and-a-half for cellar and ground floor fires. Like in the Army, it's easier, in the end, to do it by the books.

I pull the nozzle off, while Kelsey and Knipps take the two lengths. The end of the second length is uncoupled and being connected to the pumper as I walk up the three steps of the stoop. Captain Albergray and Lieutenant Coughlin watch as Nixon and Mike Runyon force open the locked door. It is a simple lock, and snaps with one pull on the halligan tool. The door opens some, and then shuts hard. Nixon puts his shoulder to the door, but there is someone on the other side pushing against him. A voice, muffled and choking, begins to moan, "I want to die. I want to die."

Nixon gives a hard shove, and the door opens wide. There is a man, middle-aged, about forty, running down the long, narrow hallway of the apartment. Toward the back. Away from the fire.

The smoke is heavy enough, but the front windows are vented, and it lifts nicely. I am on my knees, Captain Albergray beside me, and Royce behind with a mask, just in case. But, it's only one room, and I make it easily.

Nixon and the "super-probie" have followed the man. That's their job—search and rescue. Mike Runyon has begun to open the windows of the other rooms. The man has run into the kitchen, and stands like a cornered animal, with a carving knife in his hands. The "super-probie" tries to approach him, gently. But the man leaps out at him, and swings the knife. Its edge opens the super-probie's cheek. The man springs back into the corner as John pulls the bleeding super-probie out of the room.

"Go out and get that taken care of," John says as he pulls the kitchen door shut. "Have the Chief call the cops. I'll keep this maniac locked in here."

John pulls on the handle of the door, but the man does not try to open it. He begins yelling again, passionately, "I want to die. I want to die. Let me die."

The fire is out. Knipps has relieved me on the nozzle. Chief Niebrock divides his attention between controlling the fire, and making sure that Nixon is all right. The other members of Ladder 712 have begun to put holes in the ceilings and sidewalls. The Chief shines his lamp on each hole and studies them carefully, until he is sure that the fire has not extended.

Two policemen enter the hall, guns drawn. "Where is he?" one of them asks.

"That way," the Chief says, gesturing toward the end of the hall.

John releases the doorknob, and says, "Watch out for him—he's psycho."

A policeman kicks the door open. The man is still in the corner, still yelling that he wants to die. Both cops are cautious as they enter the room, stepping slowly and gingerly. One of them commands, in a strong, direct voice, "Come on, drop that knife."

The man releases an insane, diabolical scream, and runs at the policemen, the knife poised above his shoulder. A cop shoots. The man trips to the ground, dropping the knife as he falls. The man is still screaming, but he lies in a fetal position on the kitchen floor grabbing at his leg. The bullet hit him just above the knee. One cop picks up the knife from the floor, while the other puts his gun back in its holster, satisfied that he just saved the man's life.

Nixon cuts the man's pant leg, as Runyon places the first-aid kit down beside him. The man is quiet now, except for intermittent sobs. John bandages the wound, taping it lightly in consideration of the nurse who will have to cut it away. One of the policemen writes about the incident, as he remembers it, in his logbook. Bill Finch, Chief Niebrock's aide, writes the information in his notebook. *"John Wilkes, Age 42, attacked fireman Arthur Mazarak, shot in left leg by patrolman Hillery of 41 Precinct."*

"That's all the information I need," Finch says to the patrolmen. "Thanks."

The policemen decide to take their prisoner to the hospital in the squad car, rather than wait for an ambulance. The man is handcuffed and has stopped sobbing. He is quiet now—almost catatonic. We lift him onto a kitchen chair, and carry him out. A crowd has gathered in front of the building. Tired, worn, unhappy black faces, talking amongst themselves, and wondering what the problem was.

The "super-probie" is sitting in the Chief's car, his face bandaged, waiting for an ambulance. The Chief says a few words to him, he climbs out of the car, and walks resignedly to the squad car. The squad car wails away, the "super-probie" in the front seat, his attacker in the rear.

The hose taken up, our job finished, we start back to the firehouse. As the pumper begins to turn the corner, I notice the glazed blue and white street sign attached to the lamppost. Freeman Street, it says. I think about just how inappropriate that name is as the apparatus rolls down Intervale Avenue.

It is five-thirty. Eddy Penan walks across the apparatus floor. He has his rubber coat and helmet in one hand, and his boots in the other. He reaches the back end of the fire engine, and puts his boots on the floor. He lifts my helmet and coat with his free hand, and throws his own gear on the hose where mine had been. I am standing at the kitchen doorway, drinking a cup of coffee. He sees me, and says, "You're relieved, Dennis."

"Thanks Ed," I say taking my gear from him, and hanging the coat on the wall rack. I place my helmet on the shelf above.

"What kind of a day you have? Busy?"

"Yeah, we had a couple of jobs," I say, picking up my boots.

"Oh yeah? How are the masks?"

"They were used," I say, putting my boots on the boot rack, "but, Cosmo and Vinny cleaned them and changed the cylinders."

"Good," Eddy says as he walks into the kitchen. "See ya." He stops, and asks, "You working tomorrow?"

"No, I'm off."

"Have a nice day," he says.

I'll take a shower now, and then go home and help Pat prepare for the company tomorrow. Easter will be a nice day for me. It will be a civilized day.

8

I'LL never escape from tenements and cockroaches. The names and the geography may change, but conditions are universal when people are without money. Mrs. Hanratty who lived down the hall from us in my youth is now Mrs. Sanchez; the O'Dwyer For Mayor sticker in the vestibule wall now reads Father Gigante For Congress; and the cry "Tueres animal, Rodrego" now airs through the courtyard in place of "Jesus, Barney, can't ya ever come home ta me sober?" The smell of dried garbage and urine haven't changed, but the vomit on the unwashed marble stairs is now mixed with heroin instead of ten-cents-a-shot Third Avenue whiskey. Each apartment still houses an unwanted cousin, or aunt, and the family members try to be kind and considerate, but it never works out, because there are too many people in too few rooms.

Like chalk to a teacher, roaches are part of my past, and now part of my work. They are under me or on me as I crawl down long smoke-filled halls. They scurry helter-skelter as I lift a smoldering mattress, just as they scurried between the tin soldiers on the battlefield of my living-room oilcloth. As a child, I would shiver and run from them as I do now, but I was just fearful of them then; now, I resent them. More than anything, they represent poverty to me. More than anything, they are the one facet of my youth that I was forced to accept—the ugly, brown, quick-darting companions of the poor. My mother would whisper that she cleaned and sprayed, but it didn't help much because they were put in the walls by the builders many years ago, because they had a grudge against the Irish and the Italians. And, anyway, no matter what she sprayed around, the little creatures would learn to enjoy it. I learned that they could be fought, but not defeated. I, as they, adapted.

The July sun is now directly over the firehouse, and it seems as if it is as close to the earth as it has ever been. It is almost noon, and I am lying on a bed thinking of the fire we have just come from. The tenement on Fox Street was recently abandoned, and the day's heat penetrated the garbage piled in the center hall so that the odor was worse than I had ever experienced. I couldn't hold my breath long enough as I climbed over it, dragging the hose behind, and the smell made my stomach turn. The fire was on the fourth floor, and routine. Only two rooms were going, and Willy Knipps advanced the nozzle easily. When the fire was out, and the smoke cleared from the apartment, I noticed the roaches on every wall of every room but the burned ones. They were on the floor and the walls of the long, narrow hallway. I told Willy, and Benny, and Lieutenant Welch that since there was not much to do I would wait in the street until Chief Niebrock gave us the word to take up.

The garbage smell rose through the stairwell, and there was no escaping it on the trip down. In the street again, I felt a strange sense of freedom, like being released from years of penal servitude. I stood in front of the building, not knowing where to go or what to do, yet profoundly relieved, and happy that I was no longer where I had been. I felt curiously fresh in the hot, muggy air of Fox Street.

The air ducts above me purr smoothly, and the cool air blankets the sixteen beds in the bunkroom. The floors are clean, the walls newly painted, and the beds tightly made and lined symmetrically. The second floor of the firehouse reminds me of an army barracks—it's a place to rest. But even as I lie here I think of the tenements of Fox Street. The fire we just fought tired me, and the sucking temperature exhausted me as I uncoupled, drained, and repacked the hose. I want to rest. Relax. I light a cigarette, and choke on the first drag. If I were a policeman, a plumber, a schoolteacher, or a businessman I would quit the ugly habit. But why quit smoking when each fire I fight is more deadly than a thousand cartons of Pall Mall's. Smoke. Relax. The day is half over. But, I can't relax. I think instead about the tenements of Fox Street, the people of Fox Street, and Tina deVega.

Tina deVega is eighteen years old. She was born in Puerto Rico, and came to this country with her mother and three sisters and four brothers when she was a child of six. Tina doesn't know much about the South Bronx. She doesn't know that the detective squad working around the corner in the Simpson Street Station House investigates more homicides each month than any other squad in the city. She doesn't know that the men in the firehouse three blocks away—my firehouse—respond to more false alarms, and fight more fires than anywhere else. She doesn't know that the V.D. rate, and the infant mortality rate, is three times greater than that of any other section of the city. What Tina knows is that she is a five dollar trick, and lately she's been forced to go for four. Times are tough, and even the whores on Southern Boulevard feel the inflation bite. The Boulevard is busy with girls, but there aren't enough slow-cruising Ford sedans and Chevrolet station wagons to go around. Even the tired forty-year-olds are back, walking the Boulevard in matted sweaters and sagging nylons.

Tina rises at eleven each morning. Each day is like the one

before, and she searches out her man, and hits him for a taste. The heroin is stabilizing, always, and her appetite builds. She then goes to Amillio's Bodega for a breakfast of Pepsi-Cola and Drake's Doodle-dogs, and back to her apartment where she watches the afternoon soap operas, and nods.

The apartment Tina lives in is in a building next to the abandoned building where the garbage is piled high in the vestibule, the one we have just come from. I was sitting on the fender of a derelict car, waiting for the order to take up, when I saw her walking slowly towards me. It had been years since I last saw her, but her face is unmistakable. Unmarred dark skin, and the delicate bones of a European aristocrat. Thin lips, graceful narrow nose, knowing eyes. But her eyes don't sparkle as they used to; drugs make the lids droop. They used to radiate happiness, or at least pleasantness, but that is all lost. She is wearing a short white nylon skirt that clings to her thighs, and a thin red polo shirt that fits snugly around her breasts. In another time, another place, people would say she was developing into a smart, chic young woman. Her feet are bare and sandaled, and her calf muscles are strong and appealing. The only unbeautiful things about her are her eyes, and her pin-scarred arms.

"Denise, Denise," she calls, her accent making my name sound like its female equivalent. "How are you?" Her voice is dull and drawled, but genuinely happy. "Man, eets good to see you." She brushed her long black hair away from her face, and put her hand on my arm, with such simple, easy grace that a Vassar graduate would find the gesture in a style to be duplicated. How ironic that a five dollar trick from Fox Street would have the soft, natural class to make a Vassar girl envious.

We didn't talk long, but she held her hand on my arm all the while she spoke. She told me she shared her apartment with two other girls, and four kids. One of the girls is on welfare, and the four kids are hers. Tina wants to go on welfare, but she just hasn't gotten around to applying. Anyway, she really doesn't need the money, because her man gives her enough of her earnings to make her happy. The apartment she shares has two bedrooms, a living room, a kitchen, and a bathroom. There hasn't been any hot water since Tina has been living there, which has been five months, and a pot of water is always simmering on the stove. I asked her if there were many roaches, and she said, "Sure. And the mouses too." She told me too that she has tried to kick the drugs, but it didn't work. Maybe someday. And she talked of shooting up with a pathetic resignation that convinced me that she knew as well as I that the dope would kill her someday.

Benny and the others returned to the street, pulling the wet hose behind them. Tina took her hand from my arm and offered it to me to shake. I held it, as she said, "Well, good-bye Denise. I see you. O.K.?" I answered a positive, "O.K.," and Tina walked slowly away, nodding slightly. I called to her, but she didn't hear me, at least she didn't acknowledge that she heard. I called, "Take care of yourself, Tina."

And now as I lie here in the cool comfortable secure regimented confines of the firehouse bunkroom I think of how stupid that must have sounded to her. "Take care of yourself." But that's what she is doing. Tina is taking care of herself. She is surviving in the best way she knows.

When I first met her four years ago she was a shy, sensitive fourteen-year-old high school freshman. She lived on Home Street then, with her family. Her little brother liked fire engines, and one day she brought him into the firehouse. I was on housewatch duty, and I spoke kindly to her. I asked what school she attended, and if she liked her studies. I played with her brother Fillipo. After that, she and her brother came the short block from their apartment to the firehouse regularly. She would ask for "Denise," and the guys would rub me about being the idol of the under-sixteen set. And soon she told me that she hated living at home with all her brothers and sisters, and she hated school, because she couldn't read very well, and she wanted a job so she could buy pretty clothes, but she wasn't old enough to quit school yet. She had the same problems as millions of other adolescents in America. She was growing up, and trying to become a person instead of another mouth to feed, or another body on the living room pull-out couch, or another English-as-a-second-language voice in an English-as-a-first-language school. After two or three months—I can't remember exactly—Tina stopped coming to the firehouse. I had forgotten her completely until she walked up Fox Street this morning. And I can't help but think of all the other people who must have forgotten her somewhere along the road—the short road of three blocks from Home Street then to Fox Street now. I wonder if a school counselor ever talked to her, or a teacher? I remember that her mother was on welfare, and wonder if some social services official knows she exists, or existed. Wasn't there even one person with some sense who talked to this shy, sensitive young girl? Someone to tell her that there are ways to unravel the emotional entanglements that human beings experience as they grow. Wasn't there someone who knew at least something about guidance, direction, goals, self-motivation, self-esteem? But, maybe that's not it at all. Maybe it has nothing to do with counseling or direction. Maybe it has to do, simply, with living in a tenement. How can you talk to a child of self-esteem when she is forced to wear her older sister's outgrown clothes? How do you talk of self-motivation to a child who has never known the privacy of a room, or the quiet of a home? How do you talk of goals to a child who has never experienced a ten dollar pair of shoes, or to a child whose only trip in life has been from Puerto Rico to America?

I was fifteen when I unofficially quit high school. I just didn't go. My mother was asked to bring me to the school guidance father. The priest told her, and me, that he got where he was by studying hard, and that I should do the same. I told him that I didn't much care for being where he was, and I didn't care either about being a failure in life, for that's what he told me I

[138]

would be if I refused to knuckle down. I tried to make him, and my mother, understand that it wasn't that I was tired of being slapped by the Irish Christian Brothers, and that I didn't mind being locked into a building for six hours a day, or about the reams of homework I was assigned daily, but that I had the prospect of this great job delivering flowers. I was going to be paid fifty dollars a week. Fifty a week. I could do whatever I wanted on fifty a week. But they didn't understand, and my mother cried, and the priest told me that I was an insult to a good Catholic mother.

I was fifteen, and my pockets were empty. The country was enjoying the prosperity of the fifties, but I was still wearing six dollar shoes. With forty-two dollars take-home a week I could buy a pair of London Character wing tips. But nobody understood that I was wasting time in school. Time was fleeting irretrievably by in a classroom, when I could be earning money to save for a new one-button powder blue suit. Man, would I make a hit at the Police Athletic League dances with a powder blue suit, a pink shirt backgrounding a black knitted tie, and London Character wing tips. And shekels in my pocket to take a girl for a pizza after the dance.

I got the job in a Second Avenue florist shop, and I told the people I wanted to impress that I was studying to be a botanist. I walked the streets of Sutton Place, in and out of buildings that housed the richest people in the country, like I belonged there. It was only a matter of time before I would stand camel-haired in the lobby waiting for the starch-collared doorman to hail me a cab. And I would forget the dim, concrete floored, brown-bricked corridors of the service entrance.

The forty-two dollars didn't go very far. I gave my mother ten a week towards the rent, food, and laundry, and I bought my own clothes, and stopped meeting girls in the movies and started to pay their way. I ate lunch at Riker's every day, and since I started smoking I had to buy cigarettes. And since the guys in the gang I hung around with were either still in school, or out of school and not working, I had to pay the freight for a lot of Friday night Cokes and French fries. As I think of it now, I'm sure I would have stayed in school if someone would have offered me twenty a week to be there. At least in school we had Saturdays off, but the florist was a six-day operation.

Like Tina deVega I searched for, and found, my own way of survival. After a time I became unhappy in my job, but it is always better to have money in the pocket when unhappy, than to be unhappy and broke. I kept on working. I rang the back doorbells of the "earth shakers," and delivered the orchid centerpieces, and the maid would thank me as she pocketed the fifteen cents tip that she would tell the boss she gave me. And on Saturday nights we drank beer down by the river, and watched the blinking Pepsi-Cola sign on the Queens side, and got drunk. We made out with girls in sleeveless blouses and long, crinolined, felt skirts, playing "trust me." A nervous hand on a felt-covered knee, and an anxious voice saying "trust me," and after an apprehensive nod the hand moves to the thigh, and with each nod another inch up and around the leg until the mysterious excitement of holding a female's buttock is realized. And satisfied with that we got drunker, until our bodies rejected the strange dizzying liquid. And we vomited, and the girls ran home, and we staggered through the streets abusing anyone we thought cowardly enough not to reply. And all the while we forgot about the stifling crowded tenement rooms, nagging mothers, and drunk or gambling or cheating fathers.

Someone on the apparatus floor is hammering the fire bell on the Chief's car, the signal that lunch is ready. I ditch the cigarette in a sand bucket, and slide the pole to the street level. Cagey Dulland has cooked roast beef, and the kitchen walls steam with the heat. The air-conditioning unit we bought for the kitchen was second-hand, and didn't last long. The comfortable coolness I was feeling a minute ago is gone, and I can feel the perspiration beads building on my forehead.

Thin strips of roast beef lie across warm toast, covered with a hot brown gravy. The heat of the gravy steams over my face as I lean over the lunch, but I am hungry, and I don't let it bother me. Willy Knipps is complaining to Cagey that he should have had better sense than to cook a hot meal on a day like this.

"And for eighty-five cents," he says, "for chrissakes, I could eat roast beef in the Stork Club for that price." But Cagey just utters a few words about inflation, and lets it go at that. He knows that the guys are grateful that he took the time to cook for us, and the wisecracks are as natural as the rising sun.

I am sponging the gravy from the plate with a piece of white bread when the bells interrupt. At least we got to finish our lunch. "Southern Boulevard and Fox Street," the house-watchman is yelling.

Box 2787. We were just there. "I bet it's that abandoned building again," Benny Carroll says.

"Well, of course, what else?" rejoins Willy Knipps as he puts the three-pound helmet on his head.

"Listen Willy," Benny says, with a sly smile on his face, "since you had the nob at that job this morning, I'll take it if we have a job now, O.K.? I mean you must be pretty tired and all."

"That's no on two counts," Willy replies. "I'm not tired, and I won't give ya the nob."

"Say no more," Benny says, pretending indifference.

The clock on the firehouse wall reads 12:45 as the pumper screams out of quarters. Ladder 31 echoes close behind. We can see the dark, dancing clouds of smoke as we roll up Tiffany Street. "What did I tell ya?" Benny says, pulling his boots to his thighs. I swing my rubber coat on, and I realize that it is going to be hot. The coat insulates the skin pores from the air, and I can feel my shirt already sticking to my chest. As I look over the side of the rig to get a view of the fire, I can see Bill Kelsey strapping the thirty-pound air pack to his back. The smoke is high and wide in the sky, and that tells me that the job is going to be a tough one.

The people of Fox Street have left the midday heat of their apartments, and have gathered in the middle of the street to watch the fire. Billy Valenzio is driving the pumper today, and he is hitting the air horn wildly as he tries to drive through the crowd. The mood is like a Mardi Gras. The people cheer and shout as they cross to either side of the street to make room for the pumper.

Why can't the city tear these buildings down fast enough, I wonder, as we approach the same abandoned building we had earlier. Whoever set the place up this time didn't feel like climbing the stairs to the fourth floor, because the fire is jumping out of all the windows on the second. The pumper stops in front of the building, and Lieutenant Welch yells to stretch the inch-and-a-half line as he runs into the building. Bill Kelsey jumps from the side with a face mask in his hand, and Vinny Royce comes from the other side to help with the stretch. Knipps has the nozzle in his hand, and is crossing over the garbage heap in the vestibule as the men of Engine 94 reach the back of our rig and start to stretch a second line. Chuck Radek, Billy-o, and the others from Ladder 31 have entered the building to ventilate, as Cagey Dulland goes into the adjoining building to cross the roof. As Valenzio moves the pumper to a hydrant, I can see Ladder 48 careening up the street. They'll search the floors above the fire.

There is not much for me to do on the second floor, except hump the hose in. Lieutenant Welch and Knipps start to make the apartment on the left side of the hall, and the guys of Engine 94 start to push their way into the apartment on the right. Soon, Willy Knipps crawls into the hall, his chubby face covered with sweat. He wipes his running nose, and spits.

"God, it's hot in there," he says. "The smoke wasn't too bad, but the heat was murder. I could've made it, but Kelsey had the mask, so I figured what the hell." Yeah, what the hell, I think, and I hope the day will come when all firefighters will refuse to enter a burning abandoned building unless they have a mask on.

"Give us some more line," Vinny Royce is yelling from the doorway, and I hump the hose forward. There is a guy next to me doing the same with Engine 94's line. Both companies are progressing through the rooms at an even pace. I can't help but think of Tennyson's poem. There is fire to the left of me, and fire to the right of me.

The fires in both apartments are extinguished quickly, though. Gasoline must have been used to create so much fire, but it hasn't been burning long enough to get through to the floors above. Chief Niebrock walks calmly through both apartments, checking each corner beam and crevice with his portable lamp. He radios what he sees to the 6th Division Deputy Chief, who is standing in the street supervising over-all operations.

The smoke has cleared, and I look around for roaches, but there are none, for the walls are now burnt black and blistering. Bill Kelsey takes his mask off, and sits smoking a cigarette in the hall. The rest of us join him, for there is nothing to do now until Ladder 31 pulls the ceilings down, and strips the window and door frames. And all the walls have to be opened to check for fire. I can watch them work from where I am squatting in the hall. Billy-o is using the pointed end of his halligan tool to release a window frame from the wall. He struggles briefly, and with a final yank the three part frame loosens and crashes down. Cagey Dulland and Horace Brewster pull the lath slats down a bay of beams until the ceiling disappears, dropping and smashing to pieces on the floor. The room is filled with plaster dust, which sticks to Cagey's wet face, and which makes Horace's handsome black face appear white. And they occasionally spit the dry chalk from their mouths as they work. There is not another group of men in the world who could strip a room to its skeleton as efficiently as these men. This is heavy work for them, but it is not hard work. They perform this overhauling work well, but the hard work, the work they do best, is getting in and around a burning building where a life is in danger.

Chief Kelsen, the Deputy Chief, orders Engine 94 to take

their line up, and return to their Seneca Avenue quarters. He then radios Chief Niebrock that he has to respond to another "all hands" fire down on 138th Street. Chief Niebrock is back in charge of the fire, but there is only the final wash down left.

Much of the water we used has found its way down the stairs, and the cooled garbage doesn't smell nearly as bad as we return to the street. The police are on the scene now, and are trying to control the crowd as best they can. But there are too many people, and only three cops. Ladder 31's rig is covered with kids, but we are used to that. The truck is a mobile jungle gym set in a parkless neighborhood.

The apparatus radios blare, "*A second alarm has been transmitted for Box 2188—Brook Avenue and 138th Street.*" The Captain of Ladder 48 asks the dispatcher if he is assigned on the second alarm. The radio answers that Ladder 48 is assigned on the third alarm, and the anxious troops of Ladder 48 are disappointed.

I pull the empty hose to the back of our pumper. The men of Ladder 31 and Ladder 48 help us uncouple, straighten, and drain the hose.

"What do they have goin' down there?" someone yells to Valenzio.

"They have an occupied tenement," he returns, "but I didn't hear how much fire they got. It must be goin' good, though."

Vinny Royce is on the sidewalk, across from the abandoned building. He has put his wet gloves on the fender of a parked car, and he is trying to get himself prepared to repack the hose. We are all hot and sweaty, but Vinny has just helped Bill Valenzio uncouple the six-inch connection from the hydrant, and he appears to be sapped of strength. Suddenly, as Vinny begins to remove his heavy rubber coat, a garbage can hits the ground next to him with a deadly thump. It hasn't missed him by more than twelve inches. Vinny moves quickly to the security of a doorway. The people in the street scatter, and the kids jump off the truck and run down the block. The street is a valley, canyoned by six-story tenements from end to end, and all our eyes turn towards the roofs. Benny Carroll screams, "LOOK OUT," and runs to join Vinny huddled in a doorway. A volley of two-inch iron balls hits the street, one shattering the windshield of Ladder 48's rig. The cops run into the buildings, each cop taking a separate entrance. Some of the men from Ladder 31 and Ladder 48 follow them to the roof. One of the balls has bounced off the rig next to where I am standing. I pick it up, and run to Benny and Vinny for cover. It looks like a sawed-off end of an antique school-desk leg. I put it in my pocket, and then remember my Uncle Tommy coming home from Germany in the forties, his pockets filled with spent shells.

The cops and the guys of 31 and 48 return to the street. Whoever was up on the roof has disappeared, into a friend's apartment, down a fire escape into their own apartment, or over the rooftops and down a safe hallway. Whoever they were got away with it this time, as they did the last time we had trouble in this street. I feel so desperately helpless as I think that they will in all probability get away with it the next time too.

We return to the street and look at the garbage can that flew from the roof. It is on its side, and it was filled with ashes. God, I wonder, would they be caught if Vinny were killed? This was attempted murder, but nobody was killed, no one even hurt seriously, and it makes no sense to press the issue. My insides scream, "A full fucking garbage can." And here is Vinny, still shaken, his head moving slowly from side to side. The world couldn't ask for a more beautiful guy. How ironic that Vinny, who has been in more fires than almost any other fireman, came so close to getting it with a can of ashes.

Lieutenant Welch makes a call for more police assistance, as we hurriedly repack the hose. We all keep our eyes on the roofs as we pull the hose forward and onto the fire engine. Three squad cars come wailing into the block, and we feel a little safer. The hose is packed and we drive quickly from Fox Street, never taking our eyes from the roofs. That's it. Lieutenant Welch will make a report of the incident when we return to the fire-house, and that will end it. The fire marshals may phone to get the complete details for their report, but nobody will actually go into Fox Street and question people. That takes too much time, and, anyway, nobody was killed. I can't help thinking though, that if it were Mayor Lindsay standing there instead of Fireman Royce, the guys who threw that garbage can from the roof would spend tonight in jail.

As we are returning to the firehouse we are redirected to Boston Road and Seabury Place. Engine 45 arrives at the location before us, and transmits a signal 10-92—a false alarm. Once more in the firehouse, I run to the second floor, and the air conditioning. I remove my shirt, and dry my arms and chest with a beach towel. I take a clean shirt from my locker, and think of my wife as I look at the well-pressed sleeves. And I think of my kids, of the kids on Fox Street climbing on the apparatus, of sitting on a rainy stoop in my youth, not wanting to climb the steps to my apartment, yet not knowing of anything else to do, of school-desks falling from the sky, of picking buttercups with my children on soft, green mountainsides, of walking with my beautiful wife through a calm starlit night, and of talking with a beautiful whore on Fox Street. I should wash up a little, but the newly-washed shirt makes me feel clean enough.

Benny and Vinny come into the bunkroom. They wash up, and change their shirts. I am lying on a bed, smoking, and listening to the radio. The music is the easy, popular kind that is usually piped into offices and elevators. Benny and Vinny, clean-faced and clean-clothed, lie on beds on either side of me. We talk some about what has happened, but we all agree that it is difficult to make any sense out of it. Benny says that it could be an organized guerrilla warfare, and Vinny says that it is just a part of the lawless times, and I say that it could be both of those, but it is also due to a sad loss of respect for human life. The people on Fox Street may feel that they have good reason to hate us, but that's not the issue. I hated plenty of people when I was a kid, but I never thought of killing them.

I used to believe that people who threw rocks at firemen were motivated by conditions—the lower depths of American society. I used to believe that the fundamental problems were housing and education, and that people would stop throwing rocks if they had a decent place to live and were given equal educational opportunities. But I don't believe that anymore. That, to me, is prescribing for symptoms. The disease is more seriously latent, more pernicious than uncaring landlords, or bureaucratic, apathetic school officials. The malignancy lies in the guts of humankind at all levels. We have unlearned the value of a human life.

The bells ring out an alarm: Box 2737. But Vinny, Benny, and I relax when we hear the three bells follow the seven. We know that's not for us, and we lie calmly as we listen to Engine 85, Ladder 31, and the Chief roll out for Hoe Avenue and Jennings Street. In a matter of minutes, the signal 75-2737 is transmitted. All hands are working at Hoe Avenue.

We slide the pole to listen to the department radio. Whatever they have must be hot enough, since Chief Niebrock doesn't sound an "all hands" alarm lightly. From the doors of the firehouse we can see the high spiral of smoke rising to the northeast. Vinny turns the radio up as the dispatcher asks Battalion 27 if the Field Communication Unit and another Battalion Chief are needed at 2737. The reply is a laconic "yes."

"The dispatcher is supposed to send those units automatically," Vinny says. "Why the hell is he asking if he should send them?"

But, before anyone can answer the bells start ringing. Three bells, then three more. Then there is a long pause, followed by Box 2188. A third alarm has been sounded for 138th Street. Now we know why the dispatcher asked. He'll have to call another Field Com Unit from Queens. The dispatcher's office must be a madhouse of noise, bells, and men running to find available companies, and making sure that no section of the Bronx is at any time completely stripped of fire protection.

The radio begins to squawk again: *"Battalion 27 to Bronx."*
Now we will find out what kind of a fire they have there.
"Bronx to Battalion 27—go ahead."
"Transmit a second alarm for Box 2737."
The dispatcher will have to send companies from Queens and South Manhattan for this fire. He needs three additional engine companies and another ladder, but some of the assigned companies are operating at the third alarm on 138th Street.
"Can you give us a progress report?" the dispatcher asks.
"We have a large body of fire on the fifth and sixth floors of 1994 Hoe Avenue. It is a six-brick," [six stories made of brick construction] *"100 by 100,"* [dimensions in feet] *"occupied building. The occupants are being removed. Surrounding properties are, 1) A street,"* [in front of the fire building] *"2) A six-brick 40 by 80 multiple dwelling,"* [the building to the left] *"3) A rear yard,"* [behind the fire building] *"and 4) A six-brick 40 by 80 multiple dwelling"* [the building to the right]. *"We have one line in operation on the fifth floor, and two lines are being stretched. Doubtful at this time"* [it is doubtful that the fire will be controlled with the present assignment of companies].
"Ten-four, Battalion 27," the dispatcher signs off.
"That must be that big, H-type building in the middle of the block, there," Benny says.
"Yeah," Vinny replies, "and if the fire gets in the cockloft they're gonna be there all day."
The Tactical Control Unit, Ladder 712, pulls in front of the firehouse. It is three o'clock, and their day is just beginning. As Johnny Nixon backs the rig into quarters, he stops and points to the smoke above Hoe Avenue. He says, with a wry smile, "That's one of the few we missed around here."
"You may end up there yet," I say to him.
He replies, laughingly, "I'm not afraid." And I know he isn't, for Johnny Nixon has been fighting fires in the South Bronx for the past twelve years.

There are so many bells coming over the system that I stop counting them. Each time a company is special-called to a fire, or relocated to cover another fire district, the signal is telegraphed over the bells. I make a mental note to visit the dispatcher's office someday. It must be interesting to watch them organize such confusion.

Bill Kelsey is on housewatch, and he is yelling "Get out eighty-two, and seven-twelve. Boston and Seabury."

It is probably another false alarm, I say to myself as I grab the handrail on the back of the pumper.

A young boy waves us on at the intersection of Boston Road and Seabury Place. As we approach, he runs down Seabury, turning occasionally to make sure we are following. There is a large crowd gathered in front of the Diaz Bodega. Benny Carroll yells over the siren, "It must be an O.D." The pumper stops, and the crowd makes room for us. I am the first to reach the object of attention, and see a guy in a crimson-stained yellow shirt lying in a mass of thick blood spread evenly over the sidewalk. I can hear the faceless voices of the crowd uttering in broken English, "Someone tried to off 'im, man. Some bad-ass thought he made peace with hisself. Who the man who cut 'im? We gonna get 'im." It seems strange to hear the black's dialect spoken with a Spanish accent.

The Chief from the Seventeenth Battalion has been special-called, and as he looks about him he tells his aide to request an ambulance and police assistance. The man is lying on his side, with his head on his forearm. He is about thirty-five years old. His eyes are open, and he seems to sense our presence. He moans painfully as I ask him where it hurts, and mutters something in Spanish. Johnny Nixon puts a blanket under his head as I turn him over. We can see now where it hurts. His right ear has been slashed, and is swinging freely by its lobe. John opens the first-aid box, and hands me a sterile sponge. I pick up the ear, and place it where I think it belongs. I hold the sponge in place as Johnny wraps a bandage under the chin and around the head. Now if the guy dies at least he will look clean and cared for.

As Johnny ties the bandage, Benny, Vinny and the other members are holding back the crowd. But a commotion starts on the other side of the street, and the crowd deserts us for better excitement. There is a lot of yelling, and I feel a passion for blood in the air. A young man starts running up Seabury Place, the crowd following. He doesn't run fast enough, and is pushed to the ground. The crowd circles around him, and each screaming, kicking man and woman is getting even for the bandaged ear at my knees. The cops haven't come yet, and we wonder where they are. The Chief orders another request to be made— an emergency request. We can feel a sense of urgency to save this guy being beaten, but the block is filled with an easy two hundred persons. To try to interfere with this kind of mob action is stupid. We have learned from experience that this is a cop's job—he's got a gun. People have a fear of being shot, and a fear of being arrested, but they do not have a fear of firemen. Firemen are supposed to come only when needed, and it is obvious that this crowd does not feel a need for us now. This is street justice.

The people suddenly stop their punching and kicking. The man has been paid, and three men carry him into a building as the squad cars turn onto Seabury Place. We leave the injured man in the care of the Police Department, and we return to quarters, not knowing, and only casually caring about what the argument was all about.

It is three-thirty as the pumper backs into the firehouse. The sun isn't beating directly on us anymore, but the air is still, and the heat seems to radiate from the sidewalks. I go to the kitchen, and to the soda machine. The dime goes through the machine several times before it finally catches, and I follow it up with a nickel. The machine makes a short buzzing noise, and the select sign lights up. I press the Pepsi button. The machine makes a kind of wheezing sound, and I can hear the can roll through the machine and fall into the receptacle box at the bottom. I take the can and pull hard, a little too hard, on the snap-open top, and the ring breaks off. I go to the drawer by the sink for a can opener, but before I can get there the bells re-direct me. Box 2743.

We arrive at Charlotte and 170th Streets. Kids are playing in a puddle at the corner, and people walk aimlessly by. We make a search as we have done a thousand times before, and we give Lieutenant Welch the thumbs down signal. He radios the dispatcher that it is a false alarm. As we are getting back on the rig Bill Valenzio tells us that there is an "all hands" going up on Tremont Avenue. The fire is in the basement of a supermarket.

In the firehouse again I take an ice tray from the refrigerator. The creases have fallen out of my clean shirt, and there are large sweat stains at the underarms. I put the ice in a coffee cup, and pour the soda in after it. It fizzes to the top, and I stand over it patiently waiting for it to recede, but the bells come in, and I have to leave the soda once more. Box 2787—for the third time today. Kelsey is screaming with all the power in his lungs: "Southern Boulevard and Fox Street. Again. Southern Boulevard and Fox Street. The Bronx is burning. Get out Eighty-two and Seven-twelve. I bet the bastards set it up again. Get out."

Lieutenant Welch slides the pole from the second floor, but instead of running to the apparatus he runs to the housewatch desk and picks up the phone. He speaks into the receiver for a few seconds, and then runs to the pumper, explaining as he runs that he called for police protection. There is no sense going into that block today without a squad car.

As we head up Tiffany Street we can see the smoke still rising above Hoe Avenue to the north, and as we look to the southeast we can see still another column, billowing rapidly above Fox Street.

"Ya know," Benny says to me as he pulls his boots up, "Kelsey is right. The Bronx is burning up, and the sad thing about it is that no one knows it. This is an insane day for fires, but ya won't read anything about it in the papers tomorrow, and ya won't see anything about it on T.V. tonight. That's the real sad thing. We work our ass off, and nobody knows about it."

I nod my head in agreement. It is sad. But even sadder is all the families who will be shoved into welfare hotels tonight. Nobody knows about them either. One family in a small stinking stoveless, sinkless hotel room, and the immoral bastard of a hotel-keeper will charge the city fifty dollars a day for the vermin-infested room that he used to be lucky to fill for twenty a week. I think of the fire on Hoe Avenue—there must be fifteen or twenty families burned out there, and it's a good bet that most of them are on welfare. And the fire on 138th Street.

But I have a fire of my own to think about now. I pull my boots up, and throw my rubber coat over my shoulder. Vinny holds an end up as I slip my arm into it.

There is a squad car waiting for us at the corner of Fox Street. As we near the corner the cops drive slowly down the block, siren wailing. The crowd in the street makes room for us to pass. There is fire playing out of the windows of the first, second, and third floors, and we can feel the intense heat as we pull in front of the building. A small crowd of teenagers is gathered across from the burning tenement singing, "Burn, baby, burn! Burn, baby, burn!"

"I'd like to take a few of them in with us," Willy Knipps says as he takes the nozzle, and drops a length of hose from the pumper. "I'd burn baby them."

"It's all a big joke to 'em, Willy," Vinny says, pulling the hose. "Some joke."

"Listen Willy," I say, "we're going to be here for the rest of the day. Why don't you let me take the nob in a little way, and you go get a mask."

"It's all right, Den. I can do it."

"C'mon, Willy," I say forcefully, making a grab for the nozzle. Willy is a very proud man, and I know that he doesn't want to give the nozzle up. "What the hell do you want to kill your-self for," I ask. "It's only an abandoned building."

"Yeah, you're right," he says resignedly, loosening his grip on the nob. Valenzio has driven the rig to the other side of the street, and has begun to hook up to the hydrant as Willy runs to the mask bin. Kelsey is helping Valenzio with the big hydrant connection, and we get water in a matter of seconds.

"Give it a good dash from the street first," Lieutenant Welch says, and I direct the nozzle toward the first floor window; 250 gallons per minute hits the flaming room, and the fire darkens quickly.

We go into the vestibule, and over the wet garbage. It doesn't smell so much now, but it is ugly and soggy—a pyramid of waste and decay. We go up five steps, and the fire meets us at a front door of the first floor. Lieutenant Welch is saying that the Chief will have to transmit a second alarm on arrival. The truckies of Ladder 712 pass by into a smoky apartment on my left, search-ing for fire extension, and the men of Engine 94 start to go up the stairs to the second floor with a line. The fire hisses and crackles before me, and Benny and Vinny are behind me re-lieving the back pressure of the surging water. Lieutenant Welch says that we can move in, but slowly. I keep the nozzle directed at the ceiling, and I'm making circular motions with my arms as Benny and Vinny hump the hose in. Suddenly, a heavy piece of plaster falls, and my helmet is knocked from my head. I feel a long, cutting pain across the back of my neck. The melted paint is dripping from the ceiling. I let out a small yell, and Lieutenant Welch quickly grabs the nob. Benny Carroll moves up. "What's the matter?" they both ask.

"I got burned on the neck."

"Back out," Lieutenant Welch says.

"No, I can make it. Just look for my helmet on the floor." Burns are funny things. After the initial pain, they stop hurting until a few days afterward. I really feel I can make it in a little more, but Benny climbs alongside of me and takes the nozzle. Vinny

[153]

moves up, and I climb over him toward the hall door. My face feels flushed with the heat, and my nose is running over my mouth. As I reach the vestibule door, the soggy Fox Street air wraps around my face, and I take a heavy, refreshing inhalation. But I remember that I left my helmet in the fire. It cost me twenty-eight bucks, and I don't want to lose it under fallen plaster and lath.

Willy Knipps and Bill Kelsey, their masks donned, pass me. They are rushing into the fire, and don't notice me behind them. "Hey Willy," I yell, "tell Carroll to look for my helmet." Knipps turns, and seems surprised to see me in the hall, but he says "O.K." and enters the apartment on his knees. The smoke is banking down now, and rushing for the oxygen at the door. I start to cough, and crouch low to get beneath it, but the smoke follows me down. What, I ask myself, am I doing here. I return to the street, and sit on the fender of the derelict car—just where I sat when I saw Tina this morning. Firemen are racing past me, either dragging hose or carrying hooks and halligan tools. The street is filled with hose—like arteries on a highway map. Sirens are wailing the arrival of second alarm companies.

I put my gloves in the pocket of my rubber coat, and feel the back of my neck. The blisters have risen across the full length of my neck, and I can feel the rough surface of the paint still sticking to the swollen skin. It doesn't hurt at all, but it will be tough moving my head for the next few weeks.

Benny and Vinny appear, dripping wet, in the doorway of the abandoned tenement. Benny has my helmet in his hand. There is nothing for me to do now but wait for an ambulance to come.

9

Every fourth year or so the city's Department of Personnel gives notice that the filing period for the fireman's examination is open. I read such a notice yesterday, and the ten years that have passed since I read the first one disappeared. I have been a firefighter for over eight years, but I remember the day I filed for the exam as clearly as a king remembers his coronation, or a cardinal his elevation.

It was a September day, much like this day, and the heat of summer was beginning to wane. The winter lay ahead, but I felt that somehow the coming winter, and all the future winters of my life, would be less harsh once I became a firefighter. Yes, I would be a firefighter, and for the first time in my life I saw the brightness of stability and security.

There were no flowering trees to see as I walked the seven concrete blocks from the tenement I called home to the Lexington Avenue subway. But, as I passed the firehouse on East

Fifty-first Street I felt the excitement a poet might feel upon viewing an acre of exploding crocus. The doors were open, and the apparatus stood poised and ready for the charge. There was a chromed numeral attached to the front grill of the pumper, but as I looked at the number I saw instead William Carlos Williams' "figure 5 in gold." I was ecstatic that I would soon be a part of the gong clangs and siren howls. I would play to the cheers of excited hordes, climbing ladders, pulling hose, and saving children—always saving children—from the waltz of the hot-masked devil. I paused and fed the fires of my ego. I would be a firefighter, part of this great red whirl. Tearful mothers would embrace me, editorial writers would extol me in heroic phrases, and mayors would pin medals and ribbons to my breast.

As I stood there I wished that an alarm would rock the firehouse, and men would slide, fly, down the flashy, gleaming poles, jump into their folded-down hip boots, and amid great excitement be off in answer to a call of distress. And as the pumper careened up the street, the men swinging gallantly from the back step straps would hear me yell to them that I too possessed their courage, and would soon join them.

But the firehouse was silent, the bells did not clang, the sirens did not wail. I was only slightly disappointed, for I realized it was a healthy silence. False alarms were rare in those days, and people were safe when the bells were still. I took the subway to the Personnel Department, down near City Hall, and I filed for the exam—the first step, the most important step toward becoming one of "New York's Bravest."

Now, so many years later, whatever romantic visions I had about being a firefighter have faded. I have climbed too many ladders, and crawled down too many grimy hallways to feel that my profession is at all glamorous. I have watched friends die, and I have carried death in my hands. There is no excitement in that, no glamor.

The National Safety Council has told me that firefighting is the most hazardous occupation in the United States—more hazardous than underground mining, or quarrying, or construction. I live in a country where the rate of death by fire is twice that of Canada, four times that of the United Kingdom, and six-and-a-half times that of Japan. Over twelve thousand persons died by the terrible swiftness of fire last year in this country.

I hope that the young men joining the fire departments around the country are doing so out of some sense of commitment to the profession and to the people, not because of the excitement of the sounds of sirens and bells. Firefighting is a brutalizing business. The community will take you for granted, they will not say "thank you" often if at all, and they are rarely on the firefighter's side when the time comes to negotiate salary and benefits. Romantic visions of courage and heroism are the stuff from which novels are constructed, but the reality of courage and heroism to a firefighter is hard, dirty work. There are rewards, but they are intangible. Each firefighter must seek them in his own way.

As I stood shaving at the bathroom sink this morning, my wife came and stood by the door as she does at times. I was shirtless, and after watching me for a short while she put her hand on the long scar on the back of my neck—one of the reminders of a Fox Street fire. "That's an ugly scar, Dennis," she said. "Do you think it will ever go away?"

I smiled at her reflection in the mirror, and replied, "I doubt it, but a shirt collar hides it, so what does it matter?"

"It only matters as a warning for the next one," she said, pulling my face down and pressing her lips to my fresh-shaven cheek. Then, her eyes wet with concern, she continued, "Because in Engine 82 there will always be a next one. Oh, I know, you'll tell me that somebody has to do it, and I'm even learning to accept that, but I worry about you all the time. It will be hard for me to sleep tonight knowing that you might be in the middle of a fire, and as I lie there I'll be wishing that you were

[157]

beside me like a normal-living husband. But, at the same time, I'll be as proud of you as the boys are. They just know that their father rides on the back of a fire engine, and they're proud of that, but I know that you are doing what you think is right for all of us, and that's good enough for me."

At that very moment I felt one of the rewards of my occupation. My wife was communicating to me that she understood the nature of my job. She was fearful of the future, yet she acknowledged the importance, the value of fighting fires. I was so moved, so unduly proud of myself, that all I could think to say was "I love you." It was enough.

The September sun is setting beyond the bulging tenements of the South Bronx now. It is six-thirty, and I am standing in front of quarters, enjoying the last warm breezes of summer. I dread the thought of the coming winter—winter cold and firefighting are a hard combination. The summer has been frenzied, but we have begun to slow up. We were doing thirty to forty runs a day during July and August, but we have dropped down to twenty to thirty these September days. The neighborhood children have returned to school, and that eliminates a lot of daytime rubbish fires.

My attention is drawn to a little girl, about eleven years old, standing by the curb to the side of the firehouse. She has a pretty, round, Spanish face. Her head is lowered, but her eyes are staring up at me apprehensively. She is holding a black and white patterned notebook in one hand, similar to the kind of school pad I used as a child, and in the other hand she has a sharpened pencil. She seems to want to say something to me, but is too shy and timid to open her mouth. I walk closer to her, smiling, hoping to loosen her up.

"Hello," I say, in as gentle a tone as I can handle, "can I help you in any way?"

She doesn't move, and her head is still lowered in a way that

[158]

reminds me of the self-consciousness and underrated self-image of poor children.

"My name is Cynthia," she says, quietly, "and I have to write a report about firemen. Are you a fireman?"

I am standing next to her now. "Yes, I am a fireman, and I'll be glad to help you with your report."

She widens her mouth in a smile, and raises her head. "Are you a Chief?"

"No, I'm not a Chief, but I think I can help you anyway," I reply. I am about to ask her if she would care to take a closer look at the fire engines, but the bells are sounded. Box 2509. Westchester Avenue and Tiffany Street.

"If you'll wait here until we come back," I say to her quickly, "I'll show you around the firehouse." It is probably a false alarm, I say to myself, and we will be gone for just a few minutes. I wave to her as the pumper rolls out of quarters, and she waves back, happy that she has made a friend.

Box 2509 is normally a false alarm, but we make the usual search up and down the block. Knipps, Royce, and Kelsey take one side of the intersection, and Carroll and I the other. This is the beginning of the "Persian Market," the strip along Westchester Avenue, from Tiffany Street to Southern Boulevard, where the South Bronx whores hustle their bodies and mouths. Three girls are standing in the entrance of a closed hardware store. "Did you see anyone pull the alarm box?" I ask them. Not expecting an answer.

One, in a flaming red wig, says, "Honey, I ain't got time to watch no fire alarm box. I'm in business, and I got to make money. Now if you want to talk some busnez . . ."

Another looks at Benny, and says, "Where you get those pretty eyes?"

Carroll and I laugh as we turn and give the thumbs-down gesture of a false alarm.

Lieutenant Welch is about to radio the "ten-ninety-two" signal over the air, but he stops as he sees the Battalion car approach. Chief Niebrock is on vacation leave, and Chief Solwin is working in his place. As Lieutenant Welch walks to the car to report a false alarm, a small boy comes running up Tiffany Street. He is yelling, "Hey firemans! Hey firemans! A man is dying in the alley."

We get the address, and the pumper wails down the street. We push through a small crowd, and there, face up in the alleyway, is a young man, hardly a man, about nineteen years old. He is a light-skinned Puerto Rican, goateed, and wearing soiled sharkskin pants. He has been cut across the stomach, and stabbed in the heart.

I would like to turn away from him, away from such a sickening sight, but I know what I have to do. Royce and the others push the crowd back as Benny and I check his eyes and his pulse. We unbutton his shirt and take a close look at his stomach, and chest. Was he murdered by a junkie for a five dollar bag of heroin, or by a jealous husband, or by an abstraction called *machismo*, the uniquely Spanish need to prove virility? I'll never know. I only know that it is too late for us to do anything for him, and I shake my head. What a waste of life. In other times this sad cadaver before me may have been the healthy son of a farmer, or a hard-working clerk, or a poet. But, fate brought him to America. His life may have been insignificant, I don't know, but it was life nonetheless. And the South Bronx robbed him of it.

Cynthia is still standing in front of the firehouse, and I can see the happiness in her face as the pumper backs into quarters. I take her into the firehouse, and explain the difference between the long ladder trucks and the pumpers. I show her the equipment we use. She questions everything as a star reporter would, and scribbles furiously in her notebook. She is a very bright child, and it gives me great satisfaction to talk to her. Her apprehensiveness has changed to self-confidence, and her questions are phrased concisely and intelligently. Her speech is flawless. She is the first child of her family to be born in the States.

"Are you responsible for other things besides putting out fires or, I should say, extinguishing fires?" she asks. We have had commissioners in this job, I think to myself, who would not be capable of phrasing a question so well. I explain our building inspection duties, our hydrant inspection duties, our community relations program, and our fire prevention duties. She questions everything intensely. I tell her about our committee work, and how we keep the firehouse clean. "Oh, we have a man in our school who does work like that," she says. "He's called the custodian, but why don't you hire a man like that for your firehouse?" Very perceptive child indeed. Rather than try to answer her question, a question I have been thinking about for as long as I have been a firefighter, I ask her, "What do you want to be when you finish with your schooling?"

"Oh," she begins most of her sentences with "Oh," "I don't think about it very much. Right now I just think about getting into a good high school, like Bronx School of Science. Maybe I'll be a teacher, or a lawyer—I wrote a report about the Supreme Court last year."

I am about to ask her if she ever thought about becoming a journalist, but she quickly puts another question to me. "I really must be getting home," she says, "but I want to ask you the most important question."

"Go right ahead," I say.

"Well, what do you think I can do to help the Fire Department? What can I tell the boys and girls in my class to do?"

I know the answer to this question as well as a White House switchboard operator knows the President's extension, for each time a group of schoolchildren comes to the firehouse we try to impress upon them the importance of three things.

"First," I answer her, "you should not play with matches, or start any kind of fire." This seems like a banal and rudimentary answer for Cynthia, but she writes it in her book, and I continue,

[161]

"Second, ask all your friends never to pull a false alarm, and third, ask your parents never to smoke in bed, and to be careful of their cigarettes at all times."

Cynthia finishes her writing, puts her pencil and book in her left hand, and offers her right hand to me.

"Thank you, Mr. Smith," she says, "you have been very helpful." And then she turns and walks out of the firehouse with as professional an air as I have ever seen.

The subject of kids is usually a sad one to us, and my little talk with Cynthia makes me feel light and happy. This neighborhood is a series of garbage heaps, and the kids use the garbage-strewn backyards and vacant lots as playgrounds. They build forts in the refuse, and the enemy burns them down. Many times they set fires just to get firefighters there—a diversion in their play that gives them a chance to climb on the apparatus, making monkey bars of the ladder truck.

Talking to Cynthia has made me feel good, because I realize that there must be many children like her in the South Bronx, and she represents the future as I want to see it. It is unfortunate though, that we don't get to see many Cynthias. We see kids in filthy clothes playing in filthy alleyways, or on hot summer days swimming in filthy street-corner ponds caused by backed-up sewers. Kids that jeer at us, and throw things at us. But, we have been into their homes. We have seen the holes in their walls, the rats in their halls, and the roaches scrambling over their bedsheets. It is not difficult to understand why kids are a problem to us in the South Bronx. It simply cannot be expected that Cynthias will be nurtured in these environs. Cynthias exist on Charlotte Street, on Fox and Simpson Streets, but it will be a long time before they will be able to grow, unaffected by the deprivations and the tragedies of the streets. But, at least they exist.

With the help and cooperation of a neighborhood action group, we recently took a group of 150 neighborhood children on a day outing to an amusement park across the Hudson River. Twelve firefighters from the big house, a few concerned black mothers, two lieutenants from the Department's Community Relations Bureau, and 150 children—all learning from, and about each other. It was a grand day. We sang songs on the buses to and from the park, we rode the roller coaster together, we shared hot dogs. Friendships were made easily, and we were relatively sure that there would be at least 150 kids in the South Bronx who would think twice before setting a garbage fire or pulling a false alarm. But, the buses, the ride-tickets, and the food cost money, and the department does not have much of that. I thought it a successful day, but it does not seem to be in the cards to have another day like it for some time to come.

The city is in a financial crisis, and all department budgets are being cut. The Community Relations Bureau will be the first to go in the Fire Department. It's too bad that getting to know kids costs money because getting to know 150 kids in the South Bronx is like getting to know one fish in the ocean.

It is now twelve-thirty. We have just returned from the sixteenth alarm of the night. It was a rubbish fire in the rear yard of a building on Prospect Avenue. We had to pull about 200 feet of the booster line to reach it.

After the fire was extinguished—it was a pile of discarded mattresses, armchairs, and assorted brown paper bags—we humped the hose back through the infested darkness of the alleyway. It was covered with food waste and human excrement, and we had to wash it down before reeling it in.

Bill Kelsey was hand-cranking the booster reel, and wondered aloud why the hell the Department refuses to install electric motors on the reel. I told him that it is not a question of initial cost, but the time and money it would take to maintain a power booster. I added facetiously that his arms were in need of a workout, anyway.

Kelsey ignored my remarks, and said, "Well, I'll tell ya this—there is not a Volunteer Fire Company on Long Island or in

Westchester County that operates with a hand crank. And we are one of the busiest companies in the world. What a lot of crap."

"Easy, Bill," I said. "Don't be so bitter." He was crouched down on top of the pumper, cranking the reel as men fifty years ago cranked the front of a Model T Ford. I was guiding the hose as the reel turned. I continued, "The fact is that you don't know about every volunteer outfit on Long Island or anywhere else. We are still the best company in the world, and I don't know that for a fact either, but we think we are. And we manage to keep thinking that even with a hand crank. And if you don't like being a part of that, you know there are companies in this city that hardly use the booster reel, and you can transfer there." I could see that Kelsey was somewhat affronted, so I quickly added, "But, we would really hate to lose you Bill."

Kelsey saw an opening for a good retort, and said, "Listen, Dennis pal, I've been in Engine 82 as long as you, and I'll be here long after you're gone, so don't worry about Bill Kelsey. I'll always carry my own weight."

I was about to answer when Benny Carroll said, "Stop the bullshit and wind the crank." And Kelsey did wind, and the gears turned, and the reel seemed to eat the hose as it revolved. Two hundred feet passed through my hands—wet, dirty, one-inch hose. Kelsey was right. We stretch this hose ten or fifteen times a day, and there is no reason for not having an electric booster. It would make our work much easier, but the traditional budget-cutters, the bosses of the Fire Department, don't worry about making our work easier—not if it is going to cost them money.

I am sitting at the housewatch area talking to Billy-o who is on duty there.

"Listen Billy," I say, "Benny and Carolyn are coming up to my place next Saturday, why don't you and Cathy and the kids come up for the day. It will be a nice day. Kelsey and Knipps are planning to stop by."

"Geez, I'd really like to, Dennis," Billy-o says, "but I just made an agreement with myself that I'm not going to do anything on my days off until after the Lieutenant's test. I've gotta give this thing a good shot this time, and the only way to do it is to discipline myself."

"God, the Lieutenant's test is nine months away," I say.

"I know, but that's nine full months of studying ahead of me, and I'm determined to make it."

Many men in the firehouse feel as Billy-o does. They take a big chunk out of their lives, and dedicate it to one hundred multiple-choice questions. Carroll and Knipps are also studying hard, but they have been studying constantly for the past two or three years. They can find time to take their families out for the day.

To be a Fire Lieutenant a man must read and be responsible for about the same amount of knowledge required in a four-year college course, but a firefighter can blow it all, all that time, all those books, all that energy, in a four-hour examination. It's a bad system, but justified by the city's Board of Examiners because it precludes any kind of political patronage or favoritism.

Billy-o is smart enough to recognize the precariousness of the system, and he knows that he is giving up more than he should, but he also knows what he is forced to do if he wants to become an officer in the Fire Department. And he needs the two thousand dollars difference in salary.

Suddenly there are wailing screams coming from the street, and Billy-o and I jump from our chairs. As I step into the street I am met by a young girl. She runs into my arms, crying uncontrollably. Her feet are bare, and all she is wearing is cotton panties and a bra. The straps of her bra hang from her shoulders so that one of her breasts is free and exposed. She is covered with blood, and the red liquid runs over her deep brown skin from gashes across the side of her neck.

Her body goes limp in my arms. She is about seventeen or

eighteen years old, and slightly built. I pick her up, and carry her back to the kitchen at the rear of the apparatus floor. There, I sit her on a plastic-covered kitchen chair as Billy-o gets the first-aid kit from a side compartment of Ladder 31's truck. The girl is conscious, but her face shows great fear, and her eyes are closed in pain.

Carroll, Knipps, and Royce are in the kitchen, and I ask Benny to call for an ambulance and the police. As Billy-o returns with the first-aid kit, the bells start ringing. Box 2412. He runs from the kitchen yelling, "Eighty-five and Seven-twelve goes." Royce opens the first-aid kit, and hands me a bunch of gauze pads.

It is not only her neck that has been cut, but the top and the back of her shoulder also. I wipe the shoulder clean as gently as possible, but she winces whenever I approach one of her wounds. I stroke in short, quick movements over her small stained breast, and up over her chest and shoulder. The wounds are large, but they are not deep, and I see tiny bits of glass reflecting from them.

Knipps has gone upstairs for a clean sheet, and he returns with it. The girl is still whimpering, and tears are falling from her full, brown eyes, but she has settled down some, confident that she is being helped. "You'll be okay now, there's nothing to worry about," I keep telling her. Knipps covers her with the sheet, and she holds the end of it over her naked bosom.

"Thank you," she says, almost in control of herself.

An old woman enters the kitchen, crying, "My baby, my baby." It is the girl's grandmother, and upon seeing her the girl collapses again into a fit of tears. The old woman puts her hands around the girl's shoulder, and the girl screams in torment.

We can hear a voice from the apparatus floor, a high feminine voice repeating a litany of curses. "Dear God," the voice echoes into the kitchen, "that man is a no-good sonovabitch, and I swear to you when I see him I'm gonna kill 'im for what he done to my chil'. I swear to you God I'm gonna kill that mother-fucker."

The old woman goes out to the apparatus floor, and both

women return to the kitchen. The younger woman runs to the girl, and kisses her face over and over. The girl attempts to throw her arms around her mother, but the movement of her arms causes the glass-packed wounds to shoot her full of pain. She has let the sheet fall to her lap, and her mother picks it up and covers her.

Lieutenant Welch has entered the kitchen, along with Captain Frimes, who is working with Ladder 31. Lieutenant Welch will have to make out a report of the incident, and he questions the girl's mother. She is a handsome woman, about forty years old, and dressed attractively in bell bottomed pants and a silk blouse. She is very upset, and her voice trembles as she speaks.

"This girl is my daughter, Jenny, and my husband tried to get in the bed with her. He was drunk, and when she tried to beat 'im away, he broke a bottle and cut her with it. I started to fight with 'im, and Jenny runned around here to the firehouse. We live around the corner on 169th Street." The woman starts to cry, and she turns away, saying, "I jus' been married to him for a year, and now I'm gonna kill 'im when I see 'im, for what he did to my Jenny, I swear to God, I'm gonna kill 'im."

The police arrive, and take the necessary information from Lieutenant Welch. Billy-o tells us that the dispatcher has told him that there is a backlog of ambulance calls in the South Bronx, and we will have to wait forty-five minutes before one will arrive. The policemen decide to take the girl and her mother to the hospital in their squad car.

The girl is composed now, although still frightened. Her mother's lover loved her, and his lust is still breathing from her shoulder and neck, and Electra must rage as she sees the wounds of passion on the smooth, dark shoulder of a South Bronx virgin. Saints have been made for less pain. And now, as I watch her bare feet walk to the police car, as I watch her body move beneath the wraps of a firehouse sheet, I can't help thinking of Cynthia, and of all the Cynthias of the South Bronx. God, I think, God protect them!

Engine 85 returns from its run, and as the pumper begins to

back into quarters, the police car wails off to the hospital. The bells ring. The pumper stops at the door, the driver, Oscar Beutin, counting the signal. Box 2738. Oscar knows that signal as well as we know the signal for Charlotte Street and 170th. The men of Engine 85 retake their positions on the back step, and the pumper takes off. Their destination: Southern Boulevard and 172nd Street.

There is a blacktopped lot on the corner of Southern Boulevard and 172nd Street. We had a block party there a couple of weeks ago, a kind of back-to-school party for the neighborhood kids. The Department's Community Relations Bureau paid for the ice cream and soda. The men of the firehouse chaperoned.

It was a nice day, an end-of-summer day. Like the bus trip, the party was organized so that the kids could get to know the firefighters better, and the firefighters the kids. Captain Frimes of Ladder 31 did most of the work in preparing the day. He arranged with the owner of the property to use the lot, he met with the community groups, he asked the Salvation Army for the use of one of their trucks to dispense the soda and ice cream, and along with two lieutenants from the Community Relations Bureau he contracted for the entertainment with a steel band. Captian Frimes is a community-minded man.

A notice was put up on the bulletin board of the firehouse kitchen a week before, asking for volunteers to come in on their day off to meet with the kids, answer their questions, and generally add to the excitement of the party. Some of the men, predictably, said they wanted nothing to do with these kids. One said, "Why the hell doesn't the Department give a party for our own kids instead of wasting money on these kids."

I don't like this prejudice, but I understand it. Firefighters know that one out of seven people in this town are on welfare. They know that ninety percent of those are black or Puerto Rican. They know that half the people in this community are black and the other half are Puerto Rican. Like most lower middle-class people, firefighters cannot reconcile the fact that so many people are being subsidized for doing nothing while they work hard and can barely make the payments at the end of the month. They look at the Fire Department statistics and see that the busiest areas of the city—where the false alarms are greatest, the garbage fires greatest, and the incidents of harassment are greatest—are where minority groups live. There is no doubt that the firefighters' job is more difficult, and more dangerous, in black and Puerto Rican areas than in other parts of New York City.

What most firefighters do not know, however, is that a good case for economic determinism can be made to explain this prejudice, that those one rung up from the bottom of the status ladder traditionally resent those below them. Nor do most firefighters know that conditions make their job tough, not people. People only reflect the conditions. Poverty is manifested in fire statistics—that's a safe generalization.

But, many of the men came to the block party. Some came as a favor to Captain Frimes, some came because they were genuinely interested. Billy-o was there, and McCartty, Royce, Carroll, Knipps, Kelsey, and others. And the black firefighters from the big house, Horace Brewster, Juan Moran, Melvin Henderson, Eddy Montaign—men truly committed to developing better rapport with their brothers and sons.

The day passed quickly. We listened with black children to the dream-like sounds of soft hammers hitting steel drums, and we watched an African dance troupe move to the rapidity of the bongos. The white firefighters had a fascinating lesson in black culture, and black children held hands with white firefighters, feeling an unspoken friendship.

The time came to disburse the ice cream, and we had a terrible time trying to keep the kids in order, for where is there order when free ice cream is being given to children? There were over two hundred kids, and one truck. Those not fortunate enough to be in the front of the line refused to accept their misfortune, and crashed to the front. It was a mass of pushing children hungry for the cold sweetness of ice cream. It took

[169]

great effort to regain order, but finally, under the half-serious threat of closing the rear doors of the truck the children quieted. And then we heard the sound of the approaching sirens. In the confusion someone had pulled the alarm box at the corner—in the midst of the Fire Department's party. The firefighters who responded had harsh things to say about community relations that day, and they kidded those of us who were there unmercifully, but, aside from the false alarm, it was a day of victory for the community relations program. The children were stuffed with ice cream, and satisfied.

As I think of those anxious, laughing children now, I regret that some of the firefighters chose not to take part in the party. They let the banality of prejudice interfere with what could have been a happy experience for them. I do not understand how a man can risk his life in a blazing tenement to save one black child, and refuse to see, to be a part of, two hundred black kids eating ice cream.

10

It's hard to keep my eyes on the road this morning. The colors of summer are beginning to turn to those of fall, and the early Friday sun makes the leaves seem even brighter than they are. The annual transition from quiet greens to exploding golds and purples has been going on for a week now. It's comforting somehow that nature's changes are the same from year to year. It makes it easier to think of the world in terms of millions of years and it helps to keep my mind from the day to day nature of my existence. I have lived half an average life span, and I sometimes wonder if the other half exists. *"The signal five-five-five-five has been transmitted. All department flags shall be lowered to half mast. It is with deep regret . . ."*

I'm not really afraid of that. It may be in the cards, but all firefighters know that. Time will pass, the children will grow. I don't really think about it often, just when I'm too tired and trying to figure out what I'm doing in the South Bronx. But it's something you can't think about for long.

The traffic is heavy, and I reprove myself for oversleeping. It is seven-thirty, and I'm just passing Stony Point. It was near here that Benedict Arnold's wife charmed Washington as her husband made off for London. It is beautiful country, made more beautiful by the season. Normally, I would be passing Tappan by now, and the traffic would move freely. But the speedometer reads first 50, then 30, then 45, then 25 and from a hilltop I can see the long parade of automobiles before me, marching two by two and out of step toward the city. How I hate to drive. One of the luxuries of the very rich is that they don't have to drive their own cars, and they can watch the leaves turn as they go from place to place. The leaves are turning now, but I can't watch them. I begin to daydream.

"Oh Rodney, make a stop at Tiffany's before we go on to the office. I want to pick up a little something for Mrs. Smith. Isn't it clever of the maple to shed his leaves in preparation for the cold winter ahead."

It's twenty minutes to nine as I park the car next to Pete's Bodega, a Spanish grocery store across the street from the firehouse. Like many industrious Puerto Ricans, Pete came to this country and opened up a small bodega. Eleven years later he found he could buy his wife a new Cadillac with leather upholstery and wire wheels. Then he bought the frame building that housed his bodega, and the two buildings adjoining it. He attached a garage to protect the Cadillac from the neighborhood kids, and he double padlocked it, and built a mesh wire fence around it, and padlocked that. He never gets to drive the Cadillac though, because he works the bodega fourteen hours a day, seven days a week. His wife doesn't get to drive it much either, because it takes two to run the store. The garage proved to be a good investment for them.

Charlie McCartty is in the firehouse kitchen munching an onion roll. Most of the day crew, and some of the night crew are sitting around drinking coffee and talking idly. Charlie is standing with an elbow propped on top of the soda machine. He spots me, and says in his deepest authoritarian voice, "It's about time you got here, Dennis. I'm gettin' sick an' tired of you minute men gettin' in here just before the nine o'clock bells. The brothers are tired, and they need relief."

"Up yours, Charlie," I say dispassionately.

"Up mine, huh? Up your old lady's." He pauses, then adds, "That's probably why you can't get in here in time."

"That's probably why everyone is late around here," Jerry Herbert says.

"Listen guys," I say, not bothering to give an explanation, "it's only a quarter to nine, and the book of regulations says we don't have to start until nine. Give me a break."

"No breaks around here," Charlie says. He puts his coffee cup on the soda machine, and throws his heavy powerful arms around me.

"Lemme give ya a little hug," he says.

I feel enveloped and crowded by his husky frame, like a plastic toy being pressure-wrapped in cellophane. He squeezes with small effort, and I can feel a slight pain in the small of my back. Not a hurting pain, but one of relief, like when a chiropractor's at work.

"Listen Charlie," I yell, "love me or leave me, but don't go halfway."

He releases his hold, and laughs, "But you know I love ya, Dennis."

"So does that broad in Prospect Hills," I return. Charlie lives in a small town called Prospect Hills.

Benny Carroll is sitting at the back table reading a newspaper. He looks up, and interjects, "That broad in Prospect Hills loves everybody."

Everyone but Charlie laughs.

"Ahh, turnin' against me, huh?" Charlie says, mocking a surprised look. "At least I don't have the long gray line around my house everytime I go to work."

[173]

Benny lives near the United States Military Academy at West Point.

"O.K., Charlie. Ya got me," Benny says. "Now sit down and stop making a fool of yourself."

Malachy McKeon walks into the kitchen. He worked last night, and has changed into his civilian clothes. Charlie's expression changes from surprise to one of concern. "Did you call the insurance company, Mal?" he asks.

"No, not yet," McKeon answers. "I'll wait until after I have my coffee." Mal is twenty-six, a handsome man, with penetrating brown eyes. He is usually full of life, and giving away smiles to everyone he meets. Now though, I sense indifference as he pours his coffee.

"Why, Mal?" I ask. "What happened?"

"They purloined his automobile last night," Charlie answers. Even Malachy laughs as these words come from Charlie's mouth.

"Is that right? That's the third one in the last few months."

"The third? Who else besides me and Freddy Schoan?"

"Eddy Montaign. About two months ago. Poor bastard! It was the first new car he ever owned."

Billy O'Mann gets up to pour another cup of coffee, and says, "Well it's the goddam city's fault. They could fence off that whole area across the street, there by Pete's Bodega. It's city property, and we could fit fifteen cars there, but instead they fence off all the vacant lots so people won't dump garbage. They must have spent half a million bucks fencing off vacant lots in the last year. So the people throw the garbage over the fence, and it makes it twice, three times as hard for us to put out rubbish fires."

A probationary fireman was on the back step with Benny Carroll and me not so long ago. As we were pulling out of quarters, the probie noticed three youths sitting on the fender of his car. It was a new car, and the moonlight shone on its fenders. "Get off the car. Whatsa matter with you?" the probie

[174]

yelled over the loudness of the siren, and the pumper raced out of view of the sneering youths. It was a bad move, and I told the probie that it was a bad move. After he has worked in the South Bronx for a while he will learn that it never pays to say anything to anyone on the street unless the words are kind, or unless someone is going to get locked up. And if someone is going to get locked up it makes even less sense to say anything to him. If a guy refuses to move his double-parked car as we respond to an alarm, give him a ticket. If someone interferes with us as we try to fight a fire, have him locked up. It never pays to be less than polite, and there is no such thing as verbal satisfaction. When we returned from the alarm the youths were not sitting on the probie's car anymore, and neither was his radio antenna. And the antennas of twelve cars in front of the firehouse were broken. See, it never pays. The probie understood.

"What we really need," Billy-o continues, "is armored protection like Pete has around his Cadillac over there. A steel garage and a chain-link fence. But I'd even settle for chicken wire if the city would give us the space. But they won't, and we all know it."

"Yeah, but what can you do about it?" mumbles George Hiegman. A short, stocky man, Hiegman is a sixteen-year veteran of the job, and an Engine 85 chauffeur. He's been around the fires and the firehouses, and his opinion is respected. He continues, "The firemen always end up with the brown part of the stick. You know, the part that was dipped in human excrement." Some of the younger firemen laugh, but the older guys are used to the way Hiegman talks.

"What department," he asks, "does the mayor call on to cut its budget from year to year? The Fire Department. The traditional budget cutters. And it's our own fault. We're the dopes who paint our own kitchen to make it livable. The city buys television sets for every police precinct in the city so the cops can

[175]

watch closed-circuit training films. We have to watch training films too, but does the city buy television sets for us? Damn right they don't. The firemen like to watch television between fires so let them buy their own. And we have to pay for a subscription to a department magazine so the bosses can feed us technical information that we have to memorize if we want to pass the next Lieutenant's examination. We write in the department journals with our own pens, and we take up collections to buy an air conditioner, or a new stove, or supplies to build a decent sitting room in a damp cellar. We never make calls on the department telephone. Instead we pay a monthly bill for a pay phone. When we need paper towels, we go shake down a school custodian. When we need bandages for the first-aid kits, which we paid for, we have to con some nurse at a hospital."

I remember as George says this, Billy O'Mann walking, helmet in hand, into the emergency room at Bronx Hospital. The nurse there was having a bad day.

"Listen ma'am," he said, "do you think you could give us some gauze pads and bandages?"

"Dammit, you firemen are always coming in here and bothering us. Why don't you go to a drug store?"

"O.K., lady, you can shove the bandages," snapped Billy.

George continues, " . . . and the most important tool we use we pay for ourselves—the halligan tool. Why should the city pay for it when the firemen go out and buy it themselves?"

The companies were operating at Home and Simpson Streets. A car was on fire, and Charlie McCartty dropped his halligan tool on the street as he went to open the hood. When he turned around again, the halligan was gone. Back at the firehouse later in the afternoon, the Captain gives a kid two dollars. The kid tells the Captain that he'll find the halligan under the stairs at 987 Simpson Street. It was there.

"Why didn't ya arrest the kid, Cap?" someone asked.

"Look at it this way," he answered, "we just saved ourselves a sawbuck."

"Jesus, George," Billy-o says, "all I want is an eight-hundred-dollar parking lot across the street. You just increased the Fire Department budget a couple a million dollars with those complaints."

"Yeah," George says, "it's amazin' what wonders you can do with a flip o' the tongue, isn't it?" The bells start to come in, and everyone is silent for a moment. The first round of eleven came through. It's nine o'clock, and the men in the kitchen talk over the second half of the 11-11 nine o'clock test signal.

George is right, I think. Especially about the television set. I wish the hell we could get rid of it. I'll never forget sitting in the kitchen, waiting expectantly for Humphrey Bogart to fondle those steel balls in the greatest courtroom scene to be put on film. Here he comes. He's walking down the hall. He passes his junior officers waiting outside the court. He stops. Good old Bogey, he never lets the enemy get the edge on him. "Good morning, gentlemen," he says in that cool, polished way. He opens the door, and enters the court. I wait. He salutes the court. I am about to be rewarded for being a loyal Bogart fan. Then—then the bells toll.

I wouldn't have minded if it was a fire. But it was a false alarm. Yes, get rid of the television. I wasn't even interested in seeing José Ferrer throw a glass of champagne in Fred Mac-Murray's face. If the administration wants us to watch television training films, let them buy us a television set.

The room is quiet, but the conversation interests me so, that I do not want to see it die.

"The real sad thing about it though," I say dogmatically, stressing the *real*, "is that we know the system will never change unless the firemen in this city realize they are being duped."

"That's a grammatical redundancy," says George. "Duped and firemen mean the same thing. It's oxymoronic to say that a fireman realizes reality. Two opposite things don't match up—if we did realize reality we would not be doing this kind of work for a living. Ya gotta be nuts to go into a fire, and crazy people don't recognize reality. Ergo, 'firemen can't realize they are being duped' is a grammatical redundancy ta begin wit'."

The kitchen is filled with laughter as George washes his cup in the sink. George's hands are wet as he turns around. Cagey Dulland is at the coffee urn, and his back is towards George. "Kerchoo," George yells, and shakes off the excess water on Cagey's neck.

"God bless you," says Billy-o.

"Goddammit, George," says Cagey, wiping the back of his neck. The laughter increases as unsuspecting Dulland pulls a handkerchief from his back pocket.

The bells start ringing, and the laughter stops. Box 2295 comes in. Engine 73 and Ladder 42 are first due there. We're safe.

Billy-o returns to *The New York Times*. George makes a motion to me as if to say "Watch this."

"Listen Billy," he says, "I bet you didn't think I knew all of those big words. You know, even us guys who read the *Daily News* got some smarts."

Billy-o lays the *Times* on the table, smiles, and says, "George pal, there is nothing you could say that would surprise me. You are an idol in my eyes. But that 'oxy-something' really threw me."

"Yeah," says George, "you don't find words like that in the *Times*. Ya gotta read those little Dell books with the pictures in 'em."

Billy-o laughs in agreement as the bells come in again. Box 2404.

"Engine Eighty-five only," yells the housewatchman. George, Bill Robbie, Marty Hannon, and the other members of 85 hustle out to the apparatus floor.

The time passes quickly, and Engine 85 returns to quarters. It was the first false alarm of the day. I am drinking another cup of coffee as the nine-thirty signal comes in—two rounds of eleven bells. It's time to start our daily committee work, wash the floors, clean the tables, change the linen, make the beds, shine the poles, wash the windows, clean the toilets, sweep the cellar. It reminds me of a song from *Cinderella*.

Billy-o, McCartty, and I go to the second floor. Billy and Charlie begin to strip the sheets from the beds as I grab a toilet brush and a pail and head into the bathroom. The smell is terrible, and I open the only window. I can see someone's feet beneath the commode stall door. "Give us a courtesy flush, will ya?" I say.

"Dennis? Is that you?" a harsh voice comes from the stall.

"Yeah. Is that you Milsaw? What the hell did you eat last night?"

"I'm sorry, Dennis," Milsaw says as the water flushes down the drain. He continues, "I'm just trying to live up to what they wrote about me there over the urinal."

I walk to the urinal and read the one-line graffito on the wall. It is in two parts. The first part in red ink reads: "THE BIG HOUSE—THE BRAVEST MEN IN THE WORLD." Someone added, in blue ink: "SHAVE WHILE MILSAW TAKES A DUMP."

"I know what they mean, Milsaw," I say, walking out of the latrine. "Talk about air pollution. I'll take the streets of New York anytime."

Artie Merritt and Benny Carroll have joined Charlie and Billy-o at the bed-making.

Artie says to me, "Milsaw drove you out, huh?"

"Damn right. It's unbearable."

"I know," says Artie, "I went in there a few minutes ago to brush my teeth, you know. And, you know, I was gagged."

Billy-o sits on the edge of a bed. "You know, Artie," he says. "I know. This is what George Hiegman was talking about before when he said that being duped and being a fireman is the same thing. How the hell can we ever think of ourselves as professional firefighters when we are forced to clean toilets and sweep floors? Milsaw is in there smelling the place up, but when he's finished he has to pick up a mop and wash the floor. . . ."

Charlie interrupts, "Yeah, but in Milsaw's case it's probably the right thing to do. You can't ask a normal person to go in there after Milsaw does his thing."

The guys laugh a little, realizing that Charlie has to get a joke in on everything.

Billy-o continues, "Take a bank, for instance. The lowest job in a bank is the guy who sweeps the floor, right? And the next lowest is the bank guard, but do you think a bank guard would ever sweep a floor in a bank? Hell no. That's not his job. He gets paid to maintain security, and maybe to direct people to the right window. We get paid for fire protection and fire prevention services, but we also clean toilets, wash windows, and sweep floors. Professional, my ass."

Billy-o gets up, and throws a blanket over a bed. He tucks the ends in. I can see that he is heated, that the subject angers him. He is most effective and most convincing when he is mad, and I want to push his buttons.

"Listen Bill," I say, "you know damn well that the only way we can change any of this is through collective bargaining, and if you were so concerned you would run for union office."

"Don't give me that crap, Dennis. Mickey Maye worked in this firehouse for years, and then he became president of our union. Cleaning shitbowls one day, and having a forty-minute conference with President Nixon the next. That's what the union is all about. They don't want any real change. They want secure positions, and their positions become insecure if the boat begins to rock. You can clean shitbowls one day and be mad about it, but when the President of the United States puts his arm around you and tells you that you are a responsible labor leader, yessir, you're no radical, then you begin to see yourself as part of the responsible establishment. Well, I don't want to be a part of the responsible establishment—not if my men have to clean shitbowls. When I see the President of the AFL-CIO go to the White House to have lunch with a Republican President at a time when unemployment is at its highest in a decade, that tells me that labor in this country is on the wrong road."

Artie, Benny, and Charlie are interested, and now they are
sitting on the edges of beds.

"Well," Charlie interjects, "no matter what you say about
the union, you hafta admit that we're all happy with our job.
Some things about it may be bad, but we still like to come to
work. . . ."

"But," says Benny, "that may be because of what George said—
that we're all crazy and don't know the difference."

"I think Billy-o," I say, "that you're right about the little plumber having lunch at the White House—that was no place for him
to be. And maybe it's true that the labor movement has gotten
soft, rich, and comfortably settled in the establishment. But,
it's still true that, at least for us, the only way we can effect
change is through our union."

The other men nod in agreement. "Listen Dennis," Billy-o
says, "you go get your brush and go in there and clean those
bowls, and then tell me that the union is going to change things.
I've been talking about this for ten years now, and nothing
happened. I've written letters downtown, and I've spoken at
union meetings, but nothing ever came of it. I'm still sweeping
floors. . . ."

The conversation is interrupted by the sudden bells. Box 2743.
That's us. Charlotte and 170th. Eighty-two and thirty-one. We
get up and go. Slide the brass pole. Into our boots. Rubber coats.
Helmets. Rrhhhheeeww. Up Intervale Avenue. Up Wilkins Avenue. Up 170th Street to Charlotte. It's a rubbish fire in a vacant
lot. The lot has been fenced recently, but a large hole has been
cut into it. Benny grabs the booster nozzle, and squeezes through
the hole. I look around at the drab, overcrowded tenements.
Little kids sitting on window sills, old ladies peering from behind
plastic draperies. Someone has painted a large sign on the bricks
of the corner building. It says: "TEN DOLLARS REWARD FOR THE
SUPER OF THIS HOUSE." We have troubles, I think. But there is a
way out of ours. The people of that building can't find the man
who is supposed to clean the halls, tend the boiler, and collect

the garbage. There is no union for them to turn to. They can only paint a sign on the weathered bricks of their dirty building.

We are back in the firehouse now, and it is almost eleven o'clock. Benny Carroll and Artie Merritt are collaborating on the day's meal. Hamburgers. Artie will go to the butcher for the meat, and the bodega for the rolls. Benny will cook. Like all the other times we have had hamburgers I will take only one bite, and throw the rest away. I do not like hamburgers. When I was a child we ate hamburgers three or four times a week. My mother would occasionally mold them into meatballs or a meat-loaf, or break them into chips to mix with a sauce. But it was all hamburger to me. Like potatoes to the Irish before the famine.

The committee work is done quickly. My value to the people of the city of New York is that I keep their firehouse clean. Ig-nominious effort swept the floors, and pride was flushed down the toilet along with the coal tar cleanser.

It is noon, and the hamburgers sizzle on the grill. Jim Stack is helping Benny separate the rolls while Artie Merritt washes the cups that have accumulated in the sink. The bells sound Box 2544. Get out. The housewatchman is yelling, and men are scurrying from the kitchen and down the poles. "Eighty-two and thirty-one goes. Union Avenue and 166. Both companies are second due." Engine 50 and Ladder 19 are first due at that lo-cation.

Captain Albergray and our regular chauffeur are on vacation. Jim Stack is the spare chauffeur while Bill Valenzio hustles a second job instead of going to Florida. Captain Albergray has been replaced by a mild, quiet man named Collins. Lieutenant Collins was promoted from the rank of Fireman only two weeks ago, and I get the feeling that he doesn't care much for his new role. There is a two-thousand-dollar difference between Fireman and Lieutenant, and that is a good enough reason to study for promotion, but when a guy becomes an officer he is separated from the men he has worked with for a good part of his life, the men he grew to love, the men who made going to work worth while. He doesn't have time anymore to sit and laugh or argue in the kitchen, because his role has changed. He must learn to relate to the men as a supervisor, and Lieutenant Collins is finding that hard to do. He doesn't like to give orders, or to check up on firemen, but he'll get over that. He will adjust, and he will make a good boss, because he has a genuine respect for the men he supervises.

The second floor of a three-story frame building is fully involved with fire at the corner of Union and 166th Street. It is a vacant building that someone has set up to cause some excitement, or to achieve an orgasm, or to kill a fireman.

Engine 50 has stretched the heavy two-and-a-half hose, and Ladder 19 is searching the building for sleeping derelicts or unconscious drug addicts. Benny Carroll and I run to Engine 50's pumper to stretch a second line. The fire is coming out of six windows, but it doesn't look like it has gotten into the floor above yet. Kevin McMann and Cosmo Posculo, two of the younger members of Engine 82, don the heavy Air-Pac masks as Benny and I stretch to the floor above the fire. Luckily, there is a hydrant in front of the building, so the stretch is a short one.

As we reach the second floor I can see through the smoke a lifeless figure propped against the landing wall. I tell Benny to hold up a minute while I check it out. As I get closer I can see by the bulky outline of a rubber coat that it is a fireman.

The roof has been vented, and the smoke begins to lift. I recognize the face before me. It is exhausted, and has two black liquid lines running from the nose. "How ya feeling, Louie?" I ask.

Louie Minelli, the senior nozzle man of Engine 50, answers, "I'm O.K. I got the first two rooms. Mike Roberti will get the rest." That's Louie's way of saying Engine 50 can do the job.

Lieutenant Collins is on the third floor landing waiting for us. The smoke is lifting, but it is always bad above a fire. "I don't think we'll hafta charge the line," he says to nobody in particular.

[183]

Benny and I sit on our heels in the hallway. Artie Merritt comes crawling out of the apartment above the fire. He has a halligan tool in one hand and an ax in the other. It was his job to search the apartment thoroughly.

"It's clean," he says. "The walls are a little warm, but I don't think the fire has extended." Kevin and Cosmo have arrived, breathing easily in their masks. There is nothing for them to do but to join us in sitting on their heels.

The Chief from the Seventeenth Battalion passes by us. He disappears into the apartment for a short while. Upon reappearing, he says, "Take up, Eighty-two." The fire is out. Engine 50 saved us a lot of effort.

We drag the hose back down the stairs, and begin to fold it onto Engine 50's pumper. It is easy work, and we are all silently satisfied that the line wasn't charged, and there is no water to drain. I am not paying much attention to what I am doing, for I keep thinking of Louie Minelli. His eyes, heavy and watered, staring at me through the lifting poison. Tired and blank. "I got the first two rooms." His body robbed of energy, he barely mustered the strength to turn his head. "Mike Roberti will get the rest." His words, though barely audible, were filled with pride. Engine 50 can do the job. Engine 50 can put out any fire. I want to yell as I pass the limp, empty hose forward, "But Louie, the goddam building is vacant. We should let it burn." We won't let it burn though. I know that, and Louie knows. We have a tradition in this department of going where the fire is. And we know that two or three fires will be set in this building every week, until the city tears it down.

There are five Fire Department vehicles parked on 166th Street. The engines are running, and the radio volumes are at their highest. The rigs sing like a chorus as the dispatcher asks: "*Engine Eighty-two. Ladder Thirty-one. Are you available?*"

Jim Stack is sitting in the cab of the pumper, He yells over to Lieutenant Collins, "We're available. Huh Lou?"

Benny lays the nozzle over the hose, and Lieutenant Collins

nods to Jim. We can hear Jim's voice blare over the radio as we run to our pumper: "*Engine Eighty-two is available.*"

The dispatcher replies: "*All right Eighty-two. Ladder Thirty-one?*"

The Chief of the Seventeenth Battalion answers: "*Ladder Thirty-one is in the process of taking up. They will be slightly delayed.*"

"*Ten-four Battalion Seventeen. Engine Eighty-two, respond to phone alarm Box 2509. Location, 1335 Intervale Avenue. Did you receive, Engine Eighty-two?*"

Jim comes over the air: "*Engine Eighty-two, ten-four.*"

The fire engine races and wails away from Louie Minelli and the smoldering abandoned building. 1335 Intervale Avenue is right up the street from the firehouse. We could have been there in thirty seconds. Now, it will take us three or four minutes.

We can see the smoke five blocks away. Our boots are up, and we are ready. Finally, we pass the firehouse and the sizzling hamburgers. The doors are open, and the house is empty. I look over the side of the pumper, and I see the men of Engine 85 stretching into a five-story tenement house. They are not assigned at this location, and they must have been special-called since we were operating elsewhere.

The fire is roaring out of two windows on the ground floor. Benny and I, and Kevin and Cosmo are off the pumper and running before Jim Stack brings the rig to a stop. This would be an ordinary fire, except that the fire escapes are a circus of people yelling desperately at every level. There is no ladder company at the scene, and we all know without speaking that we have to think about life. Engine 85 will think about fire.

"Aqui, aqui," the people cry fearfully. The drop ladder on the fire escape has been let down, but it is not secured well, and it shakes. I make a quick wish, as I climb the thin, narrow bars, that a ladder company will get in soon. Benny is before me; the others behind. There is a man yelling in wild frenzy on the third floor, and we are trying to reach him. But the fire escapes are crowded with fleeing people. Please hurry. Hold the handrails. Watch your step. Let us by. Let us by.

The man on the third floor is holding an infant out of the window. His arms are outstretched, and it seems he is offering the baby, as even Abraham offered his son. Benny nests the child in his arms. It is in its first month of life, and cries the high violent cry peculiar to its size. The man turns and bends down to the floor. He picks up another infant, and hands it to Benny. It is the sixteen-inch twin of the first. Benny cradles it in his other arm, and begins to descend the fire escape. There is a light mist of smoke in the apartment, and a little girl coughs. She is about three years old, and she wraps her small arms around my neck as her father hands her to me. I start down the fire escape, followed by the barefooted, shirtless man.

Cosmo and Kevin have carried children down from the second floor. In the street again, the children are delivered into the warm arms of neighbors. The fire whips around the center hall of the ground floor, and the men of Engine 85 have moved out to the vestibule. George Hiegman must be having trouble with the hydrant. Did someone hacksaw off the controlling stem for a quarter's worth of brass, or shove beer cans or soda bottles down the casing?

I look expectantly for Ladder 31, but they haven't arrived yet. Benny has returned to the fire escape, and I follow quickly. The people on the street shout about children being left behind on the fourth floor. Benny goes in one window, and I go in another. The smoke is heavy now throughout the building. I am in a living room. A cheap print framed in plastic hangs on the wall. It looks like a western sunset. I look under the vinyl-covered furniture. There are two bedrooms, and I look under the beds, and in the closets. My eyes are wet, and my nose is running, but the kitchen and the bathroom are clear—there are no unconscious bodies, or frightened whimpering children.

I return to the fire escape. I am not sure now if I should continue to search the building, or go down to the street and stretch a second line to the floor above the fire. The decision is made for me as I see Ladder 31 careening up Intervale Avenue. Ladder 48 is right behind them. The "truckies" will now search and ventilate the building. I head down the fire escape thinking again about fire. It was going good, and the chances are that it has probably gotten through to the floor above. As I reach the top of the drop-ladder I hear Benny's voice calling for me. He is coming down the fire escape with a small girl in his arms. I meet him between the first and second landing. "Take her down for me, Dennis," he says. "I found her in her crib. I'm going back up." His face is black with smoke, and a heavy cylinder of mucus hangs from his nose. The child is crying, which is a good sign.

There is a woman waiting at the bottom of the ladder. She is shrieking hysterically "Maria, Maria." Another woman holds her shoulders as she takes the baby from me. I can see through her tears the happiness in her simple, unadorned eyes—that true happiness that is unique in a mother's love for her child. She doesn't know Benny, and I wonder if she will ever think of him, pray for him.

Lieutenant Collins, Cosmo, and Kevin are in the street taking orders from Chief Niebrock. The Chief's walkie-talkie is blaring and squawking, and the transmission is broken up. The only words that are understandable are *"roof,"* and *"the bulkhead door."* The Chief speaks into the transmitter in his slow, confident way, *"Please repeat your message. You are coming in broken up."* And the radio just squeals in reply.

The Chief looks at Lieutenant Collins and the rest of us. Engine 45 has already started a second line to the floor above, and Chief Niebrock orders us to help them with the stretch. The second line should have been ours, but we have all been thinking about other things. Lieutenant Collins, Cosmo, and Kevin helped carry people down the fire escapes, and they searched the apartments on the lower floors. Now, we will have to help Engine 45 stretch its line without getting a real piece of the action. We'll just squat in the hall as Engine 45 fights its way in with the nozzle.

Engine 85 is making good progress with its line. Marty Hannon and Jim Barrett are on the nozzle. They are in the apartment, but they haven't made the front room yet, and the fire is still pushing out of the windows. Bill Robbie is right behind them with a mask, but Marty and Jim won't take a blow. Captain Konak is beside them yelling the traditional words of confidence. "Beautiful, Marty, you got it. Move in a little more. Give us some more line Robbie."

Benny has gone into an apartment on the fifth floor. He makes a careful search, but the apartment is empty. He opens the hall door, and he is hit with a hard wind of heat. He drops to the floor, and the heat passes over him. The smoke is thicker than he has ever experienced it, and he coughs almost uncontrollably. His first impulse is to get back out to the fire escape and air, but he puts his nose to the linoleum floor and tries to relax. As his coughing stops he can hear soft moaning coming from the hall. He listens carefully for the direction, and it seems to be coming from the landing between the top floor and the roof. He crawls on his stomach through the hall, and up the stairs. The heat is unbearable and he feels that all energy has been drained from his body. He reaches the landing, and sees before him an incredible mess of human beings. They are piled on top of one another, and some are thinking the last conscious thoughts of life while exhaling the sighs of death.

The landing is an inferno. There are seven people—five adults and two children—lying there. They tried to flee the burning building, and they went to the roof door. But the roof door was chained closed to keep the drug addicts from entering from the roof, and the heat from a fire five floors beneath them had nowhere to go. And seven human beings lay there with the heat, before a chained bulkhead door.

Benny can hear the desperate thump of the axhead hitting the halligan tool as he grabs for the nearest body. A two-inch hole was cut into the bulkhead brick and into the steel-covered door, and the chain was run through both holes, bound by a lock on the inside. The links are heavy, and the firemen on the roof cannot break them. They work instead on the hinges.

Benny has a two-year-old girl in his arms again, but this one isn't breathing. He carries her down into a fifth-floor apartment. He closes the door behind to keep out the smoke, and lays the girl gently on the kitchen floor. He wants to give her mouth-to-mouth resuscitation, but he has to think also of the others on the landing. He blows two hard, hopeful puffs of breath into the girl's mouth, and returns to the landing. There is a large woman there, made even larger with a pregnancy. He grabs her under the arms and pulls, but she is heavy and Benny is sweating a last resurgence of power. He is pulling hard, but it is of no consequence. He is close to collapse, and gasping with the heat and smoke. Then, like a *deus ex machina* redemption, he feels an arm swing around him, grabbing the woman's arm. Artie Merritt has vented from the roof, and seeing the door chained he came down the fire escape from the roof to search the floor. He and Benny drag the woman down the stairs. She is still breathing, but badly burned. They leave her next to the baby in the kitchen and return to the landing. Artie cannot control a coughing seizure, but he partially lifts a man, and drags him down the stairs. As Benny lifts the other child the bulkhead door swings open, and hangs down, caught by the chain. The heat and smoke rush out to the midday air, and the firemen fight their way down the stairs. Benny and Artie know now that the worst is over, and they minister to the people whose lives were worth more than their own.

Engine 45 is in the apartment extinguishing the fire that has come up through the walls. We are waiting in the hall, but we know that the men of Engine 45 won't need us to relieve them. Kevin, Cosmo, and I follow Lieutenant Collins to the street, where he confers with Chief Niebrock. The Chief wants us to make a secondary search of all the apartments in the building.

As we re-enter the building a man stumbles out. He is burned on the face, and bleeding heavily from the mouth. A large black man, he is wearing a light cotton shirt that is now red with blood, and he has only one shoe. He falls in front of us, and I catch him before he hits the ground. The others go in the building, and I stay with the man.

About fifteen minutes have gone by, and I have tried to clean the man as best I could. I used my handkerchief until Oscar Beutin, one of the men of Engine 85, brought me a wet towel. The inside of his mouth is gashed. He must have fallen down the stairs. I have loosened his belt, and placed my boot under his head as a pillow. The man is not in any real danger, at least as far as I can tell, and I try to make him as comfortable as possible. A call has been put in for ambulances, and they should be here soon.

A large crowd has gathered in front of the building. One man is agitated, and he shouts, "Why don't you put that man in a fire engine and take him to the hospital?" He speaks clearly, without any trace of the black dialect or the ghetto localisms. I ignore him, because I know that he doesn't understand the workings of an emergency service. We don't take people to the hospital because it ties us up. We deal in seconds and minutes. Seconds and minutes determine life and death in our business. But this man doesn't know that. He only knows that a man is bleeding on the street, and there are no ambulances to take him to the hospital. He yells again. "You motherfuckers don't care about black people. If that man was white you'd have him in a hospital soon enough." Many in the crowd nod in agreement, and others stare with interest. I look at the man on the ground, and then look at the intruder. I would like to tell him about the kind of work firemen do. I would like to tell him about people in this very neighborhood who are enjoying life only because of the actions of firemen. But it won't make any sense. This man doesn't want to like me. Not here. Not now. Another time, perhaps, I can tell this man that I care as much as he about the bleeding man at my feet. Even more important, I can ask him why he thinks I don't care.

Four ambulances turn the corner at Intervale Avenue—the disaster unit from Bronx-Lebanon Hospital. The Chief radios the word into the building, and firemen begin to carry the victims out. They are in chairs, or on stretchers. An attendant brings a wheel chair to me, and we lift the bleeding man into it. The attendant rolls the chair to the ambulance, and the driver assists us as we lift the chair into the antiseptic confines of the truck.

No one ate hamburgers in the firehouse today. They were ruined, but even if they were not burnt and dried out I don't think anyone would have felt like eating. It is after six now, and I'm sitting on a bed by my locker, putting on a clean pair of socks. The Chief called the hospital, and they told him that three of the victims were dead on arrival. The large woman was dead. She was eight months with child. Two men were dead, but Benny puffed life into the baby.

And now Benny is lying in a bed in the men's ward of Bronx Hospital. He collapsed finally, after bringing the small, breathing girl to the ambulance. The men's ward at Bronx is a dingy place, and I've seen many firemen recoup there after they brutalized their bodies in the course of their work. There are sixteen beds in the square, dim-gray room, and lying next to Benny is Joe Mazillo who was one of the men who fought his way down from the roof. And next to Joe is Lieutenant Connell who supervised the roof operation. The department medical officer has told us they will remain in the hospital for at least three days, for rest, blood tests, and X-rays. But Jim Stack will have to stay a little longer. He is across the hall in the intensive care unit, suffering dangerously high blood pressure and nerve palpitations. He felt a shocking pain as he helped George Hiegman connect the pumper to the hydrant. And Artie Merritt has been transferred to the Manhattan Eye and Ear Hospital where he will spend the night. He cut the cornea of his eye as he hit a table corner while crawling through the smoke. Three human beings are dead, and ten are hospitalized for a fire that should have been routine.

I wonder what all this means. Is it ontological proof—that what God gives, He also takes away? Or does it mean that if there were no drug addicts in New York City people wouldn't have to put chains on roof doors?

11

I was twenty-one when I filled in the blanks on the fireman's application form. I didn't know what the job was all about then—I only knew that it was a mark of success for a neighborhood boy to become a fireman or a cop. They were secure jobs, and much respected by our elders who had lived through the depression. The nuns in the school I attended as a child never spoke to us about becoming doctors, or lawyers, only about becoming President of the United States, or a fireman, or a cop. Any of us could become President, it was our birthright for we were all second generation Irish or Italian, but we could become firemen or cops only if we applied ourselves, and managed in one way or another to get through high school—a great achievement in those days.

The day of the civil service exam was bright and summer-hot. I borrowed my brother's old '51 Chevy, and drove to a high school in Greenwich Village where schoolteachers were going to earn time-and-a-half by proctoring the firemen's test. There were no parking spaces, so I double-parked the car—after all I was about to become an official of the City of New York, and no policeman would dare to ticket it.

A thousand young men, armed with real or equivalency diplomas, were gathered in classrooms to answer the hundred questions and to compete for the job. A legion of hopefuls in plaid shirts and gabardine trousers, all hunched over ink-stained desks, squirming in the seats built for men five sizes smaller, and trying to remember the who-whom rule of seventh-grade grammar. It was a hot day, and I remember sweating anxiously.

Eight thousand men competed that Saturday morning in schools throughout the five boroughs of the city. The list would be promulgated a few months thereafter, and two thousand would be eligible for Department jobs over the next four years. The firemen's test is traditionally the most difficult of all the tests for the uniformed services. More men apply to become firemen than apply for any of the other services, and because there are fewer job openings the examiner makes the test harder to pass, ensuring that the city will get the cream of New York's employable youth. The men who failed the test that day, or who did not pass with a grade high enough to be within the two thousand selected, would seek other city jobs—the Police Department, the Transit Police, the Housing Police, the Sanitation Department. I was lucky. I passed. But I found a ten-dollar tag on my car. I decided it was a small price to pay.

I was investigated thoroughly, and my moral character was ascertained. A firefighter goes, in the course of his work, into banks, jewelry stores, and people's homes—an applicant with a criminal record is not considered for obvious reasons. I took a strenuous physical examination in which we ran obstacle courses, climbed over walls ten feet high, lifted weights of 110 pounds and more—the more weight one pressed the higher the mark—broad-jumped a minimum of six feet, and did sit-ups while holding a minimum of forty pounds behind the neck. The physical examination was also competitive, and the grade was averaged with the written mark to give the applicant a final score.

Then there was the medical examination. Flat feet, missing digits, being less than 5 feet 7 inches in height, having less than 20/20 vision or less than perfect hearing, an even slightly imperfect cardiogram were all automatic disqualifiers. I passed again, and two years later, in 1963, I was appointed to the rank of Fireman in the New York City Fire Department. I was engaged to be married then, and in my first year of college.

The swearing-in ceremony was brief, and after a few gratuitous and banal remarks about courage and dedication by city officials I was given the three-inch chrome maltese cross that is the badge of a firefighter. Badge number 11389, NYFD. It was a symbol of security and importance to me—and it saved me the fare each time I rode a city subway or bus. It would act in place of a ticket in many of New York's movie houses—it is always nice to have a firefighter in the house, a kind of cheap insurance policy—and it represented a ten percent discount in many of the city's shops and department stores. If stopped by a policeman after running a red light, or speeding, it usually meant that the cop would not write the ticket. It was a free meal in many of the best restaurants, as long as the meal was eaten in the kitchen, and a room at half price in the hotels if there was a girl friend.

Merchants were good to firefighters then, because they expected firefighters to be good in return as they made their annual, semi-annual, or monthly fire inspections. But, the system has changed now. Firefighters are perceiving themselves as professionals, and they perform inspectional duties with the diligence of a woodpecker pecking at a soft tree. Violation orders are written if the proper number of portable fire extinguishers are not hung on the walls of factories, and summonses are issued for locked exit doors. There is no bargaining for future discounts, and there are no promises of free merchandise. Firefighters

[195]

know that a conscientious inspection can mean the difference between life and death. Souls are not sold anymore for a ten percent discount, or a two-dollar movie ticket, or a ten-dollar dress for the wife.

I was inspecting a restaurant recently. It was housed on the ground floor of an old two-story wooden frame building. The place was clean, but I noticed that the ducts over the oven were coated thickly with grease. I began to write a violation order. The owner folded a twenty-dollar bill and laid it on the table. He didn't offer it to me, he just let it sit there beside the salt and pepper. "Listen, I'll get the ducts cleaned, but I don't want a record of the violation," he said. A double-sawbuck is a night out for my wife and me, or new shoes for the kids, or a hundred other things we need that twenty dollars can buy. I earn $10,950 a year, but it doesn't go far. I pay my bills, and that's all. I have no savings account, no investments in stocks or bonds. The only investments I've ever made were in a house and a car. If my boys want to go to college, I have to pray that they will be smart enough to pass scholarship exams. Twenty dollars is a lot of money to me. But it doesn't take much heat to ignite grease, and when it ignites in the confines of a duct it spreads fast. The duct metal radiates the heat until the building is on fire. The people living above the restaurant would be burned out, if not burned to death. And even if there were no people living above, there is an insurance company that would have to cover the building loss. I handed him the violation, and said, "We'll be back in two weeks." Of course, I could have reported him for an attempted bribe, but I understood that he was operating in an old system. I did not want to jail the man, but teach him.

The swearing-in ceremony was held on a Saturday, and we were ordered to report to the department's training school the following Monday. It was a humid June morning as I rode the bus from Manhattan to Queens. The iron expansion plates of the Queensborough Bridge sang as the bus wheels rolled over them.

It was a happy day for me—the beginning of a new, stable, secure life. From the bridge I could see the training tower of the Fire School rising high on Welfare Island, a two-mile strip of land in the middle of the East River, between Queens and Manhattan. I took another bus from Queens to Welfare Island, and there my career as a firefighter was born.

We began each morning, Monday to Friday for eight weeks, with forty-five minutes of calisthenics, push-ups, sit-ups, pull-ups, jumping, and running. Then, there were three hours of classroom work—learning building codes, inspection procedures, fire laws, first aid, building construction, the science of fire, the science of fire control, and about building fires, car fires, ship fires, chemical fires, explosions, implosions, the telegraph alarm system, bell-signal codes, community relations, arson investigation, and a hundred other subjects as diffuse and difficult as any college course I've taken.

Then there was a forty-five minute lunch break, and a hundred and fifty probationary firefighters would unwrap the sandwiches made for them by wives or mothers, or bought earlier in a hero shop, and talk about the job, and how nice it would be to have a beer with the sandwiches. But, it was against regulations to leave the island at any time during the work day, so all managed to satisfy themselves with the only available liquid—water or canned soda. We ate quickly, and rested in the sun for the remainder of the period, talking excitedly about our futures, about studying for the lieutenant's exam, about our families, and girl friends, and relentlessly projecting our coming assignments. Would we go to a firehouse in a ghetto area, or a slow house in Queens or the upper Bronx? A truck or an engine company?

In the afternoons we had three hours of field work: stretching hose up stairs, up fire escapes, up aerial ladders; crawling past fifty-gallon drums filled with burning wood scraps in the heat room, crawling through controlled smoke conditions in the abandoned buildings of the old State Hospital on the island, breathing the first whiffs of the poison that we would soon

[197]

get to know as a doctor knows death; chopping through floors and doors with eight-pound axes, forcing locks with halligan tools, ripping down ceilings with six-foot hooks, connecting pumpers with water hydrants; lifting, carrying, and placing twenty-five-foot ladders, lowering ourselves down the outside of a five-story building with a rope and a life-belt, being lowered by others from the roof, stopping to pick up a simulated victim at a windowsill—the victim invariably a firefighter bigger than the rescuer—jumping three stories into a life net, aiming for the red bulls-eye in the middle of the white canvas; carrying victims in stretchers, in chairs, over the back, making inch-by-inch searches in smoky rooms looking for a dummy well hidden by a diabolical instructor, and when returning without it being ordered to crawl back and find it; bandaging foreheads, splinting legs, climbing from floor to floor up the outside of a building with a twelve-foot scaling ladder—but safe, always safe, with a net below. We learned everything about being in a fire, the heat, the smoke, the quick exhaustion of strength—everything but what it is like to be in the uncontrolled madness of a real fire. We would soon learn that.

The awaited graduation day came, and our Department Orders. Like soldiers huddled for mail call in a World War II movie, we grouped expectantly as a Lieutenant read the assignments. "Dennis E. Smith, Engine Company 292." I was happy with that. Engine 292 was in Queens and, since I would marry within the month, I would be moving to Queens anyway, so it would be convenient traveling. Engine 292 responded to about a hundred alarms a month. I liked that. Not too fast. Not too slow. I intended to return to college, and I didn't want to be overworked. I needed time to read, and on my days off I needed to be rested to attend classes at New York University. Yet, Engine 292 was busy enough so that I had a piece of the action. I was being paid to be a firefighter, not a student.

Three years passed quickly in Queens. My wife bore two sons, and I had managed to get through my sophomore year in college. But I still had a long way to go for a degree. A thousand novels lay before me, and the hours of my life were carefully rationed: so many hours in a quiet Queens firehouse, so many hours in school, and just so many hours at home with my family. It became a terrible, boring grind. Boring because no one thing demanded the total commitment of my mind and body. I was doing something worthwhile in that Queens firehouse, but I felt I just wasn't doing enough. I needed a change in the tempo of my life. My whole future seemed bounded by an incarcerating triangle. I loved my wife and family and I realized they represented the one immovable angle of my dilemma. I didn't want to quit school, because the diploma had become important to me. The choice left was to either quit being a fireman, or transfer to another firehouse. Since I had no other means of supporting my family, and since I liked being a firefighter, I decided to transfer to another firehouse, another company.

I did not know where to go. I had friends working in Brooklyn companies and Manhattan companies, but Brooklyn was difficult to get to from my apartment in Queens, and there was no place to park a car in Manhattan—I dislike riding the subway.

I picked up a copy of the Fire Department's annual report, and turned to the statistics page. The company listed first under "RUNS" and "WORKERS" was Engine Company 82. That's where I'll go, I said to myself. If you're going to make a change, make a full change. Go to the busiest engine company in the city, the one at the top of the list. It was a decision I'll never regret. That was 1966.

I am in the bunkroom of the firehouse now, lying on a bed, absentmindedly counting the nails in the ceiling, and wondering why I'm here. There are conversations floating through the air around me, but I try not to hear them. Dust has settled on the ceiling, and because the paint is heavier over the plastered

[199]

nailheads the dust has not stuck to the surfaces there. I can count the series of round, lighter marks. There are 39 marks to a row, twelve inches apart. I'm tired. I should be home like the rest of America on this hot Sunday night, watching *Lassie*, and the *Ed Sullivan Show*, or reading the Sunday supplement.

Over five years have passed since I transferred to Engine 82. Five summers with the length of five long winters. What would Wordsworth have said of the South Bronx? He wouldn't write of hedgerows hardly hedgerows, but of people hardly people. I worked last night, and I'm tired. We had no fire of consequence, only burning rubbish and false alarms. False alarms at five in the morning, at six, and at seven. A rubbish fire at eight. It doesn't make any sense. The people are killing me, and I don't know why. Five summers with the length of five long winters, and I'm tired. I went to my mother's house this morning, to rest, but I didn't get much sleep. I had breakfast, and my mother asked, again, "What do you keep knocking yourself out for?" I didn't sleep well, because I tried to answer her. Nothing I said made sense. *Somebody has to do it!* Perhaps I need to sit in the North Bronx and write. . . . Lines Written a Few Miles from Charlotte Street. Get away, and think about it. It does no good thinking about what I'm a part of. We went in and out of the firehouse thirty-two times last night, rubbish and false alarms, and I can't explain it. People in the South Bronx—many of them —are unhappy. I understand that. They pull false alarms. I understand that. But is there no end? Five years. And I'm tired.

It is six o'clock. The evening is still bright, and I will work through the night, watching for the morning horizon all the while. In fifteen hours it will be 9:00 A.M., Monday, and I will be relieved of duty. Then I'm off for three days, but I will sleep through the first. The first day after a set of night tours is not really a day off. On Tuesday I will relax, read Steinbeck or Mailer again, and practice the guitar. I will play the bagpipes, and when the neighborhood children hear the piercing tones of the pipes they will gather on my back porch entranced by the foreign music—thirty little eyes, shy, and unsure of their welcome. They will squirm playfully, and poke the small bodies around them, watching carefully for signs of my disapproval. I will pack the pipes away, and and ask them if they would like to learn a folk song or two. Half, perhaps, will run away, afraid, or simply not interested in a more personal interaction. And I will sing with the remainder until they, or I, get bored. The night will come, and my biology will begin to function normally again after having been imbalanced by my work schedule. I will hold my wife, and love her furiously, knowing that she has been denied because she married a firefighter.

Wednesday will be much like the day before, except that I plan to work on an amendment that I want to submit to the membership of my union for a change in our Constitution. I will take the boys to a nearby lake to swim, and because our waters should be free to all, I will curse the money I will have to pay for the privilege. Later, I will play tennis or basketball with friends on the courts behind the town high school. After a shower, dinner, bedtime stories for the boys, a soft hour with my wife, I will sleep, and I will return to duty, Thursday and Friday, nine in the morning to six at night.

The powerful voice of Charlie McCartty awakens me from my wondering. "I heard three rings, men."

I sit up in the bed, and listen for the housewatchman's voice. It could be for Engine 85, but the command travels up the pole-hole from the floor below: "Eighty-two and Seven-twelve. Chief goes. Fire at the corner of Home and Union."

"So long suckers," Charlie says as men move to the poles.

As I slide down the shining brass pole, I can hear Bill Kelsey say, "You're just jealous it's not for you, McCartty."

Bill slides the pole, but Charlie's voice, deep and raspy, follows right behind him, "Listen Sonny, I have more time sliding this pole than you have in fires, and don't you forget it."

We are all laughing on the back step. Kelsey insists that

Charlie would follow us down Intervale Avenue in order to have the last word, and the chuckling continues. But as Valenzio turns the pumper up Home Street the faces on the back step become serious. There is an abandoned one-family, wooden frame building on the corner of Union and Home, and the second floor is completely ablaze. The fire is so intense that it has reached out and burned the overhead electrical wires in the street, and a line lies on the sidewalk in front of the building, arching, and leaping.

There is a wooden crate in a lot beside the burning frame, and John Nixon rips a side off to lay across the exposed wire. Chief Niebrock is here, and he orders a man to stand watch by the fallen hotline, as John rushes into the building to make his search. But the man is more interested in the fire than baby-sitting over a wire, and another fireman almost steps on the thing—500 volts strong. Fortunately, Chief Niebrock sees him, and cries a desperate warning, as I pass by dragging the hose. The fireman, a man from Engine 50, redirects his step, and Chief Niebrock scolds the man who was assigned to stand watch.

The fire is going in three rooms, but the large amount of water pouring from the two-and-a-half-inch hose makes easy work of it. Kelsey has the nozzle, and is moving in fast. The smoke is dark and putrid, and the inevitable mucus flows heavily from our mouths and nostrils. Lieutenant Welch begins to cough, and realizing the effort Kelsey must be making orders Willy Boyle to the nozzle. Knipps, Royce, and I hump the hose from behind, where the smoke is not as bad.

Kelsey bails out to the lighter air, but as he passes through the hall Kenny Hing pulls back his halligan tool to take a swing at a rear door. Kelsey is hit with the end of the weighty, metal tool, and his eyelid opens up.

The fire in the last of the rooms is out, and the room steams. The men of Ladder 712 enter to pull the ceilings. Tony Indio walks to the far corner of the room, but the flooring gives way. His six-foot hook flies to the ground as he tries to catch a beam, but he isn't quick enough, and disappears to a room below. Nixon and Mike Runyon hustle out of the room, and down the stairs to where Tony lies.

It is eight o'clock now. Knipps is cooking breaded veal cutlets for dinner—McCartty calls them motorman's gloves, and Boyle calls them elephant's ears. Kelsey is still at the hospital getting his eye stitched, and we heard that Indio has two broken ribs.

Knipps is cooking the cutlets by threes in the deep oil fryer. As he lays three finished products into a brown-paper-lined pan, he announces to all in the kitchen that there is just enough food for the meal, and if he catches anyone trying to steal a piece of knosh he will cut their hand off.

"You can shove your meal," someone remarks, but Knipps overlooks it. He has never experienced sincere gratitude for his cooking, but thank-yous come in other ways, like "Shove it."

I climb the stairs to the bunk room, hoping for an hour's respite, but the bells intercede as I reach the top step, the twenty-third step.

We are at Charlotte Street again, and it is a false alarm. The men on the back step say nothing as Chief Niebrock radios the ten-ninety-two, the signal of a malicious false alarm. Knipps, Boyle, Royce, Valenzio, Lieutenant Welch—all of them are conditioned to accepting false alarms as a way of life, like climbing into pants in the morning, or stopping at an intersection for a red light. Things that must be done. False alarms that must be answered. But will it ever stop? Almost ninety thousand of them last year in this town, and the number rises from year to year. I am enraged. I won't accept them as part of the job, not until the courts decide to send even a virgin child to jail for the malicious act. If a judge and his family were immolated in a downtown fire because firefighters were answering a false alarm elsewhere, then the judiciary would think of false alarms as a problem. But, it never happens that way. It happens here in the South Bronx, where people are poor, and not important enough to be concerned about.

Calm. Be calm, I tell myself. There are less tragic hypotheses to make. Think about the wear and tear of the pumper's tires, and the cost of diesel fuel. Think about a burned and forgotten roast smoking in an oven, or a sparking chimney, or an overflowing bathtub. Things less serious than death.

I am looking at the bunkroom ceiling again, but I don't bother to count the nails. I close my eyes. Each minute's rest seems like an hour of sleep. It is eleven o'clock, and I have an hour before I begin housewatch duty.

We almost ate the elephant's ears uninterrupted, but a woman stopped by in passing, and told of a garbage fire around the corner. Lieutenant Welch called the dispatcher, and we took it as a single unit call. The men of Ladder 712 were satisfied that we would extinguish the fire before someone pulled the alarm box, saving them a response. The pumper has left quarters seven times since we were at Charlotte Street. Three were false alarms. Two were abandoned cars, derelict, stolen, and stripped, and two were garbage fires, "*outside rubbish*" as they are called on the fire report.

Engine 85 and Ladder 712 caught a job on Longfellow Avenue. They were washing dishes and cleaning pots as the alarm came in. Chief Niebrock transmitted a second alarm on arrival, when he saw three frame houses afire. Fire in wooden frame buildings spreads like a fire on a dry prairie, and the flames soon grew to three-alarm intensity. But they held it to a third. Eighty-five will be there most of the night, and Seven-twelve will go off duty at twelve-thirty, their tour completed.

The hour passes quickly. I do not sleep, but the sixty minutes of inaction purges the fatigue and gives me new energy. Vinny Royce's voice echoes from the apparatus floor, "You got it, Dennis." I arise swiftly, and slide to the floor below. It's time to begin my housewatch duty—three hours of recording bell transmissions, and answering telephones. From midnight to 3:00 A.M.

Vinny picks up a pack of cigarettes from the housewatch desk, smiles an appreciation of relief, and heads for the kitchen, free from the confinement of the housewatch area. I sit at the desk, the eighteen-inch department journal in front of me. The last entry logged in the book was *"Engine 82 and Ladder 712 in service from Box 2700—MFA"* (malicious false alarm). Directly under it I write the time in the margin: 2400 hours, midnight in military time. Next to the time I write, *"Fireman Smith relieved Fireman Royce at housewatch. Department property, apparatus, and quarters in good condition."* I don't know for sure that anything is in good condition, but the department regulations mandate the entry. If anything is stolen or broken now, everyone but me is covered. I am responsible for the next three hours, until I yell to Willy Knipps, "You got it, Willy," and Willy puts his name in the book.

There is nothing to do now, but read and wait for the alarms to come in. In the desk drawer there is a book of Ellery Queen mysteries. I start to read it, but my eyes begin to strain at the second paragraph. I replace it in the drawer, reflecting unhappily that my eyes are not as strong as they used to be. I am still a young man, but I am beginning to sense a feeling of agedness and weariness. This is a young man's job, but it's making me old. I am thirty-one years old, and at times I feel fifty.

The South Bronx has taught me much about people, about misery and deprivation of all kinds, but I have paid well for the lesson. I live a five-day week, and chalk the other two up for rest and recuperation. The day after my day-tours and the day after my night-tours do not belong to me, but to the South Bronx, to the false alarms and the garbage fires.

I am tired, yet I don't want to transfer to a middle-class neighborhood, where false alarms are surprising, and garbage is piled neatly in cans. Not yet. I still feel I have something to give where it is most needed. I am a professional firefighter,

[205]

I know my work, and the South Bronx needs men like me, Royce, Carroll, McCartty, O'Mann, and the rest. We have developed the necessary mixture of moxie, skill, and self-reliance that makes us firefighters, and gives us the responsibility to protect where people are victimized most. It took us years to develop that combination of skills that permits us to challenge the unknown of fire, to crawl breathlessly into a whirling darkness, a deadly nightshade of smoke, knowing all the while that the floor or the ceiling may collapse, yet confident of victory, assured that only we can do the job. We, New York's front line of defense, will get the job done. Firefighters. New York's Bravest. Anyone can be President, the nuns taught us that; but they were wrong about firefighters. It takes more than study and hard work to be a firefighter. Sometimes it takes more than anyone has to give.

The bells start to ring. I brace myself attentively, and write the signal in the journal. *"Received telegraph alarm, Box 2291.* I open the drawer labeled Alarm Assignment Cards, and finger the cards until I come to 2291. The location is Prospect Avenue and 153rd Street. The first alarm assignment reads *"Engine 73, Engine 41, Squad 2, Ladder 42, and Ladder 17."* Engine 85 is assigned on the second alarm, and Ladder 31 is assigned on the third. I holler through the apparatus floor, "Okaaay," and return to my thoughts.

No, I don't want to transfer from Engine 82. I have grown to love the men I work with as much as any man can love another. We have been through much together—from being caught between an extended fire, huddled on the floor, flames jumping before and behind, and unsure if we would be able to fight our way out, to consoling each other in hospital emergency wards, to drinking hard in the North Bronx bars, hard, like the sun wouldn't rise again, to picnicking with our families by a calm upstate lake. Between us there is a mutual admiration and concern that can only be found among men whose very lives depend on each other's quick, competent, and courageous actions. It is a good feeling, this dependency, a proud feeling.

The harsh clang of the bells makes me jump, and I poise for the count—Onetwo onetwothreefourfive one onetwothree. I record the signal in the book as I yell "Get out Eighty-two and Thirty-one. Box 2513. Prospect Avenue and 165th Street." The telephone rings the three short rings that indicate added information. The dispatcher gives me an address, and I relay the information to Lieutenant Welch.

The troops are already standing on the back step, and I have to hustle to put my gear on. The pumper begins to move out, and I take a running jump to catch it. Knipps and Royce reach out to grab me as I land.

Ladder 31 is behind us as we reach the Prospect Avenue address. Lieutenant Welch runs into the building, as we begin to drag the hose from the pumper-bed. There is no excitement, no discernible fire or smoke, but we stretch the hose just in case.

Billy-o and McCartty are on the fouth floor. Billy-o has his halligan tool wedged between the door and its frame. McCartty is whacking the end of the halligan with the base of his ax-head. The noise has awakened the neighbors, and the building becomes a chorus of excited, questioning people.

Richie Rittman goes through the alleyway to the rear yard. There is a girl, about ten years old, lying on the rough concrete, her face distorted by pain. Richie begins to kneel by her, but he hears screaming from above—the high-pitched desperate screams of children. Richie knows his job is not to comfort this girl. Not now.

There is an iron gate on the fire-escape window on the fourth floor. Next to the fire escape is another window, but it is too far to reach. Three little boys are leaning over the sill, gasping for air, and crying fearfully. Thick smoke is pushing out of their apartment, over their small anguished heads, and between them. "Just stay right where you are boys, I'll get you out," Richie yells, over and over.

The fire-escape window is broken, and Richie forces the iron gate open. It takes all his strength before the brackets snap. Behind the gate there is a chest of drawers. Richie kicks it over, and enters the room.

The room is hot, the fire from the adjoining rooms is beginning to sweep in. The boys are in shock, and they don't want to leave the window. Richie picks two of them up and carries them to the fire escape. As he returns for the third, he can hear me open the nozzle at the front of the apartment—first the air gush, and then the powerful stream of water.

There are three rooms going, and we have to get on our bellies to escape the ever-lowering heat. We push in, Lieutenant Welch saying "Beautiful, we almost got it, just a little more," all the while, and Royce just behind humping the hose, saying "If you need a blow Dennis, I'm right here." I can feel the heat sink into my face, like a thousand summer days at the beach. We reach the third room, and the fire is extinguished, defeated, dead. The smoke lifts, and the walls breathe the last breaths of steam.

I am in the street, resting and breathing short, regimented gulps of air. Men pass by and ask how I'm feeling, but I just nod to them. I don't feel like speaking. I feel like I have climbed a mountain, and although I have given up all of my strength, I will bask in the silent, personal satisfaction of victory. I have done what I have been trained to do, and in the doing I have trained for the next time. My throat is congested, and as I spit the black phlegm of my trade I realize again the price I—all of us—pay for the victory. Is it worth it, this brutal self-flagellation, this constant ingestion of black poison, this exhaustion, this aging? Firefighting is a job. It is not a spiritual vocation. Hundreds of years have passed since medieval ascetics whipped themselves for glory. No, it is not worth it. Garbage men are paid as much as we, prison guards and subway policemen reap the same benefits. We get satisfaction. Yet . . . yet, this is what we do, what we do well. We could not do anything else with such a great sense of accomplishment.

The ambulance comes, and men pass by me carrying the three boys—three shaken whimpering boys, left alone by their mother in the care of a ten-year-old girl, their sister. Billy-o passes by with the girl in his arms. She was frightened. The fire-escape window was blocked by a chest of drawers and an iron gate, and she jumped from the fourth floor window. What thoughts must have been going through this little girl's head as she climbed over the sill to jump fifty feet to an almost certain death? With good reason have Christians chosen fire as the metaphor of hell. What could be more fearful than the slow, agonizing crisping of skin, the searing of the lungs until the throat passage closes? If only someone had called us sixty seconds earlier—just one minute sooner, Richie would have been there in time to talk to her. The ambulance hurries away. Billy-o sits next to me on the warm slate of the stoop steps. "God," he sighs, "was that kid lucky. It looks like all she has is a broken leg." I look at Billy-o, at the worn frontpiece of his helmet, smoke-darkened and heat-blistered. I can just barely make out the identifying number of his company—the black numerals that were once white and bold, the number 31 on the black background that was once red, and signifies a Ladder Company. I don't speak, and he puts his gloved hand on my knee as he rises. "She hit a clothesline on the way down," he says as he re-enters the building.

The day has begun to come alive. I have watched the mist around the street lights fade as the morning light appeared. It is now 7:00 A.M., and the kitchen is filled with men and empty coffee cups. Engine 85 has returned from the third alarm, and stories are being exchanged about fires. Billy Valenzio has relieved Knipps at housewatch, and Knipps and I sit at a table talking of the first day we walked into the quarters of Engine 82. He, Kelsey, and I were assigned together. Kelsey is sleeping, his eye bandaged. Knipps will drive him home when the tour is done. Tony Indio has been admitted into the hospital.

An alarm comes in, and the men of Engine 85 move out as Valenzio hollers "Eighty-five only." Minutes pass, and the bells ring again. Box 2743, the inevitable 2743—Charlotte and 170th Streets. Valenzio yells, in an attempt at early morning humor, "Eighty-two and Thirty-one goes, you know where. Chief goes too."

We reach the corner of Charlotte Street, and see an old man lying at the base of the alarm box. His throat is cut, and he lies in a small sea of his own plasma. We are too late to help him for his head is thrown to one side, and I can see into the hole in his neck. His eyes have rolled back under his open lids, lost forever. Nothing could have helped him but the prevention of the murder. McCartty comes over with a blanket, and lays it gently over him, shielding him from the filth of Charlotte Street.

A passerby stands next to us, a middle-aged black with graying hair. His face is sullen, but distinguished and proud. "He was a nice man," he says looking down at the blanketed body.

"Do you know him?" Lieutenant Welch asks. "Do you know his name?"

"No," the man replies, "I don't know his name. They called him 'the old Jew,' that's all. He owns the laundromat, and he came here every morning with a bag of change for the machines. I guess they killed him for a bag of nickels and dimes."

Ten years ago the South Bronx was a mostly Jewish and Irish neighborhood, but as they progressed economically in the American system they moved from the tenements to better buildings in the North Bronx, or to small ranch houses in the surburbs of Long Island. As they moved out, blacks and Puerto Ricans moved in. As blacks and Puerto Ricans moved in, the less successful whites moved out to other tenements, but in white neighborhoods. There are still bars in the neighborhood named "Shannon's," and "The Emerald Gem," but they are frequented by men with black faces, and there are signs in Spanish saying "Iglesia Christiana de Dios," hanging obtrusively in front of stain-glassed Stars of David on abandoned synagogues. But, some merchants have lingered on, working hard for a dollar-by-dollar survival. Like this old man whose last act in life was to call the Fire Department, to pull the alarm that would keep him alive.

There is a trail of blood from the laundromat to the alarm box, a distance of ten steps. There are footprints in the trail, placed there by careless passersby, who pause momentarily on their way to work, ask a question or two, and continue their journeys.

The ambulance comes, and we place the body on an antiseptic, sheeted stretcher. McCartty folds the red-stained blanket as he steps from the ambulance. It will have to go to the cleaners, or to a laundromat. The police have arrived, and are talking to Chief Niebrock. Our job is finished. From the back step of the apparatus I can see the old man's keys, hanging, still and forgotten, from the padlock on the door of his business place.

It is ten minutes to eight now, and the sun begins to break through threatening clouds. In another hour I will take a shower, change into clean clothes, and drive home for a day of sleep. Right now though, there is nothing to do but drink still more coffee, and wait for the men of the day tour to arrive for work.

Charlie McCartty, as usual, is the center of attention in the kitchen. Most of us are sitting wearily in chairs, trying to relax after a hectic night tour, but McCartty is pacing up and down the kitchen floor berating a probationary fireman for not cleaning the kitchen.

"Ninety percent of this job is professional work, fighting fires, and making inspections, and all that," he says, "but the other ten percent is pure bullshit."

The probie, Frank Parris, starts to grin as he collects the empty cups from the tables.

"The ten percent bullshit," Charlie continues, "is your responsibility, and that is to keep this kitchen clean, and make sure there is fresh coffee at all times. If ya do that right, then maybe we'll teach ya about the other ninety percent."

Parris is one of the most conscientious probies we have ever had in the big house, and he knows, as well as all of us, that Charlie is just making noise. Parris wipes the tables with a sponge as Charlie continues to pace, and mutter.

"When I was a probie, I did everything I could to make the senior men happy, but none of you guys would know about that—that was in the days of leather lungs and wooden fire hydrants, when horses pulled the rigs. I even used to service the mares when they got restless. That's when a probie was a probie." Charlie is a pleasant diversion, and he has got the men laughing, and interested in his soliloquy. But, three sharp rings on the department phone redirect everyone's attention.

"Eighty-two and Thirty-one, get out." Valenzio's voice carries through the firehouse. "And the Chief," he adds. "1280 Kelly Street."

We can smell the smoke as the pumper leaves quarters. Up Tiffany Street, and down 165th Street. As we turn into Kelly the smoke has banked down to the street, making it difficult to see even ten feet away. Valenzio pulls the pumper to the first hydrant he sees. We will have to stretch around the apparatus, but at least we know we have a hydrant that works. The building is occupied, and we will have to get water on the fire fast.

Engine 73 arrives and helps us with the stretch. Between the lifts and banks of the smoke, we can see that the job is on the top floor, five flights up. But, there is enough manpower for the stretch now, so I drop the hose and head for the mask bin. Valenzio has the pumper connected to the hydrant by the time I have the mask donned, and Jerry Herbert has the aerial ladder of the truck up, and placed by the top floor fire escape. He is climbing up it as I enter the building.

The fifth floor is enveloped with smoke, and I can barely see in front of me. Billy-o and McCartty are working on the door of the burning apartment, but it is secured inside with a police lock—a long steel bar, stretched from one side to the other like the gate of Fort Apache. The smoke is brutal, and Billy-o has a coughing fit between ax swings. Charlie pulls on the halligan with all his strength, as Billy-o hammers with the head of the ax. Finally, the door begins to move, and Charlie and Billy-o work their tools, one complementing the other, like a computed machine, until one side of the door is free. Still coughing and choking, Charlie puts his shoulder to the door, and it swings inward, and out of its brackets to the floor.

Charlie and Billy-o dive to the floor, for the fire lunges out to the hall. Willy Boyle has the nozzle. I ask him if he wants me to take it, since I have the mask, but he replies that he thinks he can make it.

"Let's go," Lieutenant Welch says.

Boyle makes it about ten feet into the apartment, but it is an old building, and the plaster falls freely from the ceiling in large pieces. Boyle's helmet is thrown from his head by the falling ceiling. Lieutenant Welch orders me up to take the line. Boyle has to back out, because it is unsafe to operate in an inferno like this without something protecting the head.

Herbert has entered the apartment from the front. He can hear McCartty and Billy-o banging at the door. All but the end room of the apartment is burning, and the smoke and the fire are being drawn there by the open window. Jerry crawls along the floor, realizing that the room could go up in a second. He hears a slight moan, coming from the far side of the bed that stands in the middle of the room. The room is blind dark with smoke, and Jerry crawls to the sound, patting his hand before him as he goes. He reaches the other side of the bed, and the fire begins to lap at the ceiling above him. The smoke has taken everything from him, but he knows he can't back out now.

His hand gropes searching before him, until at last he feels the soft give of a woman's body. There is a child by her side. Jerry picks the child up and hurries on his knees to the window.

As he nears it, he sees Rittman enter, and he yells to him. Rittman takes the child in his arms, and climbs out of the apartment. Jerry knows that he is in trouble, for the fire is coming at him fast. He grabs the woman under the arms, and pulls her to the window, keeping his head as low as he can. She is a slight woman, and he pulls her easily. As he lifts her out to the fire escape he can hear the front door give way, and at that moment the room lights up completely in fire.

I am swinging the nozzle back and forth across the ceiling. The floor is cluttered with debris, furniture, fallen plaster, and it is difficult moving forward.

"Keep pushing, Dennis. Keep pushing," Lieutenant Welch says.

"Give me some more line," I yell to him through the mask, and he yells back to Royce and Knipps. We reach the front room, and as I lift my leg to get a better support, the floor gives way and my leg goes down, caught between the smoldering boards of the floor. Lieutenant Welch sees what has happened, and calls Royce up to the nozzle.

"Easy now," I say to Knipps as he helps me. "Just pull me out, easy." The smoke is lifting as Royce gets the last room, and I rip my face piece off to breathe freely. Lieutenant Welch yells back to me, "Go down and take the mask off, and check for injuries."

I start to move out, but the way is blocked by the men of Ladder 31. They are kneeling in the middle of the hall. "It's a baby," one of them says. I go to a window to get some air. The mask is heavy on my shoulders, and I want to sleep. Breathe. It's a baby. Breathe deep. I can feel my stomach moving. I had to crawl over it. In the middle of the hall. Breathe. The air tastes good. We all had to crawl over it. My mouth is full of coffee and veal. The taste is horrible as my stomach empties, and I can feel the terror of a thousand children as I lean across the sill.

A few minutes pass until the hall is clear. I go down a few

steps and take my mask off. I lay it on the stairs, and pull my pants down. I examine the top of my leg, but it's only bruised. I lift the heavy canister of air, the self-contained breathing apparatus, and carry it in my arms down the stairs.

Billy-o is sitting on the vestibule steps, waiting for the ambulance. The baby is wrapped in a borrowed bedspread, and lies like a little bundle in Billy-o's arms. A little package of dead life, never having had a chance to live.

I lay the mask on the floor, and sit below him on the bottom step. I look up, and he shakes his head. Mucus is hanging and drying beneath his nose, and his face is covered with grime and the dark spots of burnt paint chips. He feels, no he knows, that the baby could have been saved.

"How the hell can a fire get going like that before someone turns in an alarm?" He continues to shake his head in dejection. "And that police lock. What a mark of the poor when they have to barricade themselves in like that."

"What is it?" I ask him, looking toward his arms.

"It's a little girl about two years old. She never had a chance, but at least they got her mother and sister out."

"Did you give her mouth to mouth?" I ask.

"We couldn't. She was roasted so bad, the skin was burnt completely off her face. The poor little thing. She never had a chance."

I don't say anything further, nor does Billy. I look up at his eyes. They are almost fully closed, but I can see they are wet, and tearing. The corneas are red from heat and smoke, and light reflects from the watered surfaces, and they sparkle. I wish my wife, my mother, everyone who has ever asked me why I do what I do, could see the humanity, the sympathy, the sadness of these eyes, because in them is the reason I continue to be a firefighter.